MW00624347

# WEBS OF POWER.

## GOVERNMENT AGENCIES, SECRET SOCIETIES, & ELITE LEGACIES

### ERIK FORTMAN

RANDY LAVELLO
HENRY MAKOW, PHD
TOM CHITTUM
CHUCK BALDWIN
DR. LEN HOROWITZ

INTERVIEW WITH
CONGRESSMAN RON PAUL

VAN CLEAVE PUBLISHING
AUSTIN, TEXAS

Webs of Power
Copyright Erik Fortman, 2004

First published 2004 by
Van Cleave Publishing
1712 Riverside Dr. #93
Austin, Texas 78741

True First VCP paperback edition

ISBN: 0-9759670-0-2 paperback

Library of Congress Cataloging-in-Publication Data
Fortman, Erik
        Webs of Power: Government Agencies, Secret Societies, and Elite Legacies/
        Erik Fortman
        Includes bibliographical references and index
        ISBN 0-9759670-0-2 paperback
Library of Congress Control Number 2004109773
For additional cataloging information, write Van Cleave Publishing

Cover Design:  Scott Wade
Interior Design: Erik Fortman

Printed in the U.S.A.

# Table of Contents

Author's Note

# Author's Note

This book is comprised of editorial analysis. This is not pure news, though the topics were researched using television, books, the Internet, movies, interviews, pamphlets, and government documents. I call it editorial because opinion is inserted. For those who gush adulation when it comes to the United Nations, the Republican Party, the Democratic Party, and anyone else who likes the idea of globalization...well, this book is going to upset you. In the end, what I hope to have done is bring the scattered information that now abounds about the New World Order, and assimilate it under one title. A mini-global agenda reference guide, with opinion added for spice and style, was my ultimate goal. Last but not least, several great authors contributed wonderful essays and commentary, bringing the book an added variety. Randy Lavello, Henry Makow, PhD, Tom Chittum, Dr. Chuck Baldwin, and Dr. Len Horowitz deserve a 'shout out' for wonderfully written essays. I'm not responsible for their content, but I do fully endorse their right to publish their opinions.

As a political columnist with a libertarian bent, I inevitably end up discussing government with just about anyone who will debate. I was completely unaware of the CIA mind-control projects, FEMA's interment camps, and the other, more spectacular policies and agencies inside our government until after the September 11 attacks. Within a week after that fateful day, accusations of prior knowledge and possible cover-ups began, as did my own new journey into the truth concerning the United States Federal Government and the looming Global Super State. First, I had to decipher the new terminology that was inherent in the conspiracy subculture. "Illuminati," "New World Order," "Rothschild;" all are necessary vernacular for any real dialogue to occur. And almost at once, quagmire. I had to research and identify which ideas, and therefore which terms, were conjecture by people on the fringe of the fringe, and what was real information. Not to mention it is common knowledge that the government has endorsed a disinformation campaign to veil their evildoing. This is evidenced in recent admissions that Washington insiders waged a false campaign of UFO discoveries at Roswell, as well as other nefarious accounts by "experts" that the government had made some kind of contact with aliens. I believe this disinformation campaign began with H.G. Wells' now infamous "War Of The Worlds" radio program, which was reported to have created a mass panic. The legend is Americans were terrorized because they really believed aliens had landed. It was one of the first modern renditions of the Hegelian Dialectic, or Problem/Reaction/Solution. They create the problem. We react with alarm. They provide a governmental solution, eliciting power by their fear campaign in return for a semblance of security. Only, now it was being done on a mass scale, and in instant synchronicity.

Before I discovered that our monetary system is out on loan to foreigners by our Congress, I was still trying to assimilate facts about the government to better understand the depth and breadth of that mythical, mystical Beltway. I kept repeating tidbits to an accountant-friend, Nifer, who was interested, but completely unacquainted with most of the rudimentary facts of the governmental mechanisms. Legislative ignorance is common among public school graduates, and she thought a "Government For Dummies" book might be in order so that she could better understand my espousals. I searched around, but oddly enough, I couldn't find many books exclusively dedicated to overviews of our ruling government organizations. My investigative instincts were aroused, and so I began looking through current high school History books, but to no avail. A sentence or two about the Internal Revenue Service is usually printed, but no real information. "What was going on here? I wondered. I knew that almost 50% of our income went to taxation, and that a large percentage of this enforced tithing was used to fund our federal agencies. Why, then, was not a portion of this money used to educate the public about the government itself? As we will see, our government's subterfuge makes perfect sense not because they are protecting national security, but to cloud the coming tyranny.

I decided to do the research myself and provide my accountant-friend with my own interpretation. It would give us an equal point of reference. Now, I am admittedly a cynical man. A belief in the Constitution and a distrust of government was instilled in me by my old-school conservative Father, and a grandfather who saw family farms and ranches disintegrate throughout the 20th Century due to government intervention. Both men are my heroes. My father was sent to Vietnam for an unjust cause which was lied about by our leaders. I saw the devastation war wreaked on my father's psyche, even unto today, more than thirty years after he was sent home from Nam's killing fields. Both my father and grandfather would tell me of my great-grandfather, who came to America from Germany to avoid conscription by totalitarian leaders. What is ironic about that is, one hundred years after my great-grandfather left Germany to avoid an unfair draft, my dad was conscripted by the American military.

I was not prepared. I knew the government was steadily becoming too intrusive. That could not prepare me for the appalling lengths our government goes to ensure adherence to its agenda. Paul Joseph Watson, a freedom compatriot located in England, began to publish my essays on Alex Jones's prisonplanet.com, infowars.com and on Watson's own highly acclaimed propagandamatrix.com. In fact, even though I listed reputable sources and authors in my columns, mainstream media wouldn't print the incredible information. Even interviews with dissenting Congressman Ron Paul were blacked out by the leftist *Austin Chronicle*, and the more conservative *Austin American Statesman*. One editor wrote me: "You are obviously a good writer, but some of your facts are unsubstantiated. For instance, there is no proof of an 'Illuminati.' Paul Joseph Watson commented that

Illuminati was located in the Encyclopedia Britannica, for starters. Not to mention that the Order of the Illuminati, a German Freemason lodge, was an historically real political instigator with verifiable origins linked to Rothschild money. The information blackout regarding our government was becoming apparent. The corporate owners of cable news, talk radio, and print media - members of the same clubs that the politicians and energy barons belong to - were definitely not going to report that their buddies were passing laws 'rearranging' the Constitution. These same lawmakers continue to allow individual corporations to own larger and larger pieces of the broadcasting pie. Today, you can count the ownership of media on both hands, practically. Because of the successful propaganda campaign to place a 'conspiracy nut' moniker onto anyone relaying this very real data, other news sources have become afraid of being tainted by publishing the compelling information.

I thought I was finished. I was wrong. I wanted to know what these families had in common besides wealth. Irrefutable proof that they are acting to end individual and national sovereignty with a one world government would have been nice, too. But, alas, they are always one to one hundred chess moves ahead of us. One correlation was that the most powerful men of the Earth have always loved to meet in secret to discuss the future of their herds. From Ancient Babylon to Modern America, secret societies have been one of the ways the elite have hidden their true motives. The second section of this book deals with these secret societies under the title "Shadows of Power." This was, admittedly, the most difficult to pen due to the cloaked nature of these groups.

"Webs of Power" began as a gift to my friend. Unfortunately or fortunately, depending on which way you look at it, I stumbled headfirst into the truth during my research. What began as a basic overview of our governmental infrastructure has become public exposure of the blatant corruption in government and the impending probability of martial law. I decided to expand my work to include a "Legacies of Power" series, which was a summary some of the elite and their family histories. Rockefeller, Rothschild, Bush, Windsor: their lineages have held dominant power for decades, generations, centuries. They were and are instrumental in the formation of U.S. and World foreign and domestic policies. These families have been harbingers of war, decided national economic fates, and preached a philosophy of death. Speculation as to the number of families in the highest echelon of wealth and influence range from 3,000 to as few as ten. While investigating the Federal Reserve, the FBI, and other agencies, certain names continued to come into the peripheral. Therefore, I found it prudent to further delve into a summary of these families.

"Politics in G Minor" is a montage of chapters, meant to tie some of the loose ends together. I present three of these chapters on different aspects of mind control. Randy Lavello adds to that theme. Henry Makow gives some incredible information on the Rothschild history, which is inexorably intertwined with world history. Another that I wrote gives my opinion on how we might defy the New World Order nonviolently. Tom Chittum lashes scathing commentary about our "nation of suspects," and includes some great information about the Knights of the Golden Circle. Another fire is lit when Chuck Baldwin reveals the truth to Christian Conservatives about their "anointed" President Bush. Len Horowitz reminds us through research that the global conspiracy and a "Jewish Conspiracy" are not one and the same.

Finally, and most importantly, Congressman Ron Paul was kind enough to take time off of his busy schedule to grant me an interview. Ron Paul, for those who don't know, is a patriot, a Texas Representative, an Obstetrician, a military veteran, and an American hero. He ran for President in 1980 under the Libertarian mantle and is one of the only members of Congress that adheres to a platform of strict constitutionality. I don't understand why he is not on more television and radio programs. He is one of, literally, a handful of Congressman that voted against the

Patriot Act and Gulf War II. He answered candidly my questions concerning guns, gold, and globalism. His startling answers add credence to the building howl of Americans who think the Republic has been diverted from its intended path.

None of this material is meant as a definitive work, and is, of course, subject to my interpretation. I would require that all true Americans research this information on their own. Sadly, most do not even know the names of their two Senators...or that they only have two. I use brevity in my summations. This is to make the reading easy and informative for those who are unaware of the depth of corruption in our government. Too many numbers, dates, etc., would mire the layman in statistical data that would be gibberish and useful only on a trivial basis. Hell, as a layman myself, I think most interpreted statistics are nonsensical. My basic format was to lay out the official mission statements and histories released by our government and the propaganda. Then, I would try to find out if the stated mission had been accomplished, or if the history had been revised. What I found out was that in most cases the official mission statement was not the true mission, and that the Illuminati had set the agenda to bring about a One World Government. Highly decorated military heroes, lawyers, and politicians are risking job termination and even death to tell us that our government has stepped over the line and sold us out. Sold us out almost 100 years ago, when the International Bankers were given control of our money supply, and the IRS was created to ensure payment. These men and women who bravely admit the deceit...These are the whistleblowers, a very important aspect of the research. Also important, declassified documents. They are problematic, especially prying them from government's stingy hands. When the documents are finally released, they usually support the whistleblowers' stories. The stage has been set for a domestic and World military takeover. Will this happen? None can see the future. One can suppose using evidence and fact. It is my foremost hope that my countrymen will learn by rote this information. It may not stop the passing of draconian laws, but with an informed public, the implementation of these laws will become less likely.

At least for now.

**Special thanks**:

Mom - I owe you my creativity and my love of books

Dad - You taught me to question

Amy - Thanks for being patient as I wrote this

Paul Joseph Watson - propagandamatrix.com.

Alex Jones - infowars.com, prisonplanet.com, & prisonplanet.tv.

David Icke - davidicke.com

Randy Lavello - Randy Lavello is a political journalist. He deftly analyzes difficult subject matter, including mind control and language interpretation. Randy Lavello welcomes feedback at paintbox17@aol.com

Henry Makow, PhD - Inventor of the board game, Scruples, and author of A Long Way to go for a Date. He received his Ph.D. in English Literature from the University of Toronto. He welcomes your ideas and feedback at henry@savethemales.ca

Tom Chittum - Military and political analyst and satirist. He is the author of the book, Civil War II. Tom Chittum welcomes your comments at t.chittum@worldnet.att.net

Dr. Chuck Baldwin - Dr. Baldwin has dedicated his life to God. He received degrees from Christian Bible College, and went on to minister to prisoners for over 35 years. He is the host of the radio program, "Chuck Baldwin Live." Mr. Baldwin has written two books, and is an active political commentator. He is currently running for the Constitution Party's Vice-Presidential candidate in 2004. Visit Dr. Baldwin's website, chuckbaldwinlive.com

Dr. Leonard G. Horowitz - Received his doctorate and two masters, he has worked in the health field for many years. Dr. Horowitz is the author of several books, including a bestseller, <u>Emerging Viruses: Aids & Ebola - Nature, Accident, or Intentional</u>. He was awarded "Author of the Year Award" from the World Natural Health Organization. To contact, visit his website at tetrahedron.org.

Thanks, also, to the following:

Scott Wade
U.S. Legacies
Illuminati-news.com
Portland Independent Media Center
freespeechradio.net
Anti-Communitarians
&
Texas National Press,
and
Nifer

# Part One

# Webs of Power

## Webs of Power - Chapter 1: The Federal Reserve

In uncovering truths pertaining to the New World Order, it becomes necessary to study its power structure. This encapsulates a web-like base of operations that extends across the globe. Many people embrace government organizations because of the security that they profess to offer. This offer is almost always untrue. If the New World Order plans on a fascist World Super State, then there are primarily two areas of opposition: The United States and the Middle East. The reasons are many. First, we both have very fundamentalist religious systems. Neither the Christian Right nor the Islamic Fanatics will ever throw away their respective religions. Also, both regions are littered with personal firearms proliferation. The big bad American Army took two months just to rout out al-Sadr's militia in Najaf and other cities (April and May, 2004.) All this information is much more bred in the Deep South of the U.S. Guns and God, baby. Another similar attribute with the South and the Middle East is resentment toward centralized government. Certainly, the Middle East is several years, possibly decades, possibly centuries behind American politics. The similarities are there though. A belief in an exclusive God, who has granted the right to defend, and a history of decentralized control, all can be likened to forces in the U.S.A. and the Middle East. The thing is, Middle Easterners have not allowed themselves to be disarmed. They have much more firepower against the N.W.O. than do citizen Americans. Of the two, it is the Arabs that make the U.N. the most nervous. After they use U.S. power to put the Muslims into line and bring them into consumerism and secularism...well, at that time the globalists will look more seriously at Americans and their weapons.

We are fortunate in that, even in the current state of oncoming oppressiveness, we are aware of the meaning of individual sovereignty. This knowledge encompasses the benefits, privileges, and responsibilities of freedom. The

2

fortune that we were born free also makes it our duty to study the power structure of our country, and the world. In the following series, "Webs of Power," this author attempts to write a simple, basic compendium of America's ruling entities. It is my hope that these articles will provide even a few pieces of data and other insights into the organizations that run our lives.

**The Federal Reserve System** - The Federal Reserve is the entity that oversees and regulates America's money supply. Congress instituted this system in 1913. There are seven members on the Board of Governors and twelve Reserve Banks located in America. The Board of Governors are appointed by the President and confirmed by the Senate. The official Fed Website states, "The primary responsibility of the Board is formulation of monetary policy." However, it goes on. "The seven-member Board represent a majority of the twelve-member Federal Open Market Committee, the group that makes the key decisions affecting the cost and availability of money and credit in the economy." It seems that these board members are not appointed by our elected leaders, but by officers of the Bank, and simply approved by our leaders in a hollow, senseless ceremony.1 Many of the board members are also involved in other organizations. For example, the New York branch's president, William J. McDonough, is a member of the Council on Foreign Relations and the Trilateral Commission. Both of these organizations advocate the New World Order.2

Those interested in learning the actual intent and purposes of the Federal Reserve would be well served to read the book Mullins on the Federal Reserve. Eustace Mullins served in WWII and was educated at several American and overseas Universities. The book Mullins wrote was commissioned by Ezra Pound, a great American poet and writer held without trial as a political prisoner for thirteen years due to his criticisms of the Fed and his opposition to entering WWII. F.D. Roosevelt indicted Dr. Pound on the orders of Alger Hiss, both of whom were later discovered to have many Communist connections. Pound guided Mullins in

3

the writing.  No American publishing house initially accepted the book, and 10,000 copies were burned in Germany, which was lauded by James B. Conant, then President of Harvard University.  Eustace Mullins now enjoys full circulation of his book, which he researched and updated almost continuously for 50 years.3

What Eustace Mullins discovered was that a secret group had convened to plan the writing of the Federal Reserve Act.  The executors met at Georgia's famous Jekyll Island to draw up the plans for instituting what would become the Federal Reserve System.  Mullins writes, "I found that notwithstanding the successes in the Wars of Independence of 1812 against England, we (America) remained an economic and financial colony of Great Britain…we located the original stockholders of the Federal Reserve Banks and traced their parent companies back to the London Connection."

Mullins, in his exhaustive research, has come to the conclusion that the Federal Reserve "is not Federal; it has no reserves; and it is not a system at all, but rather, a criminal syndicate."  These are harsh words against the entity that runs all of the United States' monetary and credit policy.  The Federal Reserve is the organization that American taxpayers pay debt to, known as the American deficit.  The Fed has always been cloaked in secrecy, even from the first meetings by international bankers at the turn of the 19th century on Jekyll Island, Georgia.4

The Federal Reserve Bank of America is not a government entity.  It is a private corporation with stock owned by shareholders.  A majority of these shareholders are not American.

The prior paragraph is common knowledge by economists and professors, and can easily be found with minimal research.  With that knowledge, I will record a list of assaults against our Country implemented by the Federal Reserve and their elitist directors.  According to Mullins, the Fed is responsible for America entering WWI, the agricultural depression of the '20's, the Black Friday Crash of Wall Street in 1929, the Great Depression, WWII, the conversion of America's assets from real property to paper assets in 1945 which has caused America to go from the most prosperous nation in 1945 to the largest debtor nation since 1990. Knowing this, might it also be possible - nay, probable - that the Fed was also instrumental in the decision to go to war with Iraq? Time shall tell.

For many years, America was run on a debt-free money system. I have read that the American Revolution was not fought over taxation so much as it was a war over this monetary system. England and the international bankers wanted us to use their banks, and thus owe them debt and pay their interest. Americans had been printing Colonial Scrip money, which was debt-free.5 Our first Congress was divided on this issue, and the War for the Fed was waged. Besides a few attempts to establish central, monopolized banks, Americans, with the help of leaders like Jefferson and Jackson, were able to stave off a central reserve. Sadly, the bankers finally won in 1913. President Thomas Jefferson was a vicious and vocal opponent against this Federal Reserve System, and it would be prudent to quote his writings at this juncture pertaining to the Federal Reserve Bank. Jefferson said that the institution of a central bank was undertaken for these, among other, reasons.

*"1. To form the subscribers into a corporation.*
*2. To enable them to receive grants of land; and so far is against the laws of mort main.*
*3. To make alien subscribers capable of holding lands; and so far is against the law of alienage.*
*4. To transmit these lands...to a certain line of successors; and so far, changes the courses of descents.*
*...7. To give them the sole and exclusive right of banking, under the national authority; and so far is against the law of monopoly.*
*8. To communicate to them a power to make laws, paramount to the laws of the states..."*

Jefferson ends this full list by stating that his guiding light is the 10th Amendment, which all Americans should know. "That all powers not delegated to the United States, nor

5

prohibited to it by the states, are reserved to the states or to the people."

In closing, Jefferson: *"The incorporation of a bank...has not been delegated to the United States by the Constitution."*6

Another discovery made while researching the Federal Reserve was a Website entitled "Congressman McFadden on the Federal Reserve Corporation..." After perusing this, I recommend that all Americans read the full page (type "Astounding Exposure" into any search engine.) It begins: "On May 23, 1933, Congressman Louis T. McFadden brought formal charges against the Board of Governors of the Federal Reserve Board System, The Comptroller of the Currency and the Secretary of the United States Treasury for numerous criminal acts, including but not limited to, Conspiracy, Fraud, Unlawful Conversion, and Treason. The petition for Article of Impeachment was thereafter referred to the Judiciary Committee and has yet to be acted on." Yes, an elected Congressman essentially filed petition for a jury hearing stating the Federal Reserve was an unconstitutional and, furthermore, criminal institution. Yet, to this day, those charges languish without answer.7

Presently, there are many hints and rumors about the Fed. William J. McDonough, the Governor of the New York branch of America's Central Banking Web, is due to be replaced soon. In the Inner City Press it is stated that so far all appointments have been declined. If no one accepts the position, the first vice president, Jamie B Stewart Jr., will receive the post and is not granting interviews. Mr. Stewart was formerly a vice president of the Mellon Bank Corporation, with the Mellons being affiliated with the Rockefellers and the Rothchilds. The Inner City Press continues, "we were informed last week by the Federal Reserve Bank of Boston that 'you should be aware that the Federal Reserve Bank is not an agency of the federal government and is not subject to the Freedom of Information Act...'" This Inner City Press also quotes William Ryback, associate director of the Fed's Banking Supervision and Regulation (BS&R) division as saying that they have detected a lack inside the Fed in enforcing the anti-money-laundering laws.8

On the current deflation worries, Greg McBride, CFA points out in his column to the fact that the Fed is NOT worried about deflation, but wants to create an environment for long-term, low interest rates to encourage mortgage refinancing and corporate borrowing.9 This would cause more money to be owed to the Federal Reserve, therefore boosting their privately held shares. With the IRS as their policing agent, the Federal Reserve is bleeding the common taxpayer to enrich itself and fund its campaign to own every single cent of the money that it prints.

Another very interesting story is that of Navy Captain Gunther Russbacher, in his article "The Short Road to Chaos and Destruction: An Expose of the Federal Reserve Banking System." In the editor's note, we are privy to a short bio on Russbacher. He served three decades as a Naval Intelligence Officer and covert operative. "In 1980 Captain Russbacher flew then Vice President George Bush to a secret meeting in Paris in what has become known as 'The October Sunrise Scandal.' In 1989, Russbacher was to marry a reporter researching the scandal. He was told by his superiors not to wed her. When he did, he was immediately arrested and incarcerated until December, 1993. He was essentially a political prisoner during the first Bush administration. In his writings, Russbacher asserts that 300 families rule the world. It seems information was leaked to Russbacher about the then new American currency that caused him to begin to study the Fed. (Russbacher states that Congressman Ron Paul was also asking questions about the new printings.) Russbacher further claims that several countries at the time were planning new currency. These currencies have several similarities, including a filament strip that is detectable at airports. "Rumor had it that these currencies would later receive a common image linking them together in an international monetary system." He also wrote from his prison cell, that "the chance of bypassing the new currencies and going directly to an electronic (cashless) system are increasingly exponential." The cashless system will make it much easier to track us, the bankers' human resource. There is so much more in Captain

Russbacher's essay, and I recommend it highly to all.10

    Robert Gaylon Ross, Sr. is a distinguished, deaconly-looking man who writes books. During his illustrious life he graduated with a B.S. in Industrial Engineering, and served as a 1st Lt. in the Army branch of the National Security Agency, an early version of the CIA. He served in the Korean War, giving him an absolute patriotic credential. Inside the cover of his highly commendable book, <u>The Elite Serial Killers of Lincoln, JFK, RFK, and MLK,</u> former intelligence officer Ross bares the cold, undeniable truth about the Rothschild and Rockefeller's use of groups such as the Bilderbergs, Council on Foreign Relations, and earlier in history, the Freemasons. They were to foment chaos and better implant their insidious monetary policy based on a backed-by-thin-air theory to enslave Americans and the World. Ross claims that the War of 1812 was actually the Rothschild family's attempt at re-colonizing America wielding their enforcer, mighty England. Our own elected leaders brought about our "punishment." The crime? Doing a damn fine job of keeping European banks out of the country and becoming a World Power with the ingenuity and hard work of Americans. We defeated Rothschild and the other Aristocratic families of power. However, in the end, it is we who have been overpowered. To the list of atrocities perpetrated by the Fed and World bankers listed by Eustace Mullins, Ross adds the following: the Bolshevik and French Revolutions, as well as the Opium Wars and modern drug trafficking. To summarize, Ross writes, "Most of the Rothschild fortune came from financing both sides of just about every war on earth since about 1860." Again, I ask, "Could this also have something to do with the war in Iraq?" Read Ross's book to see the evidence supporting an Illuminati conspiracy to kill our great leaders.11

    In closing, it is easy for anyone with the remotest computer ability to log onto the web or go to a library and discover the corrupt, corporate, secret workings of the Federal Reserve Bank. Private, mostly foreign owners whose interests lay in a different reality than our own hold its shares. Almost every modern secret society is behind the scenes of the inner sanctum, including the CFR, Trilateral Commission, and Skull

& Bones. There are rumblings among prominent governmental and academic personnel saying that the Fed is planning to depress the United States monetary system to a point of no return. This design correlates with the implementation of the Eurodollar, which these foreign bankers would be better served to have as the leading currency on Earth. With Europe's currency trading at about 1.30 to the dollar, it seems they have been successful. As an author, a political critic, and as an American, I beseech each and every person reading this to write every one of your political representatives to rid our society from the scourge of the Federal Reserve. There will be a day of reckoning for the disastrous borrowing and spending that Americans are inclined to do. It can't last forever. Forswear credit cards. Never take out a loan except for house and car. Then, and only then, can we demand that Congress quit borrowing from the Federal Reserve.

# Webs of Power - Chapter 2: U.S. Department of Agriculture

Why is it that a small majority of the intrusive and arguably unconstitutional government agencies were created under Lincoln, Wilson, or FDR? Furthermore, why is it that these Presidents are consistently listed as the best Presidents in our History? I find it horrendous that any U.S. Presidents who would institute a gargantuan Federal Government and create organizations that essentially suspend the Bill of Rights or endorse banks that manipulate our economic system would be deemed anything other than traitors. The United Stated Department of Agriculture found birth under The Great Emancipator, Abraham Lincoln. Since that time, the family farm has become the stuff of legends and giant agricultural conglomerates have taken control of our food supply. Money is often allocated to pay these corporations to NOT plant food. Scientific knowledge that would ensure the end of starvation is NOT implemented. For, what would a Web of Power be without an office to control our agricultural destruction with the farming and ranching profits lavished on a select, chosen few.

USDA.gov is the Department of Agriculture's tax funded website. The USDA was created in the 1860s under Lincoln, and since its meager beginnings has grown into a bureaucratic behemoth that has put thousands of family farms out of business while allowing the acquisition of land by the government and elite farming corporations. I have seen it first hand, first as my Grandfather had to sell off most his land piece by piece to pay the ever increasing property taxes and obey new legal restrictions. Now, as my Dad tries to raise a few head of cattle and a meager crop, I watch the yearly battle with the tax office and his grumbling about price fixing amongst the larger companies. The U.S. Department of Agriculture touts its failed welfare programs, their illegal acquisition of real estate (30% of America is owned by the Fed, by their own number,) the unsuccessful safekeeping of

10

meat and poultry, and the outright lie to keep an open market for the U.S. in their list of accomplishments. This is acceptable, due to the disclaimer at the end of the USDA's site. "Effort has been made to provide accurate and complete information. However, we cannot guarantee that there will be no errors."1

The United States Department of Agricultural oversees a multitude of other departments, including the Foreign Agricultural Service, Food and Nutrition Service, and Economic Research Services. And, once again, almost every branch has been involved in some alleged corruption or another. On July 27, 2000, the Inspector General of the USDA, Roger C. Viadero, testified that USDA graders had been manipulating the produce marketing through bribery and extortion.2 Also, the USDA has levied a hog tax on Midwest farmers that is so debilitating, a petition of almost 20,000 people was signed and taken to Congress. In a typical slap in the face of America's backbone, Congress said they must verify petition votes before hearing the farmers at all. Unfortunately for the farmers, Congress has no process to check and insure all signatories of a petition are hog farmers. Thus, Congress won't even answer to the redress of grievances.3, 4

Tad Williams of the Americans for Democratic Action Education Fund published a few telling statistics. There were more than 6 million farms only 60 years ago. Due to the rise of the quasi-monopolistic farming conglomerates, that number has dwindled to fewer than two million. I estimate a loss of over 600,000 farms per decade. My family's land has produced beef and produce for over 50 years under the Fortman name. Yet, it is destined to become a statistic, unless I decide to enter into the fray of small town politics, unjust property taxes, federal regulations, and the like. Williams goes on to write that "the bulk of agriculture's profits accrue to only a few hundred super farms." In fact, most if not all of food sector industries are controlled by a few corporations. He concludes a fact that I have witnessed first hand in rural Texas: "As the companies have flourished, rural communities have suffered economic, social, and environmental effects of concentration, merger, and vertical integration."5

I will skip right to the point, and give factual documentation to support my theory: the USDA is another extension of the North American branch outposts of the New World Order. There are only two reasons that a ruling class would want their cronies in agriculture to own vast percentages of American and Global food supplies. One, to make money. Two, to have agents already enmeshed in the supply chain so that when FEMA legally enforces its right to control our staples the process will be streamlined. To control food and water, one must subjugate landholders to the status of vassals in a fiefdom. And, the hard facts prove that that is what is happening. The despicable Farm Bill of 2002, signed into law by President Bush, allocates vast amounts of taxpayers' dollars into the bank accounts of a small group of conglomerate farmers, most of who are already millionaires.6 I can assure you that my father, Edwin K. Fortman, and his tiny ranch didn't see a penny of that compensation. What's worse, he is a disabled veteran of the Vietnam conflict, living on a pension of not quite middle class means. He insists that he would give up all the money that he has earned by being wounded while serving his country if only our government would end the unjust taxation of everything except air.

Racially speaking, African-Americans have been discriminated against in agriculture, as they have been in most industries. In 1964, a study commissioned by the Johnson Administration revealed an almost blanket discrimination against black farmers by the Department of Agriculture.7 Regrettably, as recently as 2000, the Land Loss Prevention Project and Black Farmers and Agriculturalists Association plan on filing a class action lawsuit against the USDA for discriminatory practices. Black farms have declined approximately 70% in the last 25 years. In 1999, the USDA settled a lawsuit with black farmers, but by then, it was too late. Most their farms had been lost. So much for forty acres and a mule.

Investigative journalist Che Green sets forward a not-so-new premise in his LiP article.8 He says that the U.S.

Department of Agriculture is in fact run by the same CEO's that own the conglomerate farms and ranches. Therefore, they have presented a flawed food pyramid so that we will buy the products they are growing. In particular is the USDA suggestion that three servings of milk a day should be standard. Yet, Amy Lanou Ph.D., the nutrition director of the Physician's Committee for Responsible Medicine asserts, "Beside prostrate cancer, milk has been linked to asthma, anemia, allergies, juvenile-onset diabetes, obesity, heart disease, and ovarian and breast cancer." So, the stuff they pump us up with is in actuality a steady diet of cancer-giving poison. I can attest to the fact that once dairy left my diet two years ago, my gastronomic and overall health has improved greatly. This would mean that their insistence that red meat and milk are good when it is actually detrimental to our health is a ploy. It is a ploy to keep us sick and our minds malleable. From fluoride in the drinking water to milk for our cereal, they are making sure that we are not healthy, physically or mentally.

Also in the news, the USDA seems to be remiss in imposing sanctions on meat plants that do not follow Animal Cruelty Laws.9 This from the Washington Post.9 The U.S. Department of Agriculture has also made groups associated with Freemasonry immune from being scrutinized for animal cruelty and use of illegal exotic animals. The Shriner Circus and Shrine Temple is an economic generator and purportedly a pagan house of worship. At Freemasonry Watch, it is given as fact that only 1% of the Shriner Circus's profit was donated to medical research or children's health. The majority went to funding Freemason syndicates. Nor are the Shriners held to the same standard as filmmakers or zoos when it comes to animal cruelty, as can be seen behind the scenes of one of their events.10

The USDA does not only discriminate against people of color. Employees at the Forest Service, an affiliate of the Department of Agriculture, have brought accusations of a hostile work environment being provided for Christians. They have been ridiculed, ostracized, and generally harassed. Sadly, this is not the only government organization charged with a detrimental environment to Christian heritage.11 The Federal Government has a duty to never endorse religion or lack thereof, but does not have the right to stifle free speech. Blatant discrimination is another matter all together. Could it be that Freemasonry's overt denouncement of Christianity has subtly found a place in the USDA, an organization with many past and present members being involved in Freemasonry? Are Zionists involved, as America saw the 2003 Christmas (or should I say X-Mas) bring about the criminality of Christian scenes and icons, even as a huge increase in the viewing of other religious icons and symbols was deemed acceptable. Furthermore, I contend that many segments of the higher government have been on a campaign to secularize the country. Throw Daniel into the lions' den.

I recently read a great article by Randy Lavello entitled "The Great Deception".12 He manages to take several complex subjects and put them into simple terms, making the concepts much easier to understand. One of the enlightening subjects that he was able to bring into focus for me is the dichotomy of individualism versus collectivism. In essence, what he wrote was that a collectivist believes the group is more important than the individual. Of course, an individualist believes the opposite. There would be no group without each individual; and each individual entering or leaving the group affects the group dynamic. Lavello further puts these two philosophies into ideological concepts. An individualist believes that each person is the most sacred part of society, and therefore government is mostly instituted to protect the individual. Collectivists, on the other hand, believe that a group must be formed to overcome all obstacles. The bigger the obstacle, the bigger the group. So, a world government is the answer to the biggest problems, by a collectivist's theory. At least until we meet alien life, at which time we will need to form our first intergalactic government to solve cosmic problems.

The problem with collectivism in regards to politics is this: collectivist-style governments create obstacles. They do not overcome them. The larger the group, or government, the more obstacles it sets up, whether inadvertently or no. We can't get the city council of even the smallest communities to do their job: roads are in disrepair, taxes are too high, social services are too low. As we progress up this chain, we come to the state level, wherein ineffectiveness and corruption become compounded. In my own State of Texas, it seems we can't even get the Democrats and Republicans to meet at the same place due to supposed differences in zoning theories. (My opinion is that the Democratic walkout of 2003 in the Texas House was a directive ordered by someone in the White House. Bush is from Texas. This kept the media and United States' eyes off of Iraq, and perpetuated the old Donkey versus Elephant trick to divide our nation once again.) The next stop on the elevator of collectivist politics is national government. Our U.S. Government is not different than other countries' governments. It is riddled with deceit, lies, corruption, family aristocracies, secret societies, and just a general ineffectuality in administering anything to the public besides fear and brainwashing.

This brings us back to the United States Department of Agriculture. As the belief in collectivism took hold slowly throughout the 20th Century, people began to clamor for bigger government to solve their problems. As proof of that, just look at the rise in American welfare and handouts starting with the New Deal. Many farmers welcomed the USDA as a means of stabilizing sporadic markets and defending against falling crop prices. Unfortunately, after over 100 years, the USDA has compounded the problems of the average farmer. They are, in fact, making the average farmer extinct. Why is this? you might ask. The average farmer is an INDIVIDUAL. They are one person, working the land, making a living. Would it not be better, the collectivist logic implies, if we took all of the farms and turned them over to a large group, and created one large American farm? Possibly so, if the large groups and this farm could elevate agricultural output so as to stop starvation and bring a stable market. Well, the USDA has not done that. They have given us untested bio-engineered staples, while still a majority of the World continues to go hungry. The CEOs of the farming companies ante up millions of dollars to campaign coffers. Then they are appointed to the

Department of Agriculture's hierarchy. After that, the CEOs, under the guise of federal employees, pass laws that benefit their crops, their farms, and their bank accounts. They spray the food with whatever chemicals they can without alerting too many of the public. They experiment with genetic alterations using the population at large as a vast resource of human guinea pigs. They continue to underpay their workers, fail to provide insurance or medical coverage except to themselves and the other affluent, connected administrators, and employ a largely illegal workforce. The list goes on. Could not these conglomerate farm owners cum USDA board members have something to do with Bush's proposed amnesty policy. It would give them 14 million legal indentured servants. Ghastly.

While I'm writing this, another family farm goes bankrupt in a manipulated economic downturn. A friend of these manipulators will buy that farm and add it to his vast collection of other little farms across the country. What does he care of rising taxes and idiotic government restrictions. He does not adhere to these rules. And the individual farmer and his family pack it up and leave. They fed us, yet no one will feed them. This downtrodden family may or may not be educated; but, they are skilled labor. They know seasons and seed, farming equipment, and animal husbandry. Yet, there are no jobs such as these in the big cities they will be forced to live in in order to eke out a meager existence. The United States Department of Agriculture was remiss in not stopping this phenomenon. In actuality, the USDA has enabled and even steered things. We are going down their chosen path, and for the United States Department of Agriculture, there are no surprises.

## Webs of Power - Chapter 3: Federal Emergency Management Agency

The Federal Emergency Management Agency (FEMA) was an independent Federal entity until the U.S. Government under the Homeland Security Act incorporated it in 2003. Officially, FEMA is responsible for "responding to, planning for, recovering from, and mitigating against disasters." It would behoove our Country to have such a department, for the United States has its own fair share of disasters, both natural and synthetic. Until 2003, the U.S. had simply passed fragmented legislation to confront natural disasters as they came up. The actual history of a first FEMA-like Bill was the Congressional Act of 1803 that provided help with a fire in a New Hampshire town. This piecemeal lawmaking continued until 1979, when Jimmy Carter authorized the joining of several independent disaster agencies, thus creating the Federal Emergency Management Agency. It was at this time that civil defense responsibilities were bequeathed to the new agency. This information is published by FEMA. No mention is made in their literature as to why President Carter allowed the newly created FEMA to become an independent Federal agency, or why it was given a more militaristic role during his administration.1

Most government agencies have had accusations of corruption and claims of unconstitutionality levied against them. The Federal Emergency Management Agency is no exception. This is complicated by the fact that because FEMA was autonomous until 2001, it was not required to disclose information to the public. Political journalist, Harry V. Martin, reports in the Free America journal. "(FEMA) has the power to suspend laws, move entire populations, arrest and detain citizens without a warrant and hold them without trial, it can seize property, food supplies, transportation systems and can suspend the Constitution." These are serious charges. Martin states that the sole purpose of FEMA is to save top-ranking politicos and their family members during any unforeseen chaotic future. Unlike the CIA and our Military, the Federal Emergency Management Agency was not responsible to Congress until it became part of Homeland Security. However, the Homeland Security Department is simply a nationalization of our police forces. Furthermore, the police are melding with the military. As proof that FEMA has the power to forego the Constitution, Martin lists the Executive Orders associated with FEMA. In addition to the aforementioned charges, which are allowed by Executive Orders, are other atrocities to the Constitution.2

*"Executive Order 11000 allows the government to mobilize citizens into work brigades under government supervision.*

*Executive Order 11002 allows the Post Master General to operate a national registration of all persons.*

*Executive Order 11051 specifies the responsibilities of the Office of Emergency Planning and gives authorization to put all Executive Orders into effect in times of increased international tensions and economic or financial crisis.*

*Executive Order 11921 Allows the Federal Emergency Management Agency to develop plans to establish control over the mechanisms of production and distribution, of energy sources, wages, salaries, credit and the flow of money in U.S. financial institutions in any undefined national emergency. It also provides that when a state of emergency is declared by the President, Congress cannot review the action for six months."*3

To summarize: Through a series of Executive Orders (i.e. not voted on,) the President may simply dictate a state of emergency which is not subject to critique or question for half a year. At that point, FEMA will be allowed to take over everything, including the day-to-day functions of our lives. We will have to register with a local census weekly, accept food doled out by the government, work in enforced work crews, adhere to curfews, and yield to major infringements on our civil liberties. Martin concludes that during a state of emergency declared solely by a President, FEMA would become the most powerful entity in America.

Apparently, the Federal Emergency Management Agency is to administrate martial law for any President who is willing to invoke its vast powers. However benign the executive orders were (and I now believe that these orders were anything but benign) - however benign they may have been, the orders are dangerous, were not voted on, and if exploited would bring about the total eradication of life as we know it.

Probably the hottest topic regarding FEMA right now is the agency's supposed erection of empty interment camps in America along with appropriated funds to operate a civilian labor force inside these camps. On August 8, The *Wall Street Journal* reported, "the Goose Creek, South Carolina facility now has a special wing to house about 20 U.S citizens if the government were to deem them enemy combatants." Under the recently passed Patriot Act I, 'enemy combatant' is esoterically defined. Enemy combatants can be held without charges, or a court hearing. Jonathan Turley, a professor of constitutional law and defense attorney in national security cases, insists that "the proposed camp plan should trigger immediate Congressional hearings and reconsideration of Ashcroft's fitness for important office." It should also be noted that Turley defended Ashcroft in his highly debated appointment as Attorney General.4

Al Cuppett is a retired military officer, decorated with the Bronze Star and Purple Heart, and spent six years on the Joint Chiefs of Staff. He has presented documented proof that FEMA was placed under Homeland Security through orders from the Trilateral Commission, and will be the reigning agency during a predestined state of emergency. He proves that the Federal Emergency Management Agency has been given interment prison facilities and the power to round up U.S. citizens to fill them. Cuppett presents the official government policy report, State Department Publication 7277, entitled "Freedom From War: United States Guideline for General and Complete Disarmament in a Peaceful World."

This policy, written by top-ranking military hawks and politicians from both sides of the aisle, proposes to completely dismantle the U.S. Military and disarm all civilians. All weapons will be forfeited to the United Nations. It allows for an armed national police force - much like the proposed Homeland Security - to keep the public peace, while answering exclusively to the U.N. It will be necessary for these enforcement agents to fire on Americans. Cuppett claims that Chinese, Russian, and European forces have been quietly disseminating throughout the United States under the U.N. umbrella for this very reason.5 Chinese and Russians, it seems, would have no problem taking away our guns under threat of death. Alex Jones videotaped foreign military performing urban assault "exercises." During the practice, these soldiers went into houses, rounded up Americans, and put them in pens. They ignored the cries from the prisoners. "This is against my constitutional rights!" Why were the foreigners trained in America with these kind of exercises?6 Cuppett and Jones assert that one of the planned advantages of a secret police force in Waco was to get the public used to masked officers, therefore making it easier to hide foreigners" identities while posing as law enforcement. Pertaining to actual numbers, Michael F. Rivero has written a list of all confirmed executive orders pertaining to FEMA. He asserts that 43 interment camps are already up and running. In total, each camp could house over 30,000 Americans. These camps are already manned with guards, but are currently empty. Why? And why would retired Officer Al Cuppett, *former member of the Joint Chiefs of Staff*, try to warn Americans of a coming police state? Is he angry with his former employers? He did not need money. The Illuminati's military-industrial complex had already paid him very well, indeed. Furthermore, too few Americans care to read dissenting views for him to have made much money. Maybe he loves his country. Maybe he is willing to risk ridicule and threats because he wants us to know. With the elites' past, Cuppett must realize that assassination was and is a distinct possibility for any opposition.

Through a wealth of independent reports by a diverse

array of authors come words of impending martial law in America. This author does not profess to see the future. Certainly, laws have been incrementally passed that would make martial law much easier to establish. The passing of Patriot Act I definitely allows our government to completely sidestep the Constitution if they so desired. Why would Congress pass such laws? As stated prior, many of these laws are Executive Orders, so the President used exclusive power without Congress's consent. Republican Ron Paul, one of the only members of Congress to vote against the Patriot Act, said that our Representatives were not even allowed to read the legislation before a vote was taken.7 Congressman Paul is of the opinion that all proposals must past a test of Constitutionality. How does one test for anything if one isn't allowed to even read the scheme? Thus was Paul's vote nay. In theory, if this hodgepodge of Executive Orders and Laws united under Homeland Security were to be utilized by a President, a completely fascist, Hitlerian, Communistic state could be imposed on America in a relatively short period of time. This is not news. A character on the X Files spoke these telling words during one episode. Scully turns to his partner and declares. "FEMA allows the White House to suspend constitutional government upon declaration of national emergency. It allows creation of a non-elected government. Think about that, Mulder." Think about that, Mulder.8

In reference to actual natural disasters, reports of the Federal Emergency Management Agency's incompetence abound. The amount of money spent on disaster awareness pamphlets must have been immense, though. There are lists of things to do that citizens can read to be aware of options during a disaster, little of which includes the assistance of FEMA. Lagging response times and unavailability of information are the two main complaints. In fact, it seems that at present, besides building concentration camps, the only thing FEMA does is hand out money for public buildings after a disaster actually happens. Also available are tax dollars for crisis counseling. Brian A. Dominick reported as early as 1998 in *Peace Newsletter* that only 6% of funds earmarked for disasters were actually used for disaster relief. The remaining balance is spent to gather information on political dissidents, to build prison-style holding facilities, and to undertake martial law exercises. He reports that since 1998 Congress and FEMA have discontinued any disclosure of expenditures by hurriedly moving talks into "reserved sessions."9 James Bovard, in his book <u>Feeling Your Pain</u>, writes that $712,000 was given to 200 FEMA paraprofessionals to go door-to-door and listen to victims of the North Dakota Floods of 1997. The professionals were and are gathering data to be stored in DARPA's citizen information banks.10

The United States would definitely be a more unified and sympathetic nation by helping our disaster-stricken countrymen. The Federal Emergency Management Agency is hailed as the savior of this cause. Unfortunately, too few of our tax dollars are spent on the effort to provide shelter and food to natural disaster victims. By Executive Orders, FEMA has become a tool by which a fascist America can bring about martial law. Prisons have been constructed to house Americans under this agency. Foreign troops have been imported under this agency. Training exercises have been practiced in which a mock national police force raids U.S. citizens' homes and takes them into custody without warrants. Strategic planning has been devised so that the government, through FEMA, will be able to take over business, money, and labor in America. All the ingredients are being put into place for a hostile takeover. It is this author's opinion that the next step will be an assault on our 2nd Amendment rights. Our right to bear arms is sacred, yet we are clearly aware that our government can infringe upon this right. Recently, President George W. Bush endorsed the current Clinton assault rifle ban, against the wishes of one of his largest supporters, the NRA. This ban also includes most military apparatus needed by state militias for protection against a foreign force attempting to dispose of the Constitution by suspending the Bill of Rights and rounding up Americans for forced labor camps. To add insult to injury, the NRA was implicated in a deal that would pledge the group to a registry for handguns. In exchange, they will be precluded from litigation for gun responsibility. I have been unable to prove this, but the word on the ground is not good. Make sure and write your national and state headquarters to make sure the National Rifle Association continues to be a harbinger of justice to the plight of the 2nd Amendment and gun ownership in America.11  Or, do what I did, and join a more dedicated group. I became a member of Gun Owners of America, the "no compromise" gun lobby.

It is probably acceptable for FEMA to give priority to saving the President, both Houses, and other senior officials during a national crisis. However, under no circumstances should American citizens be detained without being allowed the due process of law. Simple things. For example, the right to defend ourselves in front of a jury of our peers, and to have representation should never be curtailed. Patriot Act II - blocked in part by widespread public sentiment against the infringement of too many civil liberties - would finish the job Patriot Act I set out to do, and destroy the 4th Amendment. Under part II, it would be illegal for officers or agents to inform anyone of your whereabouts if the police state were to take you in. So, you can be kidnapped, detained, executed. All without a trial. In fact, if any of the police that took you in tells that they took you in, that police officer will be incarcerated or executed.12, 13  These are draconian laws meant for places like Russia and China, not something to be considered by the Home of the Brave and the Land of the Free.

In conclusion, it is pertinent that we petition our Representatives to overturn all executive orders that give FEMA power other than disaster relief. Also, as a government entity under Homeland Security, public disclosure of all economic and civil activity should be reported yearly by FEMA. Finally, the Federal Emergency Management Agency, as a federally funded entity, must be made to swear allegiance to the protection of every American citizen under any and all circumstances.

# Webs of Power - Chapter 4: Department of Defense

Logic would suggest that the Department of Defense (DoD) is the federal agency charged with defending America. It is, in fact, in charge of our military, not necessarily defense. The DoD is housed in the gargantuan building/city, the Pentagon. The infamous Donald Rumsfeld currently heads it. That is what I knew when I began to peruse the "DoD 101" section of the Defense Department's historical literature. The first four bullet points on the site tell a different story about the Department of Defense than merely defense. It claims it is the...

*"Oldest Company*
*Largest Company*
*Busiest Company*
*Most Successful Company"*

I'll say.

The Defense Department's evolution begins with the creation of the Army, Navy, and Marines in 1775, until all armed forces were morphed into a the Department of Defense in 1945. In total, the DoD claims 1.4 million on active duty, over 650,000 civilians employed, 1.2 million guard and reserves, and 2 million veterans and their families garnishing benefits. It brags of 6,000 bases and 30 million acres "used." It has locations in 146 countries encompassing almost 90% of available global landmass, with a half million people either overseas or afloat. The Department of Defense has the world's largest budget and revenue; with Wal-Mart, Exxon/Mobil, GM, and Ford straggling behind. They state that they are accruing the country's best and brightest minds. At the moment the chief CEO of the defense "business" is President George Bush. In the words of the Defense Department: "Who we work for...Chief Executive Officer...The President of the United States of America."[1]

So with all this money, with all these intelligent employees, with all this land, and with control of all these countries - what are we being defended from? I know that conservatives will argue all day that we need this humongous military to protect ourselves. (Again, I ask, from what specifically?). I don't buy it anymore. So, what has the Department of Defense done during its tenure?

The military was first created to fight the tyrannical English forces. During the Civil War, federal troops were used to keep the nation united and to free slaves. In WWI and WWII, it seems that we fought to help England and to save the Jews. This has been refuted, but we will accept the statement for now. By the time of Vietnam, our soldiers were demoted to the role of "peace keepers," killing to protect U.S. interests, otherwise known as oil and rubber. Lyndon Baines Johnson was proven to have had millions invested in drilling off the coast of Southeast Asia.2 Kind of like the Cheney/Halliburton/Iraq deal. I'll dedicate a paragraph or two to the DoD's Central and South American forays, later. Those atrocities deserve special attention. By the '90's, our military was fighting under the globalist NATO banner in Yugoslavia, siding with Muslims to destroy Christians! Finally, Phillip K. Dick's pre-crimes unit has come to life on a military scale, with the Department of Defense's preemptive attack against Iraq.

It would be prudent to explore the DoD's involvement in the Americas. Canada gets a pass, possibly because they are white, and have a global voice. Mexico, too, receives much benefit from being bordered next to the U.S. Unfortunately for the rest of Central and South America, the American military has become more than a nuisance, and in some cases the "peace keepers' have been involved in not quite war; nevertheless murder, and human rights violations. If I were Hispanic, I would hate my country and me.

Throughout my travels, it seems that Americans have a unique sense of revenge that is not exercised by Latin cousins. Lucky for us. Many U.S. citizens have a hard time understanding that our military has participated in the coup de tats of democratically elected Socialists (Socialist, a definition that could be given to many of our own politicians.) These coups are beneficial in many ways to "American interests." (I love the term "American interests." As if 97% of middleclass and poor Americans ever benefit from bloodshed during the protection of American interests.) Many people have a difficult time understanding that our military demolishes governments instituted by the citizens of other countries. I know it seems strange to us that other nations would actually vote in a populist, or Communist leader. What we don't get is that Communism, in its purest form, should benefit the people. I disagree with the philosophy. But that doesn't mean I want my country to stage bloody battles to oust Communist Presidents that were elected by a majority. The film "Salvador" by Oliver Stone is a fine example of the arguments for and against staging wars in Central and South America.3

So, who are these puppet leaders that we prop up to enforce "democracy" after we overthrow democratically elected regimes? Well, by and large they are men who have shown leadership abilities inside their respective borders. These men are sent to a very fine training program that teaches American policy and tactics for holding power. The training comes from the School of the Americas (SOA), an academy provided by the Department of Defense. The School of the Americas teaches things like how to assassinate your elected opponent; the best ways to terrorize your citizenry; how to corrupt your cabinet and military. Sound outlandish? Well, it's true. School of the Americas Watch is a group dedicated to ending the despicable training of the academy. They report that the SOA name was changed in 2001 to darken the spotlight that has been shining on the school more and more. The new name is Western Hemisphere Institute for Security Cooperation, but School of the Americas Watch refers to them as the "School of Assassins." SOA was originally located in Panama, but was expelled the first year that country was given back its autonomy. Today, they train at Fort Benning, Georgia. School of the Americas Watch claims that over 60,000 men have been trained by our military at the academy, including Qadafi, Noriega, and lesser known scoundrels. They add that the sniper, counter-insurgency, and PSYOPS training have been consistently used "to wage war against their own people. Among those targeted by SOA graduates are educators, union organizers, religious workers, student leaders and others that work for the poor." The populist professors and activists they target for reeducation or death sound like far-left Democrats to me. Can you imagine training people to harass and kill Democrats in America. Ridiculous. That is what we, America, through the Department of Defense, are endorsing against our Latin neighbors. Yes, I believe that Democrats are misguided, and shouldn't give away the money of hard-working middle-class. But, I vote against them. I don't train men to take them out. "From the beginning, the mission of the SOA has been to protect the interests of multi-national corporations" and the assets of a few, select, rich elite in America, says SOA watch. Clinton raised Columbia's status to one of the largest foreign recipients of tax dollars ($1.3 billion) when he provided aid for the Drug War. Always that nasty Drug War. Human Rights Watch has documentation proving that Columbians trained at the School of the Americas are committing atrocities against their own countrymen. Repeat that for Guatemala.4, 5

The History Channel ran a show on their series "The Fifties", about Eisenhower, the military, United Fruit and Guatemala. Our military staged a coup of the elected Communist leader and put in someone who would keep profits of Guatemalan bananas going to United Fruit instead of the Guatemalans. The military even went so far as to videotape staged battles and other events to dupe the American public, and to garner favor at home. It worked. The country side was ravaged, the elected leader was ousted, and relatively little flack was taken by our military for disregarding human rights, democracy, and just plain good sense. A list of crimes by SOA members can be found quite easily. The crimes many School of the Assassins candidates have been alleged, charged, and found guilty of are drug trafficking, torture, kidnapping, assassination, murder, rape, mistreating prisoners, issuing unconstitutional decrees, and on, and on, and on.6, 7

Another Department of Defense monstrosity is the Defense Advanced Research Projects Agency (DARPA), established in 1958. This is an agency used to test new systems and technologies for the military, and to keep us ahead in the killing game.10  Some of the ideas coming out of the department are just plain crazy, though.  In 2003, a plan for DARPA's Terrorism Futures Market was uncovered.  On "Wall Street Week", Geoff Colvin called the scheme "placing bets on how you think things will turn out...whether a war will start by March."  The program would allow "experts" to speculate on what terrorist acts may happen in the future and gain money for being correct, much like a sports bet or the stock market.8  What no one mentioned, and the problem I had with the system, was this: If you allow elite to bet on terrorism, won't they have a vested interest in making sure that the predicted act will happen.  If Muhammad or Ian has $1 million speculating that the U.S. Embassy in Beijing will be hit with a truck bomb within a year, all he has to do is pay Momar or Randall ten percent, $100,000, to plant the bomb.  Then they win a million.  Now, if I can come up with this scenario, why can't the intellectuals at DARPA?  The Information Awareness Office (IAO) is a new department launched by DARPA under the DoD umbrella.9  The original logo for the Information Awareness Office had the Illuminati symbol of a pyramid with the all-seeing eye, looking down over all of planet Earth.  Like the disappearance of this powerful, Freemason symbol from the American Dollar, IAO has deleted their logo.  Too many conspiracy theories, I guess.  One of the goals of the Information Awareness Office is to create a database for every member of the Union, keeping tabs on our health, criminal, and financial histories.10  Even the tiniest details are being data-mined for IAO, including every economic transaction you ever partake in, your television and movie viewing habits, and what magazines and books you read.  An offshoot of IAO is TIA, or Total Information Awareness.11  George W. Bush appointed former Admiral John Poindexter to head this department.  He did this despite the fact that Poindexter has been convicted of at least five felonies, including fraud.  I don't know about you, but I don't like the idea of a felon and a defrauder looking over my life with a fine tooth comb.  Even Bush was forced to terminate Poindexter after his exposed futures market scheme. But, the fact that our President would appoint such a man tells us much about Bush, his administration, and the Department of Defense. Total Information Awareness is designed to keep records of all Internet activity, among other things. Of course, this caused an uproar. Now the office is called "Terrorism Information Awareness." As if changing one word changes the entire meaning.

The Department of Defense absorbs 2/3 to 3/4 of America's entire yearly budget.12 With that kind of money, it is not so easy to keep up with the thousands of projects they have taken on. There is a definite need for a military, and for the defense of America. No one refutes that. The first directive of the Federal Government is to protect us. I believe that if we cut the annual budget of the Defense Department by approximately one half, we can build a stronger, more defensive military. That would mean that all projects or operations designed to benefit the elite or designed to take away civil liberties should be terminated. We will be able to cut the cost and scope of the armed services. We should bring soldiers home, where they can protect our shores and borders, not the borders of Iraq or Afghanistan. The extra money can either go back to the middle-class and poor working people of America, or we can use it to pay down the debt. If we were to do this, we would again be a country with a savings account instead of being in debt up to our eyeballs (past our eyeballs.) In conclusion, though, the most important reason that we should discontinue the unconstitutional programs of the DoD, like the School of the Americas and Total Information Awareness, is that Americans are going down in the History books as a bunch of wasteful, apathetic villains.

Is that what we want the world to know about us in one hundred or one thousand years?

## Webs of Power - Chapter 5: Bureau of Citizenship and Immigration Services

The Bureau of Citizenship and Immigration Services (BCIS) is a morphing of the two departments formerly known as the Immigration and Naturalization Service (INS) and the Border Patrol. Furthermore, this BCIS was absorbed, along with several other agencies, by the new Homeland Security Department. This was a directive from President Bush on March 1, 2003. There is good reason for the department to change its moniker. In fact, because of inhumane and unjust actions, the BCIS has formerly had many different aliases. The roots of the Bureau of Citizenship and Immigration Services can be traced to racist soil. Even the BCIS publicly admits that the genesis law for the department was "the Chinese Exclusion Act of 1882 and Alien Contract Labor Laws of 1885 and 1887." The BCIS confesses that these laws "prohibited certain laborers from entering the United States." Some people do not believe in discriminating when allowing individuals into our country. Give us your weary. For those that want closed borders, I say this: no immigration law or agency has decreased the rising number of immigrants that cross our borders every year. None has protected either U.S. citizens living adjacent to Mexico or the unfortunate refugees crossing north for economic freedom. While I am not advocating an open border, I am asking for a review of the policies that are now in place.1

Once again we reach a victory of collectivists over individualists. Regrettably, the individualists are in the right but have lost. As I understood from reading the columnist Randy Lavello, collectivists seek the answers to problems by forming groups, or collections of people. The bigger the problem, the larger the group should be. Individualists believe that the larger the group, the higher the chance of corruption and ineptness. History proves the latter to be true. However, the Bush Administration has decided to pursue the collectivist course and create the behemoth Homeland Security

Department and the Bureau of Citizenship and Immigration Services. I live in Texas, and have been involved in real estate and the restaurant industry. I can assure you that the INS has never, since 1986 when I started working, cracked down on immigration. To the contrary, illegal immigration has risen. The laws have gotten more restrictive and the agencies larger, yet illegal and legal immigration is a mess in the U.S. Let us try to make things simpler and more practical, less obtrusive. We should just experiment with that. Instead, Homeland Security has been instituted. We shall see the outcome, to the dismay of many who hailed it originally. As it stands, the INS never employed more than 8,000 agents until the 1970s. Now, there are over 30,000 BCIS workers. Why has the flow of immigration not been dammed in direct correlation? If this were a business, we'd be searching for the break down, and then retraining. Termination would be waiting for those that could not show results. There are plenty of people who would love a government job with a cushy retirement and medical insurance.

To make matters even more complicated, Homeland Security's Border and Transportation Security was formed. This department will enforce the laws, absorbing Border Patrol agents and employees from the U.S. Customs Service. The Bureau of Citizenship and Immigration Services will concentrate on the administrative duties, such as finding American jobs to give away and helping immigrants use taxpayer money for housing and education.

The Bureau of Citizenship and Immigration Services and the Directorate of Border and Transportation Security have only been operational for a few months. Therefore, statistics and incidences pertaining to the BCIS will be confined to records from the INS, Border Patrol, and Customs. Each of these departments has been charged with corruption. Each might have its own essay, with lengthy dissertations on abuses of power. A paragraph or two will suffice for those concerned to get the gist.

The Immigration and Naturalization Service has a FAQ site that answers many important questions. Among these are "can the I&N History Office send me records of my ancestors immigration" (The answer is no.) Then there is the always important "why aren't Green Cards green?" At Justice-Denied.net, a headline reads "terrorism friendly Department of Justice Immigration and Naturalization Services continues defending policies contributing to terrorist acts in the U.S." Heavy words, yet the watchdog group display an 'Evidence Page.' For confirmation, they have the files and testimony of whistleblower Caryl Leventhal. Mrs. Leventhal reported illegal distribution of Green Cards and has since been terminated without pay, and besieged with arrest and death threats.2 This, despite our whistleblower laws. Even the Fox News Channel and CNN have reported INS corruption. A Fox article by Matt Hayes recounts. "Long before the INS mailed Visa approvals to the terrorists who attacked the World Trade Center, it had garnered a reputation as the most inefficient of all federal agencies." Fox goes further and says that inefficiency was not the only problem. Fraud has grown rampant.3 Visas were sent to 9-11 hijackers, AFTER September 11, 2001. From the kidnapping and ransoming of INS custodians, rape along the border, and bribery within the bureau, the sleaze runs deep.

Another point: while our justice system incarcerates millions of drug users (especially minorities,) many INS and Border Patrol are allowing illicit and politically incorrect drugs to come across in vast quantities. Even Hoover wouldn't let his FBI into the drug prohibition fray, because he knew that it was certain to cause widespread corruption. Cannabis News published the following. "Three current inspectors and one former inspector for the Immigration and Naturalization Service were arrested Tuesday on bribery and drug charges associated with cocaine smuggling across the Mexican border, according to Justice Department officials." Some inspectors, such as Richard Lawrence Pineda, were not able to rid themselves of their conscience. They admitted to allowing and aiding drugs to come into America. For money, of course. Then slaps on the wrist and retirements in the South Pacific.4 So, tell me if my logic is flawed here. The government makes drugs illegal and incarcerates users. Meanwhile, drug lords and corrupt government agents make huge sums of money by bringing the drugs across our borders. With two million plus jobs lost since Bush took office, it seems that American farmers, entrepreneurs, manufacturers, retailers, and many other workers should be allowed to reap those financial profits. Yes, it comes at the cost of legalizing drugs (or at least cannabis.) But, what will that change? The supply runs at a fairly static level, never changing too much one way or the other. The only alterations are the suppliers, and much more frequently, the distributors. Anyone who wants drugs can get them now. Legalization does not have to mean endorsement. The Schaffer Library of Drug Policy writes "the corruption of Immigration and Naturalization Service and U.S. Customs Service employees along the Southwest border by drug traffickers is a serious and continuing threat."5 There is only one way to allow the drug trade money to stay in America, and that is to legalize all drugs with strict laws governing dosage, prices, taxes, and the zoning locations these drugs can be bought and applied. Use the tax money to fund rehabilitation for any that want it. An astonishing one half of our prisoners, those who have never harmed another person, would be freed, thus giving governments billions extra in dollars that we use to house them.6 The government learned long ago that treatment is inexpensive compared to incarceration, while neither approach changed the supply or demand of the drug much.7 James Bovard is a renowned author whose ideology seems to be very similar to the concepts supported by The Cato Institute. In his book, Lost Rights, his listing of government's arbitrary use of power IS the book, all 408 pages. Bovard reminds us of some cold, hard facts. "The attack on individual rights has reached the point where a citizen has no right to use his own land if a government inspector discovers a wet area on it, no right to the money in his bank account if an IRS agent decides he might have dodged taxes, and no right to the cash in his wallet if a DEA drug dog sniffs at his pant." From zoning boards to the near-monopoly Post Office, government controls every facet of every facet. Bovard: "Americans of the Revolutionary Era glorified the law because it was seen as a means to restrain government and to secure the rights of the citizen....In recent decades, support for the classical concept of the Rule of Law has evaporated...Government officials have asserted a de facto right to search almost anybody, almost any time, on almost any pretext." Which brings me back to prisons. Because, the State has to have a fear factor to enforce its bloated and rank arbitrary power.11

National Public Radio ran a report. "In recent years, officers from all three of these agencies (INS, Border Patrol, and Customs) have been prosecuted and jailed for allowing illegal drugs and immigrants to cross the border into the United States in return for bribes, sex, and other rewards. Records from INS and the Customs Service show that both of the agencies combined an open average of 53 new corruption cases a year...and those are only the most high-profile cases." NPR's John Burnett brought us that striking report.8

One of the more worrisome issues is that the INS was so incompetent in allowing known Islamic militants to legally enter the country. Carl Hiaasen of the Miami Herald adds dark humor to the first sentence of an article he wrote about the issue. "We can all sleep easier knowing that the Immigration and Naturalization Service intends to stop mailing out visa approvals for dead hijackers." The sad part is, Hiaasen goes on to explain that the statement was sarcastic, but true. "President Bush was pretty hot when he learned the INS recently sent out visa upgrades for two of the Sept. 11 hijackers." The INS's reasoning? The renewals had been approved before the attacks. Mr. Hiaasen asks why they were sent out so long after approval, or why nobody recognized the names of the applicants. No answer.9 This is more than frightening. It will eventually have tragic results, possibly more horrific than previous terrorist acts. Richard Stiennon is an Internet security research director for Gartner, Inc. He said, "If every al Quaeda trained terrorist infiltrated the U.S. in one year, they would represent less than .01 percent of all visitors."10 The INS should at least be able to not mail out visa approvals to the alleged murderers, the very ones reported to have hijacked the planes that took down the World Trade Center and part of the Pentagon on 9-11.

We shall see if Homeland Security is able to meld a

unit together that can secure our borders and protect us from terrorists. It should stop the flow of terrorists and illegal immigrants. It should rout out corruption within its ranks. It should be beholden to United States citizens. One argument over the 2$^{nd}$ Amendment is that the guns were only meant for militia units. This may be true, and we (common male populace) were the militia units then. We are giving our right to bear arms away in return for the security promised by our leaders. There are thieves, serial killers, pedophiles, rapists, terrorists, and others in our society. If these agencies are unable or unwilling to protect us, then we should revert back to the full meaning of the 2$^{nd}$ Amendment and create more community action groups. In fact, there are many people already involved in neighborhood watches, state militias, and citizen brigades. If the government never invokes the laws already in place for instituting fascism, these groups may look radical. However, if a foreign enemy did ever attack the continental United States, our citizen militia groups would be the most prepared civilians. Militias will be the only way to protect us if the Bureau of Citizenship and Immigration is not able to staunch the flowing wound of Islamic terrorists, felonious illegal immigrants, and renegade refugees. We must demand an improvement because that is what we are being promised. Who will protect our women and children? The police? Our military, gallivanting on the other side of the globe? I am willing to give the BCIS and Homeland Security a chance. Yet, we must be ever vigilant.

# Webs of Power - Chapter 6: Central Intelligence Agency

In 1947, President Truman signed the National Security Act, and in so doing first created the Central Intelligence Agency, or CIA. It is an independent agency responsible only to the President through the Director of Central Intelligence (DCI). The CIA mission statement begins with "support the President..." and ends with "...as directed by the President." George Tenet is the current Director and, in a show of uncommon bipartisanship, was sworn in unanimously in 1997.1 (As of first printing, Tenet has resigned and no one sits in the Director's chair.) The vote for war with Iraq was bipartisan, and so was the institution of the Patriot Act. Now that David Kay has refuted Tenet's evidence for WMDs, it is becoming obvious that the Repulicrats are on the same team. (Kay conveniently committed suicide.) This sudden bipartisan "friendship" that the Republicans and Democrats seem to find, always in time to institute something really nasty, is the reason that conspiracy theorists are certain that they are working for the same master.

It becomes all too clear that the Central Intelligence Agency, owing to the nature of spying, is shrouded in a veil of unknowns. As I will show, the CIA has used and abused this power to destroy the lives of innocent Americans, starting in 1947, the date of its inception. Because of the awesome power that this 'independent' agency holds, the allegiance to one man - the President - seems questionable at best. Other groups that were controlled by one man were Hitler's SS and Darth Vader's Storm Troopers. (Both these tyrants had other forces controlling them from behind the scenes, too, much like other forces control our elected Presidents.)

The talk in the Beltway and across America lately has been the amount of blame the CIA should be attributed with concerning two historical events: not having or admitting to prior knowledge about the September 11 attacks; and it's assertion that Iraq indeed had Weapons of Mass Destruction.

36

In both instances, at very least they were inept. At most, they blatantly lied to the American and World public.

The Bush Administration and the CIA's prior knowledge and possible involvement in the 9-11 tragedy are common knowledge for any that objectively study the facts. An excellent article concerning this issue is "9/11 Redux: Anniversary of Treason" at the Propaganda Matrix Website, complete with government and media sources. These sources include Associated Press and Reuters. The CIA knew that a plane attack was likely, and in fact was conducting an exercise wherein a hijacked airliner crashes into its headquarters on the morning of September, 11. The CIA was warned by Israeli Intelligence of the impending attack. The CIA has even been admonished for not using its Intelligence, from as far back as the late Clinton years, which would have stifled terrorist cells, including al-Qaeda. The Agency dutifully came out with its superior intelligence after the attacks, providing us with a list of all the hijackers. It has not proposed any evidence that would support these men being the perpetrators. It has since been reported that most of these men were trained to fly, not at rural airports, but by the CIA itself. Furthermore, there are as many as nine of these suicide-bombers are allegedly alive and claiming innocence. Lastly, most of the hijackers were Saudis, a country with known anti-American terrorist organizations living within its borders. It is Saudi Arabia that is home to al-Qaeda and Osama bin Laden. Why then, I often argued, were we 'liberating' Iraq, and not Saudi Arabia?2

More currently, the FM airwaves seem clogged with debate over Iraq and the WMDs issue. Colin Powell presented intelligence to the United Nations provided to him by the CIA that listed a plethora of biochemical and nuclear weapons sites that were up and running. It seems that the United Nation's weapons inspectors were in cahoots with Saddam, and that is why they were not reporting the sites. The problem now is that America can't seem to find any weapons of mass destruction, just as Hans Blix had been reporting to American ambassadors and hawks for months. The WMD argument was probably the deciding factor for going to war with Iraq against the UN's approval. Now we know that the CIA got it wrong. One Sarin

37

filled bomb does not a WMD make.

In both of these cases, there is ample proof that the CIA knew, even helped create these situations. But, let's take things from an optimistic viewpoint and say that the CIA had no clue that al-Qaeda was going to attack America. Let us also suppose that the Central Intelligence Agency actually thought Iraq had weapons of mass destruction; they were simply wrong about it. If this scenario is the actual one, we have a very dangerous state of affairs in our Country. The agency that has the power to do almost anything, the agency that holds fealty only to the President, is obviously an incompetent, misinformed agency. We Americans are told to depend on the CIA to protect us. They claim independence i.e. no oversight, but U.S. taxpayers should want accountability. When the Central Intelligence Agency is funded independently, they can become autonomous. Until then, they must do their job which is, in their own words, "providing *accurate, evidence-based, comprehensive, and timely* foreign intelligence relating to national security." (emphasis added)

Again, we have another supposedly governmental agency failing to achieve even the most rudimentary segments of their mission statement. For example, the CIA states in their literature that they use personal and organizational integrity while functioning. Yet, there was no integrity in providing Americans with the possibility of an attack on our Homeland or when falsely claiming that Iraq had "evil" weapons. "Accepting accountability for our actions" is another part of the Agency's credo. This will most likely have to be done in a world court due to the Iraqi, American, and other deaths directly due to incorrect information pertaining to Hussein's arsenal. Melvin Goodman is a former CIA Soviet analyst and current professor of international studies at the National War College in Washington D.C., reports Jessica Cantelon of CNSNews. He is quoted as opining, "this was not an act of war, this was a terrible criminal act." This in reference to the CIA's prior knowledge and suppression of evidence in the 9-11 incident.3

Corruption inside the CIA is evident. This is detailed not only by rogue journalists, but also by the testimonials of former CIA agents, themselves. At ciadrugs.com, there are many researched, corroborated stories revealing wrongdoings inside the Agency. In fact, they go so far as to claim, "Two of the most prominent areas in which the CIA's conduct has had catastrophic consequences for Americans have been it's 50-year history of drug smuggling into the United States, and its role in generating hatred for the United States throughout the World."4   Now, unsubstantiated, these claims are libelous. Therefore, one must search for substantiation. It's pretty simple, once studied. The people claiming that the CIA are involved in drug trafficking, assassination, corruption, lies, and generally assaulting our Bill of Rights are current or former members of the United State's plethora of intelligence agencies, including the FBI, CIA, ATF, and DEA. One must make one's own conclusion: believe these educated, morally conscious men claiming corruption; or those that claim there is no fraud in the organizations.   The latter camp is unexplainably silent in answering questions posed by the True Government, we the people.  Statistically speaking, it is a proven fact that in almost all instances that the CIA goes into a country to purge it of drug agriculture, the crop yields rise exponentially. Columbia and Afghanistan immediately come to mind. Both had insignificant exportation of drugs. After CIA occupation and armament of favored guerrilla groups, drug production and importation became the dominant industry: cocaine in Columbia, heroin in the Afghanistan. For any who doubt this "proven fact," simply use a search engine for archived articles in reputable journals such as Knight-Ridder, Reuters, Christian Science Monitor, NY Times, etc. It's not even a secret anymore.

Ex-President Bush, Sr. is a former Director of Central Intelligence. Bush's appointment was stalled because he had been involved in Watergate. Some have claimed having proof that G.H.W. Bush was involved in the tragic S&L scandal, Iran-Contra, and other CIA arms and drug debacles, and in organized crime activities.5   Finally, questions as to why Osama bin Laden and other leaders were propped up into power during Daddy Bush's administration but deemed "terrorists" by Junior are still not discussed in the mainstream media often.  These allegations have not been proven in a court of law or in the court of public opinion.  These allegations have *not been tried* in a court of law or in the court of public opinion.    Under Clinton, the Intelligence Authorization Act was signed into law.  This Act renamed the CIA compound in Langley the "George Bush Center for Intelligence."  George Bush reigned as the CIA's Director for barely one year of its fifty-year history.  As a footnote, it is interesting that the two parties, supposedly diametrically opposed in philosophy and ideology, continually vault each other into prominence.  This aligns more closely with the theory that the Democrats and Republicans are actually two branches of the same party: a party that is bullying us into the Globalists' agenda.

In other cases, the Central Intelligence Agency is charged with using it's webs of power to provide insider information to Enron and other privileged companies.6  They have purportedly been involved with jury tampering and vote fraud.7    The CIA involvement in the JFK assassination is widely believed to be true.  John Stockwell is the highest-ranking member of the CIA to ever go public.  Stockwell worked in intelligence thirteen years, and was in the upper echelon of the National Security Council under Kissinger and then Director Colby.  He claims: "I testified for days before the Congress...proving specific lies.  They were asking if we had to do with Africa, that was fighting in the country.  In fact we were coordinating this operation so closely that our airplanes, full of arms from the states, would meet their planes in Kinshasa and they would take our arms into Angola to distribute to our forces for us."8  In a lesson from history, the CIA was involved in propping up Communist governments to provide a scapegoat to later administrations, much like the current CIA is accused of propping up the after-the-Cold-War "evil doers," the esoteric "terrorists."9  Now we are supposed to want to KILL the same terrorists that the CIA armed and trained!

Many people and groups have accused the CIA of involvement in child sex scandals.  The Stop Child Rape Network pronounces that the problem is endemic and that "the 'core of rape' within our Secret Society run Government Intelligence agencies structure, has been specifically created to sexually abuse and murder our children in their Satanic Black-Occult Rituals." The assertions may or - one would hope - may not be true. And when an American is accused of a crime such as this, he has his case tried before a grand jury. Many times, Child Protective Services will take children away from families for much lesser charges.10 Why then is the CIA not taken to task, so that the Agency might prove its innocence in a court? The accusations are grand and it would seem that we would hear of the allegations on the news. It would definitely seem to be great fodder for prime-time television. Why, then, is not the media exposing these charges against the CIA, the FBI, and other organizations. These accusations bring a chilling sensation when one realizes it was the CIA that charged the Branch Davidians in Waco with still unproven child rape before they raided the private church in a military-style assault in which all the Davidians died, including the children. The CIA saved the children by exterminating them and by assaulting our Bill of Rights.

Underneath the surface, there is a subculture that believes that prominent American politicians and major government agencies have direct links to secret societies. Most of these societies are linked to Luciferianism, dark occult practices, and have cultures of human sacrifice and manipulation as a means to gain power. Rumors ascribed to the CIA are no different. This is in addition to documented reports about the CIA and mind control experimentation. MK Ultra, Project Paperclip, and other CIA operations are now public knowledge. The CIA admitted in Congressional testimony that declassified documents were correct. The CIA did use unsuspecting American citizens to test the best ways in which to control a human's mind. During a Subcommittee on Health and Scientific Research in 1977, former Senator Edward M. Kennedy was quoted as saying, "Some two years ago, the Senate Health Subcommittee heard chilling testimony about the human experimentation activities of the Central Intelligence Agency...programs which included covert drug test on unwitting citizens" and that "the records of all these activities were destroyed in January, 1973." So, the CIA used Americans to test what drugs, what mechanical and electrical brain stimulation, and even what magical arts were most effective for controlling a person's mind. Is it any wonder that media moguls often hire CIA and other intelligence offices to be the keynote speakers at functions. What better agency to learn about the finer points of mind control than the Central Intelligence Agency.11

This brief expose not only shows that the CIA is admittedly, and at the very least, an inept group; but additionally it has been, and is currently, involved in too many fiascos to list. As an American, I want to believe that our intelligence agencies are innocent. Also, adhering to the Constitution, they are innocent until proven guilty. However, those who make the charges should at least have evidence examined and studied by a grand jury to decide on its relevance and admissibility. In the past, to circumvent total collapse, when the CIA is taken to court, one or two fall guys are presented. Oliver North and John Poindexter are prime examples from the Army and Navy, respectively. They took the fall for Reagan and Bush during the Iran/Contra fiasco. North, a felon, is now a media journalist for the Neo-conservative-sanctioned Fox News. Poindexter, a five-time felon, was in charge of the newly created Information Awareness Department. Poindexter resigned after his terrorist futures market was exposed only a few days before its implementation. The Patriot Act allows the Information Awareness Department to ignore the 4th amendment by "viewing" your Web activities without a warrant, suspicion, or probable cause. Back to the CIA, there is no D.A. willing to charge these seemingly omnipotent "spooks" with the crime of drug trafficking, much less child rape and murder. The CIA is arguably the best training ground for assassins. There are too few media sources willing to even report that allegations have even been made against the Agency. Yet, through laws proposed or already legislated, if the CIA was to accuse any citizen with any of these crimes, agents could take that person's property, put him in jail without charges, disallow his right to council, and hold him indefinitely.12 We are being given only one option: to accept this reality.

# Webs of Power - Chapter 7: Food and Drug Administration

The Food and Drug Administration of the United States has simple and altruistic beginnings. In 1906 the Food and Drug Act was passed, which was intended to save Americans from the devastating effects of meat packing and other food handling improprieties. As an agency, the Food and Drug Administration was created in 1930. The FDA enveloped several other food laws and organizations formerly in use inside the government. Abe Lincoln, in his penchant to bloat the Federal Government at the expense of the State's authority, hired the first chemist to serve in a primitive FDA-style lab under the auspices of public safety. Some even quote the 1813 Vaccine Act as the actual origin of the Food and Drug Administration.1

Regardless of when the first act was passed that constituted the origin of the Food and Drug Administration, since its inception, the FDA has been the subject of intense debate. There are people clamoring that without the FDA, they would never have known what foods to eat or what drugs to take. Without the FDA, they say, we would all be dead by ill-prepared food or untested drugs. In the opposite corner, some are warning that the Food Drug and Administration has allowed improper food to enter the market, debilitating drugs to be sold, and that the methods used to make the drugs and prepare the food available are highly suspect. One of the administration's stated missions is to make sure American consumers have safe food with labels. Yet, the labels on most food show that the food itself it filled with unsafe drugs and chemicals.

Life Extension, a magazine devoted to the health of its readership, made a series of scathing accusations in 2001. They claim that the Food and Drug Administration is directly involved with the pharmaceutical companies in depriving the market of competition, promoting price gouging, and other charges that sound more apt for an organized crime ring. It all

44

starts with an FDA panel that is tasked with studying drugs and making judgments on the drugs' safety and effectiveness. "Despite all the safeguards," Life Extension published, "over 50% of the FDA's Expert Committee members are people with direct financial ties to the pharmaceutical industry." This is in direct violation of federal law and was first reported by USA Today. One must wonder how this "committee" can provide us safe drugs when so many are in collusion with the mega-rich drug company owners.2   Over 100,000 people die from unsafe legal drugs that reach our pharmacy shelves every year. This is much higher than all illegal drug deaths, which make up less than 10% of that number.3   Yet, the war on illegal drugs like cannabis perpetuate a tax burden of billions. With ten times as many deaths from legal drugs, it seems this would be the area to allocate ten times as much money. This just makes plain sense, which is a trait our federal government seems to be sorely lacking

The Food and Drug Administration is also largely responsible for the high cost of drugs on the open market. It has done everything in its power to keep drug companies (remember, many FDA members have financial stakes in these companies) from seeing any competition, thus inflating prices to much higher levels than our brothers in Mexico, or - astonishingly - even Canada, a socialist country.4  The FDA has even made it illegal for Americans to purchase drugs that they have approved and deemed safe unless we purchase them in America. The reason? If they allow common laymen and women to buy drugs elsewhere, then two destructive, tragic incidents will likely occur. One, most Americans are pretty ignorant, uninformed, and just plain dumb, so the FDA thinking goes. If given the wide array of other remedies for diseases such as cancer, diabetes, and AIDS, we would probably buy the wrong thing and thus kill ourselves. Second, countries such as Canada, Germany, and Spain have extremely inept drug oversight, and so we would probably get a wrongly labeled pill that would kill us, so says the FDA. The FDA is protecting us from rogue governments like England and France, where health standards are so low.   I'm being sarcastic, but the patricianly "I'll keep you safe" attitude of the

Federal Government is not only sickening, it threatens the virility and constitution of the Country. The real reason we can't buy drugs in Canada or England is that it would create competition for the lobbyists and PACs that fund the politicians' campaigns. That would make it more difficult for them to reap such huge profits off the backs of the American elderly who pay their own way or the young who fund socialized Medicare. More importantly, the Food and Drug Administration is protecting us from ourselves. Please, will any Republican or Democrat show me where in the Constitution that protection from our own stupidity is necessary or legal or required. What's worse, our own country is privy each year to thousands of deaths due to drugs that are simply put into the wrong bottle.5 Yet, when this happen, the FDA will not claim accountability, even while barring us from other country's drugs.

The Wall Street Journal reported on July 27, 2000, that most drug price increases were not in relation to materials or labor, but to pay doctor incentives at the expense of Medicare. Some author could, and many have, written whole books on this subject. Basically, the FDA has allowed the largest pharmaceutical manufacturers to price gouge and reap huge profits using insurance and Medicare monies, all paid for by the sweat of the middle and upper-middle classes.

Food and Drug Administration regulations are another area under intense scrutiny, and with many cries of "foul." Consumers Against High Drug Prices (CAHDP) delivers a message assigning lies, corruption, and ultimately death to many of the FDA's regulations. They claim that it now takes almost fifteen years to get a drug to market, up from 6.5 in the 1960's. Of course, that would be a good thing if the regulations and interminable wait for trial medications actually brought public health. CAHDP assert that 125,000 people die every year from drugs that the FDA has approved as safe.6 This is also found to be true in reverse. The FDA has suppressed approval of many drugs that would have added extended life for millions of Americans. Dr. Craig Cooney is a scientist who formerly worked with the FDA. He found that the FDA had shut down new drug companies working with the experimental drug, TMG. TMG has been proven to protect against heart disease in some patients. At present, these reports are proving to be correct, despite fifty years of suppression by the FDA. So, TMG might have prevented your father or grandfather from having a stroke or heart attack but was specifically banned by the FDA because it stepped on other drugs' profit margins.7

With all this information, one might ask why the current administration does not fix the problem. That becomes apparent when one realizes that many of our elected officials are the shareholders of major drug companies. It is common knowledge that Prescott Bush, the current President's grandfather, amassed huge wealth through stocks in the company I.G. Farben, one of Hitler's greatest economic generators. I.G. Farben was experimenting with eugenics, chemical weapons, and has been connected to the Jewish extermination projects, specifically manufacturing drugs and chemicals to do the actual killing. John Loftus, a U.S. Nazi War Crimes Prosecutor has this to say about the vast Bush estate. "The Bush fortune came from the Third Reich."8 This does not mean President Bush is a Nazi, only that his money was derived from supporting Nazis. Bush Sr. worked for Eli Lilly, Rumsfeld for Searle Pharmaceuticals, and Ashcroft has been a lobbyist for several drug manufacturers.9 Dr. Gail R. Wilensky is the principal author of Bush's health care plan. She holds over $12 million in the stock of health insurance companies. Conflict of interest? I should say so.

The FDA is responsible for millions of deaths due to the selection of which drugs Americans will be allowed to purchase, and due to the NON-selection of certain, other drugs. Because many members of select committees are economically involved with the drug companies in power, the reasoning behind the method for this selection process becomes blatantly obvious. They are not protecting the public, they are protecting their portfolios. Unless the complete staff of the Food and Drug Administration is fired, and a new, objective one is put into place, we will never be safe from harmful drugs, nor will we be allowed the full gamut of life-saving drugs that are on the market in Europe and Canada.

Finally, if we do not terminate the employment of members of the Food and Drug Administration who have vested interests in the pharmaceutical companies, we will continue to pay exorbitant prices. That's OK. In 2003 our "conservative" president handed out $400 billion for prescription drug give-aways. This figure was admittedly false, with the price tag for taxpayers ending up at almost $600 billion.10   With conservatives like Bush in office, who needs liberals.

# Webs of Power - Chapter 8: Drug Enforcement Administration

Before I begin the sticky process of the DEA's particular strand in the web of power, I would like to say a few words about drug prohibition, and specifically the United States' War on Drugs. There are enough arguments for and against this failed policy that it would take entire volumes to catalog them. We can look at this as a statistical issue falling into the social category of the standard political ideology chart. Chart 1A is a simple depiction of political ideology. As you can see, it is set up like a diamond. One end of each point represents more or less amounts of government control. Due south is authoritarianism, or total control. Forms of authority are communism, fascism, despotism, and totalitarianism. Due north is libertarianism, or actually, total anarchy, where there is no government power. As anarchists trend south, they allow for limited government for the common good. Neither of these political philosophies holds much sway in America. The other two ideologies, however, are constantly at war. Liberalism elects to have government control economics, but not civil liberties. The prime example of liberalism is Socialism. Democrats would have government and Unions control business, but you would be able to get high, have any kind of sex you want, etc. Conservatism would let companies run rampant in deregulation, but would keep control in the social, a.k.a. moral, sector of society. These are our Republicans. They would let business pay substandard wages to even women and children. They would, however, limit free speech, hold contempt for homosexuals, and mandate what recreational plants you may or may not grow in your home. Because of the incremental wins each makes - liberals winning government controls in economics and conservatives gaining social order - we are now more akin to an authoritarian nation. In America today, the amount of control ceded is vast. The government garnishes about 50% of our income in taxes, everyone gets some kind of handout, and almost every part of our life is regulated.  To conclude, if we draw a circle around the middle of the two lines, you have the moderate viewpoint of any form of ideology.  In actuality, this is where most Americans stand, as moderates or centrists.  Thus the term "middle America."

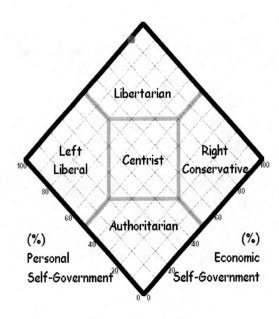

Pic. 1A

Type "World's Smallest Political Quiz" into a search engine to see where you are on this ideological chart.

With this as our guideline, the United States can definitely be placed into the moderate authoritarian category. There are many rules pertaining to business, but these rules are often ignored.  Independent, hardworking owners of small businesses are the only ones forced to follow the voluminous tax laws, regulatory infringements, and high-priced fees. Expressly, the drug issue in America falls into the category of complete government control, both as a social and economic issue.  Drugs that are difficult to regulate have been made illegal.  The pharmaceutical industry, as shown in "Webs of Power: Food and Drug Administration," is manipulated by politicians beholden to specific drug companies.  For a country that prides itself on a fair market and the freedom to pursue happiness, both these drug policies are hypocritical, at best.

The War on Drugs is largely known to be a failed program.  The drug scare reached such a crescendo, thousands of Americans have been unjustly stripped of liberty and property with only the flimsiest of hearsay.1    I do not understand why it is not a person's right to take any drug they want for whatever reason as long as it doesn't infringe on other Americans' rights.  This should not be a crime.  Now, if a drug abuser steals, drives under the influence, threatens public peace, then they have at that point perpetrated a criminal act and should be punished.  Due to propaganda, it is no longer the majority belief that we have the right to the pursuit of happiness.  Drugs are the cause of gang related violence, due to the black market created by prohibition.  The Drug War, much like alcohol prohibition, creates violence.  The drugs or alcohol are only secondary culprits in gang violence.  As with the Mafioso after alcohol prohibition, if drugs were legalized, the bloody gang battles of the drug war would diminish or cease altogether.  Dosages and purity cause overdoses in the illegal drug arena.  Whereas, if drugs were regulated correctly, this would not happen.  Another argument for legalization. Taboos constructed during the Reagan administration have created a drug culture that finds it difficult to find employment.  Yet, we know from countries where drugs are legal that addicts can and will be productive members of society in most instances, if allowed.  Dan Baum has written and reported for such reputable print media as the Wall Street Journal, the Washington Post, and the L.A. Times.  In his book, Smoke and Mirrors: The War On Drugs and the Politics of Failure, Baum provides a detailed history of America's drug war.  At the beginning of the 'war,' under Nixon, it was found that the only way to keep a heroin addict productive was to either give him heroin or methadone.  Since the government won't ever hand out free smack, methadone has successfully been used for years to keep addicts working and contributing to society.

There is nothing in the Bill of Rights that states the government should decide which drugs you can take.  There are more deaths from FDA approved drugs than all other drug deaths combined, excluding the legal drug alcohol.  Drug enforcement has been charged with organized crime activities in the production and importation of narcotics to America.  Two presidents have admitted to using illegal drugs (Clinton never inhaled; Bush had not used cocaine after 1974,) as have Al Gore, John Kerry, John Edwards and Howard Dean.  Finally, cannabis is known to have multiple uses.  These include industrial, manufacturing, agricultural, and medical applications.  The Federal government has dictated that the states can't decide whether or not to utilize the human and Earth-saving facets of grown and manufactured drugs.

Everyone knows drugs like heroin, cocaine, steroids, morphine, and the like are very bad.  Yet, almost every drug has some positive attributes.  The War on Drugs, though, has been the real problem of my lifetime, domestically speaking.

With all that said, the following is a brief overview and expose of the agency in charge of enforcing drug laws: the **Drug Enforcement Administration**.

The DEA has its roots in the Bureau of Internal Revenue, created in 1915.  Drug Enforcement was turned over to two separate agencies by the 1960's, and in 1973, Nixon unified all agencies under the Drug Enforcement Agency.  At the DEA's official website, it is shown that the rise in drug use runs parallel with the oppressiveness of drug enforcement.  The more laws they put on the books, the more users we create.  Also, on the DEA's history page, they admit that most

South American countries were not major drug exporters until AFTER the creation of the DEA. Though they never specifically give reasons for the rise in drug supplies in America, they do inadvertently correlate the creation of drug agencies from 1915 to the present with the definite rise in importation into the United States. To summarize, the DEA's own literature proves that the harsher drug laws are, the larger amounts of drugs enter the country for a net increase in users.2

Under the United States' current quasi-authoritarian governmental structure, laws dictating moralities are allowed, contrary to the mandates set forth in the Bill of Rights. As is evident, our government has been destroying the Constitution for many years. If the Drug Enforcement Agency's mission is to stop Americans from acquiring or using illegal drugs, they have failed. If they are undertaking a mission to lessen the impact of drugs on our society, they have failed. The Drug Enforcement Agency has had great success in disseminating lies about illegal drugs, as well as having been involved in abuses against the 2nd and 4th Amendments.3 They have acquired vast wealth by forcibly seizing property owned by proven and *alleged* drug offenders. When many of these citizens are proven innocent in courts, their land and assets are not relinquished. When asset forfeiture was first suggested in the 70's, it was thought to be impossible because it was in direct violation of criminal code as set forth by our Constitution. However, the government found that they could take money, cars, even real estate through a morphing of criminal and civil law. And how could they ever get Americans to accept these new draconian measures, this restructuring of double jeopardy? The evil drug epidemic. Dan Baum, author of Smoke and Mirrors, adds a little fun to his book by ending the chapters with some interesting facts. In 1969, Nixon's men allowed gross injustices to the 4th amendment, such as the no knock rule and preventative detention. Believe it or not, Americans were actually concerned about these rules that would for the first time ever allow law enforcers to break into homes without stating their name, agency, and reason for entering. But, Nixon was able to get conservatives to accept the egregious acts by instilling fear.

Fear of drugs. Were drugs such a crisis that Americans would allow for this? Baum writes,

- *"Number of Americans who died in 1969 falling down stairs: 1,824.*
- *Number who choked to death on food: 2,641.*
- *Number who died from cirrhosis of the liver: 29,866.*
- *Number who died from legal and illegal drugs: 1,601."*

Today, police storm troopers regularly canvas neighborhoods, mostly minority ones, and blanket every house in the name of the Drug War. No-knock is now "I'll bust your door down, beat you up, and take your property on the allegations of some two-bit junky punk informant who will remain anonymous." Most people who believe in prohibition are good people. They just don't know the true facts about drugs. This extends to DEA agents, most of whom begin their careers simply wishing to do their part to rid America of its drug scourge. Unfortunately, there are too many rumors, coincidences, and documents that show an abuse of power by the DEA.

As a minor example, one of the only proofs that there is anything being done to stop the crazy influx of drugs into our country are drug arrest charts issued by the DEA. The neat little charts are made to look professional and colorful, and are used so that yearly drug busts can be touted to the media and public. The problem with these charts is that they are completely imaginary. AlterNet reported "that the DEA had no documents to support hundreds of arrests…," and, "the new head of the Drug Enforcement Agency has pledged to end the agency's use of inflated drug-arrest and performance statistics." So, even the reports given to us by the DEA are lies. False reports may have been used to cover up the DEA's alleged involvement in drug trafficking. Rodney Stitch was employed by several drug agencies and has written books on the subject, exposing government corruption. In a letter he wrote to Cesar Lajud, a former Consul General of Mexico, Mr. Stitch fingers the DEA in murder, seizure of an airstrip for the purpose of flying drugs out of the country, and generally

54

aiding and abetting crime in Mexico. He is not the only investigator to make these accusations.4, 5

What is worse, the real good guys in the DEA often have their lives turned into chaotic messes simply for having the courage to blow the whistle on DEA corruption. It seems obvious that hazing and blackmail might occur by specific rogue officers who are fingered in criminal activity. The level to which these whistleblowers are harassed suggests that this hazing is an agency-wide, "unstated" code. For example: Sandalio Gonzalez was a 30-year veteran Special Agent of the DEA. After an incident where officers took ten kilos of cocaine after a bust, Gonzalez reported the crime. The San Antonio Business Journal recounts that "in addition to suffering retaliation designed to harass and humiliate (Gonzalez) and slander his character and damage his reputation," he was demoted by the Drug Enforcement Agency.6

Civil asset forfeiture laws are officially stated as being a means to punish drug users and dealers. The reasoning is that if they bought their stuff with drug money, the stuff should belong to the government. Maybe that is true, but it has not stopped corruption from taking place when land and property are seized with only rumor or innuendo as evidence. The Supreme Court has ruled that it is not double jeopardy to punish a drug offender twice: once in criminal court, and again with civil asset forfeiture. This would explain the inflated drug arrests. Asset forfeiture is highly profitable to the DEA and U.S. Government. To add insult to injury, the Court also ruled that the DEA and the government can take property used in a crime, even if the owner had no knowledge whatsoever of the crime. The horror stories are everywhere. This is what today stands as the Rule of Law, says the New York Times and The Supreme Court.

There seems to be no end to the corruption inside any of our federal agencies. The Drug Enforcement Administration is no exception. From the Schaffer Library of Drug Policy, the following is presented. "Congressional Reports on Drug Corruption and the Federal Government." Case files and testimony implicate the DEA in more serious crimes.  These include turning a blind eye and/or participating in harassment, murder, and assassination.7

Even the oppressive J. Edgar Hoover knew that drugs meant corruption.  He wouldn't allow his FBI to participate in drug prohibition.  Hoover was aware that when so much money is at stake, and with little opportunity for oversight, the illicit drug trade was destined to be rife with corruption.  In the words of one DEA agent, "Christ.  A fucking saint would go bad in this business.

# Webs of Power - Chapter 9: Internal Revenue Service

The stated mission of our Internal Revenue Service, found on their official website, is as follows: "Provide America's taxpayers top quality service by helping them understand and meet their tax responsibilities and by applying the tax law with integrity and fairness to all."1

The IRS has failed to accomplish their mission.

There has been little or no help for middle-class Americans in understanding the 54,000 pages bloating the 2003 tax laws. This page count is up from just over 40,000 in 1995.2 To understand these laws, one must acquire a very knowledgeable accountant, which is not feasible for the majority of Americans' middle-class pocketbooks. This makes only the elite privy to loophole information. The second part of the IRS mission statement, pertaining to applying tax laws fairly, is also a failed job. Remember Enron. These multi-millionaires not only took advantage of every single loophole known to man, they invented a few of their own. President George W. Bush denounced them, yet there has been far too few charges or convictions. In other words, most are getting away with it.

Every year hundreds of IRS horror stories jam the Web and FM radio airwaves. One example is the case of the Indianapolis Baptists Church, which had recently refused to be a state-sanctioned religious institution by giving up the congregation's nonprofit status. Directly after this, the IRS gave the church a tax bill, which appears to be phony upon first perusal. We will skip the point that President Bush, a professed Christian, is allowing the unprecedented seizure of a Christian house of worship.3 Yet, we know that groups like Jesse Jackson's Rainbow Coalition have defiantly refused and abused the tax system, and that the Scientology "religion" held shadowy meetings with elected representatives to gain tax-exempt status.4 In the end, the Christian church was shut down, while Scientology is now a state-sponsored, taxpayer-supplemented "religion."

Shelley L. Davis was the first and last ever Internal Revenue Service Historian. After watching as her immoral coworkers hid and destroyed documents; after several years of obvious misuse of the Freedom of Information Act; after giving her 1000% to the effort of creating a true and favorable History of the IRS; Davis wrote the book, <u>Unbridled Power: Inside the Secret Culture of the IRS</u>. The book is chock full of Davis's first hand accounts of the abuse of power by our highest tax agency. Shelley L. Davis, while being subjected to harassment at work, was still able to provide a fun and telling account of the history of the Internal Revenue Service.5

Many "patriots" consider the Founding Fathers almost an infallible lot. Yet, it is an irrefutable fact that most of the leaders of our Revolution were high ranking Freemasons. There's that "all men are created equal" part, with people of color and women not quite being "men." So, what did the old, dead, white guys think about taxes? Hell, they took us to war with England on the premise that taxes were unjust. Taxation was a symbol of economical tyranny. Shelley L. Davis writes that one of the first things the newly formed Federal Government did with their new independence was impose a tax on Whiskey to pay off debt. In fact, the author reminds us that the Articles of the Confederation were scrapped when they Federalists and elites realized it outlawed taxation! Inevitably, whiskey distillers and importers did not like the unfair tax. Federal law stated, at that time, that taxes must be imposed uniformly. There was tarring. There was feathering. Finally, a few tax collectors got fed up, and the violence escalated into the infamous Whiskey Rebellion, America's first tax rebellion. So, what did our President Washington, General of the anti-tax American Revolutionary Forces do? Davis writes, "He marched on rebellious Pennsylvania at the head of his own militia, numbering in excess of 12,000 troops - an army substantially larger than any force he had commanded during the entire War of Independence. This overwhelming authority succeeded in dispersing the enemy and in rounding up a ragtag bag of tax protestors who were forcibly marched all the way to

Philadelphia on foot, with orders having been issued to the militia to behead any rebel who attempted escape." This discovery has dropped my opinion of Washington more than perhaps anything else I have ever heard. I am a white male, from the South. It's almost genetic in our species to despise taxation. And, the fact that these men had fought with the former General to end the very limited taxation that was levied upon the colonists is noteworthy. Repeat this attack on tax protestors for Fries's and Shay's Rebellions.

As has been proven in "Webs of Power: The Federal Reserve System," the international bankers and the central banks have been one of the most dire enemies of America. Our first Treasury of the Secretary, Alexander Hamilton, was "a fierce proponent of centralized fiscal power and founder of the first central bank." Some of the Freemason elites who we call the Founding Fathers were in cahoots with the Rothschilds. That is obvious from any study of History. Even the 2$^{nd}$ Amendment is written poorly, probably intentionally. It does not say exactly that individuals should have the right to own weapons. It says individuals involved in well-trained militias should have that right. Believe me, they ain't getting my guns. But, can we think this was a simple grammatical error on the part of the Founders? Granted, many of the Founders were anti-Federalists. If it weren't for Jefferson's fight against the international bankers, we may have been put on the road to a welfare state and secularism much quicker than the 200 years it took. To all who have questions about the IRS, read Davis's book, "Unbridled Power." She was fortunate enough to attain a bird's eye view of the department, and her revelations are astounding.

The Internal Revenue, as a department, was first enacted by Lincoln to pay for war expenses. It was repealed a decade later. In 1894 it was revived, but the Supreme Court deemed it unconstitutional a year after that. As I reported in "Webs of Power: The Federal Reserve," 1913 was the year our government sold us out to the International Bankers by giving control of our money supply over to foreigners, through the corporate Federal Reserve. Oddly enough, it is the same year that the 16$^{th}$ Amendment was ratified, giving Congress the power to tax their constituents. Congress produced the first 1040 tax form right away in 1913. The Federal Reserve is the international bankers' central bank branch in America. The IRS is the enforcer for this bank and these bankers.

Bush appointed the new Commissioner of the Internal Revenue Service, Mark E. Everson, for a 5-year term on May 1, 2003. Mr. Everson has been on Cabinets in all Republican administrations since Reagan. He was a member of Yale, the birthplace of Skull & Bones, a secret society started by the Rothchilds and others. Everson worked for the Penchiney Group, from France, and has also worked for Turkey. So, the man who runs the IRS has known financial ties with France, a country that, right or wrong, consistently slaps America in the face. French businessmen are also thought of as some of the most unethical businessmen, at least in America.7

The IRS netted almost $2 trillion in 2002. They have a budget of $10 billion.

At trac.syr.edu, a nonpartisan website that acts as a watchdog for government agencies and their enforcement procedures, many IRS injustices are accounted for. According to TRAC, corporate tax fraud is rising while the amount of prosecutions continues a downward trend. Bush has not recruited investigators for the IRS despite publicly stating that he would charge and prosecute corporate tax criminals. TRAC claims that these corporate crimes were directly related to $5 trillion in stock market losses since Bush took office. In a 2002 speech, President Bush stated: "At this moment, America's greatest economical need is higher ethical standards."7 However, government documents reveal that IRS enforcement agents were never given the green light to prosecute white-collar crimes. Without prosecution of the accused, higher standards are impossible. Most Americans want the rich to stay rich. That provides jobs for the middle-class. However, we also want them to pay their fair share of the tax burden.

Most Americans do not mind paying some amount of money to the Federal Government. But, many of our countrymen do not comprehend that they pay almost 50% of their income into the tax system. The IRS takes half of this amount, with the rest going to state and local governments.

According to many economic libertarians, the IRS is an unconstitutional agency. Furthermore, many corporate, political, religious, and nonprofit organizations claim that the Internal Revenue Service has broken numerous laws. The IRS's alleged crimes include obstruction of justice, conspiracy, extortion, mailing threatening communications, engaging in monetary transactions derived from unlawful activity, taking of property without due process of law, treason, breach of fiduciary duty, and conflict of interest of federal judges. There are other alleged felonies. A full list can be found with the nonprofit group, We The People. We The People claims to have the information that would allow Americans to NOT pay Federal taxes due to these misdoings. They are also campaigning to exercise their 1st Amendment Right, which is "the right to petition Congress for redress of grievances." Bob Schulz leads this charge. After four years of petition, Congress has still not answered this legitimate, nonprofit group's queries or redresses. Schulz is encouraging all people and businesses to "legally terminate their wage withholding and filing in order to force the government to answer 537 legal questions regarding the income tax."8

Whether or not you support the Internal Revenue Service, it is unfathomable to assume that they have not broken any laws. These criminal acts are not new, simply a continuation of standard operating procedure. For example, in the infamous LaRouche case, Lyndon LaRouche and several of his ideological peers were besieged in an all out, decade-long assault which defied most of the Bill of Rights. Henry Kissinger led this politically motivated target practice. The aftermath includes LaRouche and others languishing in prison, strategic leakage of confidential taxpayer information, illegal intelligence gathering, and other crimes. It ended with a military-style offensive (i.e. assault helicopters, armored personnel, and anti-terrorism agents) to take LaRouche and company into custody, even though none had anything more serious than a traffic ticket on their records. All this was over alleged nonpayment of taxes.9 There are many stories similar to this one. Others are not so similar, but just as corrupt and unjust. The facts are irrefutable. These actions must stop, and those responsible must be charged and tried in a court of law. The IRS may or may not be a legal entity, which makes tax debt and payment debatable. The illegal acts perpetrated by the Internal Revenue Service are not arguable, and thus these crimes must be prosecuted.

# Webs of Power - Chapter 10: Federal Bureau of Investigation

It may be apparent that, as I progress in writing these very basic exposes, my cynicism becomes more pronounced. Yes, I was cognizant that there would be corruption and fiascos, though not in the amount I encountered. What is even more horrifying was another fact I am in the process of overturning. These debacles are stages in a process in which many nations' governments work in accordance with each other and at the behest of a very select group of ultra-wealthy personages. My epiphany took some time. This is due to the rewriting of my public school History books, the corroboration of elite media, and the mind control campaign these personages have undertaken, as will be proven throughout this book.

We must be thankful for the Internet. This specific technological advancement was first researched and developed extensively by the U.S. Military. No surprise. What is a wonder is why they ever let we commoners have access. Without the Internet, the Message of Freedom would have all but been completely suppressed. Might someone or some group "inside" have true morality, and thus be trying to aid us? Or is it a part of the depopulation program so often expressed by the elites?1   They WANT a few million Americans to exterminate when they uncloak their fascism.   These Americans have been fingered and named: militias, tax protestors, home-shoolers, Christians, and people who believe in the Constitution of the United States of America.2  We who write and speak out against the New World Order should make no bones about it.  We are on a list; and that list will be read off at some point in time.

Regardless of what the reasons were for allowing us access to the Internet (probably because they are greedy, and the thought of all the money they could make with e-businesses was a greater temptation than the exposure that they must have known would come about), we do have the technology.   A whole new generation is finding out about America, her original intent, her ability to adapt and change. We are finding out the true histories of our peoples.  We are finding out the truths of our subjugation.  Actually, Gen X and Gen Y were both large steps in the "rewriting history" experiment perpetrated by Rhodes followers (Cecil Rhodes is explained in the "Shadows of Power" section of the book.) There are at least two generations of Americans that were fed a steady diet of anti-American material in public schools. We (Gen X and Y) don't remember what it was like before the War on Drugs.  We can't remember when guns were for the law abiders, to PROTECT themselves from the criminals, who will obviously have guns regardless.  With this powerful tool before us - the World Wide Web - for such a short time, is it any wonder that our government is currently considering legislation to regulate Internet radio and speech?3

But I have rambled much too long.   I am procrastinating.  Exposing all this vile activity inside my own Federal Government is heart-wrenching.

## Federal Bureau of Investigation

Our Federal Bureau of Investigation embarked on its secretive, scandal-ridden life in 1908, this time under Teddy Roosevelt. J. Edgar Hoover, one of the most corrupt men ever involved in our government, joined the team in 1917. Prohibition began in 1920, after which time the FBI admits that "gangsterism" rose sharply.  With this knowledge, the government began to systematically make illegal every drug that they could not sell to their advantage, to line their own pockets.   They knew that prohibition led to gangs and the violence associated with them.  The FBI touts 1929 as the year they "captured" Al Capone.  In reality, Capone turned himself in, and the FBI flubbed the job so badly, they had to put him away for tax evasion instead of any real, violent crime.  In 1935, the division took on its current name, Federal Bureau of Investigation.  The official version of the FBI's history even goes so far as to tell us that in 1963 they were charged with the investigation of JFK's murder: charged to investigate an assassination they have been implicated in.4

Also displayed in the Bureau's official literature are the FBI's ten highest priorities. The very first one is to "protect the United States from terrorist attack." The slippery slope begins. By United States, do they mean U.S. citizens, or do they mean the land itself, or do they mean the highest-level government officials? If we assume that either of the former two definitions fit, the FBI is found lacking. For example, I cite 9-11, not to mention Twin Towers One. At very least, the FBI had prior knowledge that the attacks were probable on that fateful day in September, which has been proven by the 9-11 investigative panel despite key members' ties to the Council on Foreign Relations. If that were not enough justification to investigate the Investigators, Colleen Rowley, an FBI field agent, accused the department of shutting down the investigation of Zacarias Moussaoui, a high level leader of al-Qaeda just before the attacks.5 Joel Skousen of Rense.com reports that the FBI is continuing to cover up communications with the pilots of the hijacked airplanes.6 Where are the black boxes? Mayor Willie Brown and other VIPs seem to have been warned against flying that day.7 Deductive reasoning forces us to conclude that the latter definition of United States, i.e. chosen officials, as being the definition of what is meant when the FBI says it protects the U.S. from terrorists.

"Protect the United States against foreign intelligence operations and espionage," reads the second priority listed by the Bureau. Now that we understand what is meant by 'United States,' we see that the FBI, while not completely successful, has been actively working toward achieving their goal of aiding and protecting our figureheads. This becomes evident when even the Austin American Statesman, the mediocre (I'm being polite) city newspaper of the Texas State Capital, has published evidence of a secret Foreign Intelligence court that is able to charge, arrest, and detain U.S. citizens without a trial. The star court and their subversive warrants were even made the theme of a 2004 Law & Order episode. The FBI does not prohibit this court, and therefore the Agency only protects elite politicos from foreign confrontations and conflicts. The FBI has been implicated in murders and blackmail toward persons, including Americans, that have attempted to gather information about our elite ruling class's transgressions.8

A few other "priorities" that the FBI maintains they are striving to achieve are protecting civil rights, combating white-collar crime, and fighting organized crime. In these priorities as well as the rest, unless they pertain only to our highest echelon of leaders in government, the FBI has NOT accomplished what they have set out to do. This failure is so evident as to not be worth discussion. For example: the ongoing brutality against minorities; mutual fund frauds; and, drug cartels are all facts of American life.

No essay on the FBI, basic or conclusive, would be complete without a section on J. Edgar Hoover.9 Hoover was the mastermind and overlord of the FBI for a staggering 48 years. He set the stage for what the FBI became, and for what it is today. It seems that he was the perfect man for the job. Even before his promotion to the head of investigations, Hoover worked for Attorney General A. Mitchell Palmer. Together they misused the newly passed Espionage Act (1917) and Sedition Act(1918) to vilify persons and groups endorsing the rule of law. It is well documented that Hoover was a racist, and targeted black civil rights leaders, intellectuals, elected officials, and media. This included an apparent personal vendetta and smear campaign against Martin Luther King, Jr. Raised a Presbyterian, Hoover even worked as a minister at one point in his life. Some claim that the reason for his overt and public racism against African-Americans is that Hoover, himself, had known black ancestors. An African-American from Mississippi, Mildred Mghee, claims to be related to him. Adding to the conspiracy, many of Hoover's personal records have been altered or "lost."10

Basically, Hoover is charged with acquiring vast power for the FBI to fight the rampant crime within the country. While this did give the FBI unprecedented freedoms to circumvent the rule of law, corruption inside the agency rose, not fell, parallel to the rise in the amount of power bestowed upon it. The Director's "secret files" were a trademark of his reign. These citizen-databases allowed

Hoover to keep his job through eight presidential administrations. He was widely rumored to have dirt on just about everyone.

For those who are new to the truths that are contained herein, the seemingly sporadic jump from a government agency to a secret society may be a bit disorienting. I assure you, however, that it is not sporadic, nor is it a tangent. Interestingly enough, J. Edgar Hoover was a 33rd Degree Freemason. In fact, his 52-year tenure with the Freemason organization is lengthier than the 48 years he spent as head of the FBI. Freemasons swear allegiance to the "brothers" above all: country, family, self. A passage from the Freemason Protocols lends credence to this viewpoint. "We are the chosen, we are the only true men. Our minds give off the true power of the spirit; the intelligence of the rest of the world is merely instinctive and animal. They can see, but they cannot foresee; their inventions are merely corporeal. Does it not follow that nature herself has predestined us to dominate the whole world?" Make of it what you will.11

The current Director, as of May 2003, is Robert S. Mueller, III. Mr. Mueller's bio states that he was responsible for apprehending Noriega, when in fact the FBI backed and armed the dictator. Afterward, FBI investigators became involved in the importation of illegal narcotics in collusion with Noriega. The National Security Archive produces documented verification of the FBI's involvement with drug smuggling and in training Noriega. They cite journal entries by Oliver North, memos from Robert Owen to North, email from Admiral John Poindexter, and State Department contracts as evidence. Even Sen. John Kerry said that the FBI was involved in weapons and drug trafficking, and Kerry is a member of Skull & Bones, himself. So, what the public is not informed of is that before Director Mueller's apprehension of Noriega, Noriega had been trained in the School of the Americas, recently renamed the Western Hemisphere Institute for Security Cooperation. The military training academy is known to the unfortunate Latinos in Central and South America as 'School of the Assassins.' This "school" is staffed with FBI members and has been the breeding ground for a plethora of Latin American dictators. School of the Americas Watch is an independent group seeking to shut down this school. They state, "Hundreds of thousands of Latin Americans have been tortured, raped, assassinated, "disappeared," massacred, and forced into refugee by those trained at the School of Assassins."12 It does follow the modus operandi of the New World Order. What I have seen referred to as the Hegelian Dialectic. Problem-Reaction-Solution. Our government creates the problem (9-11, UFO's, Pearl Harbor,) we have a reaction of fear, and then our wonderful parent, the great federal government, gives us a solution. This solution provides us security, or more usually, a sense of security. And always, that solution involves more loss of individual freedom.

The FBI, today, is under the process of being reorganized, restructured, revamped - whatever - under the guidance of Mueller. The process of absorption of the Federal Bureau of Investigations with other agencies under Homeland Security, is also a stated objective of the Bush Administration. President Bush believes that if you take a bunch of broken down investigative agencies, put them all together into one massive agency, you'll have a brand spanking new, shiny, efficient agency. This holds no logic. The FBI is full of corruption. They can't even figure out when major terrorist attacks are imminent. If the federal agency can produce no intelligence and they are corrupt, there is no reason to keep the agency in existence. Began as a way to combat organized crime (a.k.a. consensual crimes and those who supply the demand,) the Federal Bureau of Investigations has ultimately at times become the warlords of that very same crime ring they purport to undo. The FBI's turf war has been fruitful, and sweet. The stakes are high. The reward is great for the FBI: they have a virtual monopoly on drugs, extortion, and assassination.

As Jane's Addiction's Perry Farrell sings in the song "1%", a loud profession, a truth that we have all come to know.

*"The biggest gang I know they call the Government*
*And The Gang is a weapon that you trade your mind in for*
*I guess you gotta be just like them*

*The Gang and the Government*
*No difference*
*That makes me 1%"*13

# Part Two

# Shadows of Power

## Shadows of Power - Chapter 11: Origin Theories, Secret Societies

At the expense of sounding too "out there," and after a year of grueling research into the governmental power structure of the United States, I was forced to turn my attention toward secret societies. This is an inherently difficult task. Before beginning, it would be prudent to define "secret society." The general consensus published by reputable dictionary sources is agreed upon. One indigenous factor is inherent in all secret clubs. The American Heritage Dictionary produces the following definition.

*"secret society (n.) - An organization, such as a lodge, that requires its members to conceal certain activities, such as its rites of initiation, from outsiders."*

A common myth for the general public is that groups, such as the Council on Foreign Relations or Skull & Bones, are not secret societies because members are fairly open about belonging. That is a fallacy. As we have just read, a secret society does not hide its members, it hides its actions, its rites, its reason for being. In other words, their true intent is hidden from the nonmembers behind a metaphoric screen of smoke and mirrors. What are these smoke and mirrors? One of the most common tactics wielded by these clandestine "clubs" is their extreme use of advanced propaganda techniques. This includes intentionally juxtaposing several unrelated stories, so as to confuse nonmembers. For instance, when the blurb about the Bush/Kerry Skull & Bones connection appeared, an AM radio talk show host - I won't mention his name, judging him ignorant, not intentionally deceiving - stated that even Clinton was in the Skull & Bones fraternity, though he was never tapped. Disinformation spirals down to the lowest levels.

It is fairly well known that the major American media news sources are owned, produced, and run by secret society members. The latter half of 2003 saw the FCC board allow even larger monopolies for Clear Channel, Time Warner, and those behind the curtain.1   Congress pooh-poohed out a whisper of dissent, but the damage will be done.   Every liberty-minded group is screaming that this will squelch third party voices. Yet, the media has run very few stories about the ruling. These secret society members that air what we watch have a vested interest in our ignorance. That explains why there are only a few, brief, biased blurbs when we see an "editorial" on the CFR or other global groups. This year, America has to confront the fact that the 2004 election is the first open Skull & Bones election. President Bush and Senator Kerry are both members.   Yet, I have heard more disinformation about S&B from the mainstream media in one week (first week of March, 2004) than I care to relate back to you.   Books about the group sell very well.   Alexandra Robbins's recent bestseller, <u>Secrets of the Tomb: Skull and Bones, the Ivy League, and the Hidden Paths of Power</u>, is a prime example.   However, Miss Robbins is a Yale elite female-secret society member herself.   Could this be her attempt to aid her alma mater, spreading her own disinformation? There is widespread appeal for secret society history and legend in America and the World, that much is for sure. These books are chock-full of true-life tawdry liaisons, fraudulent scandals, wars, and all sorts of chaos. This should make it perfect for the trashy, dumbed-down, propaganda programming dominating primetime television. Yet, secret societies are afforded only a slanted, biased, and brief documentary on the History Channel and a blip on cable news.

One note: this media blackout may be slowly changing. In March, 2004, the TRIO channel ran a series of which I was able to catch three episodes. One was a lengthy interview with Alex Jones about the Bohemian Grove Club. Another was a good one about the Bilderbergs. Also, I saw Jim Marrs on some program, but can't remember where.1a

Pertaining to the origins of secret societies, a multitude of theories are presented. There are two reasons for this. Groups like the Freemasons (who I believe are in the uppermost strata of these societies) have always "released"

72

conflicting histories, to spread confusion. Then, too, there are some kooks in the conspiracy theory field that have left a bad taste in mainstream America's mouth. It is possible, though we do have a few certifiable crazies among us, that these nuts are Illuminati plants and patsies. With vile projects like MK Ultra (explained in "Politics in G Minor - Chapter 36: State-sanctioned Individual Mind Control,") where the government used American citizens as human guinea pigs without their knowledge to test mind control techniques, the speculation for counter-propaganda is warranted. The government has admitted to this mind control experimentation. Another cloud in uncovering secret societies are the different "reality-tunnels" which make one's incorporation of data different from another's. Finally, one must be wary that everyone is trying to sell their own agenda, which obviously causes differing interpretations.

One thing seems clear: the first secret society, or at least the first one with archeological evidence, seems to have appeared in Babylon, somewhere around 2200 B.C.2 Babylon was once the pinnacle of Earth's civilization. It was in Babylon, Sumer, and Uruk - in the area now known as Iraq - that great strides in the evolution of writing, mathematics, and astronomy were demonstrated. Could this be why American military stole Babylonian relics during the first weeks of the Iraqi War? What kind of artifact could the military/industrialists have been looking for? Due to the nature of the evidence, all theories are debatable. So, without being remiss, we take a look at three of the most popular theories on the true origin of secret societies.

**Evangelical, End-Times, Revelations-based theory**

A few generations after the Great Flood, Nimrod was King of Babylon.2 He started a dark, Satanic cult that recruited and promoted many people, promising them power and wisdom. After Nimrod's death, one of Noah's sons attacked and defeated the Babylonians for their defilement of God's sacraments and for idolatry. It was after Nimrod's murder that Semiramus, Nimrod's wife, and several priests started the first secret society, so that they could continue their religious practices without being slaughtered by Christians. Their objective, of course, was an abomination to Christianity. Their group meant to spread Satanic Mysteries throughout the entire world by a series of interlinking "cells" spread across the globe and put into powerful positions.3

It is understandable that Christians would assign the general term "satanic" to the first group of secret worshippers of gods other than God, Son, and/or Holy Spirit. If the evangelical claim is correct, secret societies have an approximately 4,000-year history of spreading occult practices. Perusing documents from the higher chambers of power, it seems that this is actually a fair assessment of the truth. Many modern groups can be found to promote practices which are at best, merely anti-Christian. And modern secret societies are rife with rituals and practices that can be linked to Ancient Egypt, Babylon, Israel, and other cabalistic civilizations. The anti-Christian link is one of the characteristics that ties ancient, Dark Age, and modern secret societies together in a common, practical, spiritual, and often overlapping thread. I have read that secret society members of Babylon - Babylon, loosely translated is "heaven's gate" - worshiped Sin, god of the moon, not Satan.4 Members of the modern Bohemian Grove worship Molech, an Ancient Babylonian Owl God. The masters of the universe who meet clandestinely once a year in California's secluded Bohemian Grove have included names like Bush, Kissinger, Reagan, Gingrich, and other elite politicos. It matters little the name the secret societies ascribe to their deities. To Christians, if it ain't God, it's evil. It was this blanket "Satanism," or proclaiming someone a Satanist who merely worships a deity other than the Christian God, that has led to several holocausts: Muslims were slaughtered during the Crusades; Germanic tribes were "converted" from paganism by choice of a pyre; Jews in every Christian country in existence have been denounced; pilgrims were burnt at the stake for missing mass. One Hebrew newspaper reported that President G.W. Bush was recorded telling Sharon that "God" had told him to attack Iraq, and attack Iraq he would. Will his Iraqi War be thought of as a Holy one? To some people, it is.5

Another common tradition amongst secret leagues is the exultation of oral tradition and teaching. This is in direct relation to the need for members to keep pertinent facts away from the general public. Writing allows for proof of the groups' missions or operations or rituals. Some, such as The Cutting Edge and Bible Believers, claim that another secret society that formed during Jesus' time was the Jewish Pharisees. They are known for their rich, esoteric oral tradition. These Cabalists, as they are sometimes called, were predecessors of the Zionist movement. Calling them a satanic cult is a stretch; dubbing them anti-Christian is fair. One proof given of their evildoing is that Jesus was so violently and vehemently opposed to the Pharisees and Sadducees, while expressing toleration for murders, prostitutes, and the possessed. The worst sin to Jesus was worshipping any other than God than the true God. It seems the only people ever to make Jesus flip out were the secret elite cabal a.k.a. the Pharisees, and pre-international bankers, a.k.a. the money lenders.

Whether or not one has faith in the Bible, it should be noted that many things expressed in Revelations seem to be coming true. A one world government, one money supply, a world religion, all happening as I write this. The men who are the obvious ascendants to the New World Order throne are ultra rich, ultra educated, mostly white Europeans or Khazar Jews who proclaim they know what is best for us. Regardless of the instigators, some of Revelations' prophesies are coming true. The largest difference is that in books like <u>Left Behind</u>, Jesus Christ's Church is taken away during the Rapture. If this were to happen, that would be the first absolute proof for many me that God exists. If 20% or so of the population disappeared at any time...well, I know my Bible. I start preparing for my battle against Satan so my judgment might be reassessed after the years of tribulation. As of yet, the Rapture has not occurred, but the beat of universal-everything marches on. The concepts of the New World Order are advancing. Secret society members are promulgating a police state. One needs faith. Christians must unite to fight these elite, secret society members. For, perhaps, just perhaps, there will be no Rapture. The concentration camps are still ready, whether or not God comes. A side note about proof of God: the happiest, most sane person I know is my Mother, Jay Fortman. She is a Christian, and would state unequivocally that "with God, anything is possible."

## The Reptilian Theory.

Ziggler the Interdimensional Comic is a friend of a friend. You've met him. He is the guy with the paisley shirt trying to sell you kelp and "super vitamins." He probably has a crystal in his pocket, and does drugs frequently. Ziggler even goes so far as to say that drugs are good for you, so it does not conflict with his Vegan health ideology. That guy you know has a theory, too. Yes, Ziggler the Interdimensional Comic has a theory about the origins of the secret societies. It seems that his theory is becoming a more widely accepted concept in certain circles. It's called the "reptilian theory." Its most famous proponent is David Icke, author of several books including my favorite, Children of the Matrix.6 Icke espouses, as far as I could understand, that there are several different races of aliens. The Reptilian aliens bred with humans to create a few elite masters to control the masses, the masses being the reptilians' ultimate harvest.7

According to this subculture, one of the core issues inherent inside secret societies is the preservation of bloodlines. This is because elites believe they are more purely Reptilian than the common masses. Interbreeding and arranged marriages among the elites are pointed to as evidence of this obsession with offspring. All humans, with their reptilian DNA, can be "entered" by reptilians from other planes of existence, especially through man's use of rituals. Because of the rituals of secret societies, government organizations, and royal families, it is almost impossible that the elite can stop the Reptilians from possessing them. The ultimate goal of the Reptilians is the complete dominance of the human race. This can only be done at certain phases of intergalactic time. Icke believes that one of those times is soon. That is why they are stepping up their institution of fascist tactics and strategies. Ultimately, Icke thinks that the Reptilians are controlling the most powerful people, including Bush and Blair, and Rothschild and Rockefeller.8

The secret societies are in place to 1. Hide the truth about the reptilians 2. Bring the world under control of a tiny, concentrated power structure to better enslave us

While not as popular as the religious view, the Reptilian Theory has been honed into a viable option. There are supposed ancient writings from long ago, discovered recently, which prove the reptilian connection. These are presented as the *Emerald Tablets* and other ancient texts. Icke declares that the *Emerald Tablets* were found in a chamber of the Great Pyramid and date back an astonishing 36,000 years. Proof positive? No, but very interesting. While David Icke may have swung himself onto a highway of speculation concerning the Reptilians, his books spend most of their space explaining the power structure of the Illuminati, written utilizing meticulous research. Most of his tomes uncover well-documented proof of the Illuminati, the secret societies, and the New World Order. David Icke has perhaps deciphered the Webs of Power better than any other single writer.

**Constitutionalist Theory**

Constitutionalists are a mixed bag. Ranks include overlapping. Evangelicals, libertarians, militia members, and even super left-wing activists often jump the divide to stand together when fighting to save the Bill of Rights. Constitutionalists are generally aware that Babylon and Egypt were the birthplace of secret societies. However, to this group, the concern is not so much history as it is the societies' relevance in today's world. Constitutionalists know that they may not ever be able to prove the origin of secret societies. They want to unveil what these societies are doing right now. Evidence suggests that modern secret societies are propagating depopulation, war, a one world government, and rule by elite legacies. Unlike their fellow secret society critics, Constitutionalists seek not to find the why. They tend to search for the where, when, what, and how. These more practical questions are slowly being unraveled, by careful study of the groups in question. Secret societies have had countless U.S. Presidents, high ranking Cabinet members, mega rich financiers, media executives, and military men included in their numbers. My research into the Federal government, in "Webs of Power," forced me to investigate secret societies. From Babylon's Cabal to Britain's Round Table, secret societies are here and have been for quite a while. Their agenda becomes more and more obvious as we delve into the urban myth, conflicting quotations, and differing treatises. In famous writings by noted secret society authors Goldstein and Steinberg we read a truth that few of us want to admit. "It is absolutely necessary to understand that the American Democratic form of government came into being with the full power of the Freemasonic secret societies, which find their beginnings in the occult practices of ancient Babylon. These ancient rites mixed with Freemasonry's Germanic paganism and pragmatism and - the creation of the Illuminati, or 'illuminated ones' - have been passed down from Freemasons to others: Skull & Bones, the Zionists, and the Bildebergs, etc."9

**Erik's Theory**

After extensive research, and after finishing a book about secret societies, readers might ask what my opinion is. Truthfully, until this book was already finished, I was not able to put my theory into words. Then a friend asked me the following question one night, when we were discussing Ancient Egypt. "What do you think of this. The Ancient Egyptians were much smarter than we think, and had superior technology to what we have now. That technology has kept the same people in power since that time."

That is a very strong possibility. A strong case can be made that humans are devolving, not evolving. Also, we know the aristocrats like the Windsors, their cousins the Bushes, the Du Ponts, the Vanderbilts believe they extend from the royalty of Egypt and Babylon. As to Egyptian technology, there is some evidence to support the fact that they had radios, flying ships, and even that a nuclear weapon was dropped around 10,000 years ago.10  That may or may not be true.  It is true that the secret groups, led by members who trace their bloodlines back to Ancient Egypt, claim to be protecting the Ancient secrets of Egypt and Babylon.  I believe that they are hiding not mysticism, but advanced, unknown, "alien" technology.  "The Disclosure Project" has proposed this contention.  This is my belief with the facts that we have available to us at this time.  These people have been in power for 4,000 years, minimum.  They have almost perfected our enslavement.  The police state is here.  All you have to do is open your eyes.

The following chapters, like the essays in "Webs of Power", are only meant as brief summaries of the best-known secret societies.  I only scratch the surface.  I have attempted to take several views and find correlations.  It will be the reader's decision to decide what the purposes of the various secret societies are.  What cannot be refuted is that they exist and are in control.

# Shadows of Power - Chapter 12: Freemasonry

Freemasonry. The word evokes visions of secret rites, freedom fighting, intellectualism, and dark ulterior motives. Its members have been hailed as bastions against tyranny and criticized as harbingers of oppressiveness. They have been banned, persecuted, excommunicated, and spoken against by churches, political regimes, and by the general public. Cases can be made for all of these claims and allegations. Freemasonry boasts approximately six million members.1 There are lodges across the globe. The organization's political influence has yet to be eclipsed by any one other secret society. Freemason roots can definitely be traced back to the 11th or 12th Century, and many lodges boast of a history extending back to differing ancient civilizations. There have been over 100,000 books written about Freemasonry. In short, because of the Freemasons' unrivaled popularity and involvement in intrigue, they have been both sought for favor and avidly disavowed.

Freemasonry finds its roots in the Dark Ages, with the rise of architecture in Europe. Also, the European Continent experienced a population explosion, despite plagues and archaic medicinal practices. The Catholic Church was the State, and they dictated all. Fortunately, the clergy had the foresight to undertake great public works. This brought about a new class in the very ordered society: the Stonemasons. The Stonemasons were a skilled labor class. Great edifices were being erected, such as the great cathedrals, castles, abbeys, and libraries. Masonry was considered a "secret" knowledge, imbued with mystical properties. This was in a time when literacy was actually forbidden by Catholicism. There were different levels of masonry one could acquire. Master Masons were the top echelon. Apprentices were the bottom. Stonemasonry was an escape for young men from the rural areas and for peasants wishing to escape from mundane agricultural lives or serfdom, respectively.2, 3

At first, the omnipotent Church kept masons under complete control. The masons' days, weeks, and years were planned for them. At certain periods, kings and popes ordered civilian conscriptions for building projects. The stonemasons lived together, congregating in lodges close to the sites. This is probably where the first masons discussed their circumstances and decided to try and band together for a common good. They swore oaths to never reveal trade secrets. Concealment became a beneficial policy and trade secrets were kept, because of the skilled nature of the job. Stonemason guilds sprang up throughout Europe and became a strong economical force. Even at this early time, rumors began to spring up about the masons. For instance, London Bridge was originally wooden, but was destroyed by a fire. It was rebuilt in stone by masons in 1209, and the rhyme "London Bridge" subsequently spread throughout England. Unsubstantiated, but widely believed was that the 'fair lady' in the poem was actually a virgin walled up inside the bridge by the masons as a sacrifice to God. The term stonemason was probably from the German league's name "Steinmetzen." The organizations worked as early forms of labor unions, with all the positive and negative elements that come with them.4

At the end of the 17th Century, great bounds in science, philosophy, and economics were born. As the need for stonemasonry declined, and education rose, the mason workers allowed non-masons to enter their ranks. Many of these were thinkers, followers of the newer schools of thought. Reform, relativist, and Jacobean dogmas were debated and critiqued. Many people present Freemasons as evil because they have been excommunicated by several Popes, most recently in 1983.5 Proponents of the group also point to the excommunications as proof that the Freemasons are on the side of good, because the Catholic Church is so evil, itself. Regardless, one of the talents of the Freemason lodges was their savvy ability to curry favor from different regimes and to recruit aristocrats. Freemasons were also ousted by Hitler's Nazis, Lenin's Communists, and several other ruling parties. A side note: Hutton Gibson, Mel Gibson's father, claims that the reason he and his son split with the Catholic Church was that at that time a Freemason Pope was appointed even though the they had previously excommunicated Freemasons.6

Communist, Nazi, and Catholic denouncements have actually served to bolster perceptions of the group. This author is by no means a scholar of the craft. However, in my research I have come to my own conclusions. I believe that the original Freemasons were believers of progressive philosophies that are accepted as truths, now. All men are created equal. Government works to serve the people. These were what many early Freemasons fought for. As Freemason power swelled, the lodges became infiltrated by men who sought to use its established corridors for vile, evil purposes. Also, Rosicrucianism had a huge influence among the dominant membership. Regrettably, the Rosicrucian and Freemason belief, that eventually a universal God will be accepted by the world helping to create a global society, has been taken to the extreme. This belief in a secular God was probably in response to the oppressiveness of the Catholic Church. Today, evangelical Christians, Muslims, and others claim this universal God is meant to supplant the true (respectively) God.

In the initiation rites, not adhering to the code of silence means death. This was proven in the case of John Morgan. Morgan, a Freemason, was set to publish a book revealing many secrets of Freemasonry. The publishing house conveniently burned to the ground before the book could be printed. Morgan "disappeared." This created much ire in the American populace and led to our nation's first unified third party, the Antimasons. Loyalty to the Freemason lodge and the order are paramount, and this fact must be orated by initiates.[7] These oral statements are used for fodder against the group by its detractors. This is especially true among individualists and nationalists. It would be prudent to expand on Rosicrucian philosophy, because Freemasons adopted so much of it. The Order of the Rosy Cross, or Rosicroix, was inspired by the Hermetic writings, which are believed to hold secrets of the Egyptians which were associated with the god of wisdom, Thoth. They expounded on such things as alchemy, science, magic. Also, Rosicrucian writ describes the transference of the soul through specific spheres. A fact that lends too much speculation and conspiracy theory is that

Freemasons adopted practices from the Rosicrucians; Rosicrucians, in turn, adopted practices from the Jewish Cabalists. The Jewish Cabalists were extremely secretive, using a strict oral tradition and ceremonial rites. Cabalists opine that God is infinite light, and through meditation on His name, one can become enlightened. Just as the Freemasons were persecuted by the authoritarian Catholic elite for their more lenient secular views, Orthodox Jewish Rabbis dogged Cabalists. The charge was a false claim of unknown knowledge. Worse was alleged. Cabalists put too great of an importance on revelation and ecstasy, orthodox Jews opined. By way of a connection to Cabalism, however indirect, Freemasons have been purported to be sympathetic to the Jewish cause over the Muslim. It seems that American elite Freemasons have been pro-Zionist, as it is always the Republicans who support Israel while the Democrats endorse Palestine, generally speaking. However, Zionist does not mean Jewish.8

Freemason ties can also be found in Muslim persecutions. A portion of Freemason tradition and history can be traced to many of the holy orders of knights, most notably the Knights Templar. The Knights Templar's roots go far back, into the first Crusades. Ironically, the Knights Templar shared many attributes with the Assassins, a Persian religious warrior order first seen at the beginning of the second millennium. The Assassins smoked hashish, and ascribed credence, even sacramental elements, to the hallucinations. The Knights Templar, however, made vows of piety and chastity. It was the Knights Templars adoption of secretive rites and religious holy war that was very much like the Assassins. The Knights Templar were the deciding factor in many battles, both wins and losses. Their stated belief was the hegemony of Christianity. Their order became wealthy from the wars, and after the eventual rejection of a Holy War policy, the Knights Templar used their wealth to become the largest moneylender in Europe. They are one of the precursors to what is today generally regarded as an international banker. Rumors that circulated about the Knights Templar were not really much different than the rumors of current countries' administrations. Just recently, top level official in France were allegedly involved in child prostitution and other crimes.9 The Knights were tried for homosexuality, and worse: spitting on the cross during initiation rites. In all fairness, scrutiny of a group like the American Military in Iraq surpasses anything Dark Age minds could have fathomed. Yet, projects like MK Ultra are never revealed, never admitted to, until well after their implementation. MK Ultra was a mind control experiment undertaken by the Federal Government and CIA. They reportedly used foreigners and U.S. citizens to research mind control. In a strange twist, Cathy O'Brien is making claims that Dick Cheney, Gerald Ford, and other famous politicians bought her and used her in the most despicable ways, though most of the men she lists claim to be Christian, Freemason, and fighters of Muslim terrorists.10 The Knights Templar essentially lived their lives in the Middle East. It is possible, that the order said they were undertaking a Holy War, but in fact were raping, torturing, and abusing whomever they wanted. History shows that in most cases, left to their own devices, this is what soldiers will do. Whatever the truth, we must look to more modern times to pick up the trail of the Freemason story.11, 12

Freemasonry first recorded an instance of a unified lodge when four separate lodges started the Grand Lodge of England in 1717. As with any organization, there were members who meant well, and those that did not.

There are many strange occurrences and unexplainable coincidences in the fraternity. Some of them are myths. For instance, it is widely accepted that Freemasons have never allowed women into their ranks, which is untrue. Some European countries, such as France as early as the 18th Century, allowed women. However, this practice is still not widespread, and most Freemasons don't seem to accept women as equals. Most of our Founding Fathers were Freemason, and they saw fit to make sure women had no suffrage.

The Royal Arch began around 1750, but its exact origins are not concrete. In this Freemason rite, the name of God is revealed, and has become the name known to all

Freemasons.    Jahbulon has given Christians probably the largest argument against Freemasonry.  For Jahbulon denotes "Ja" for Yaweh or Jehovah, "bul" for Baal, and "On" for Osiris.   The spread of more pagan or atheistic morals was a phenomenon that occurred in Europe.   Nietzsche and other great thinkers were proposing new theories on a godless reality.  This necessitated a new set of morals for man.  The stranglehold that Catholic Church brainwashing infected upon humankind was deep.   Not many were able to make the refutations of God that Nietzsche made, at least not publicly. If one believes the premise that life is a fight against good and evil, then the Freemasons use of the name Baal is something to get angry about.  If one allows for freedom of religion, then it matters little what Freemasons call their God.  Whatever one believes, at the end of the 18th Century, many men were starting to look at other possibilities than those given them by the Holy Roman Church.

While Freemasons were starting a grand experiment in America, Napoleon was devastating Europe.  Napoleon and most of his council were Freemasons.  Freemasonry is replete with vile characters, just as it is with heroes.  This is another dichotomy that lends to debate over the true intention of the group.  Adam Weishaupt was the creator of the Order of the Illuminati, and was also a Freemason.  It is said the Illuminati wanted to guide history.  That is true.  Weishaupt and the Illuminati were aristocrats and elitists.  Yet, one of their most definite reasons for existing was to fight the Catholics and the oppressive Prussian and French regimes.  In fact, the Order was banned in Bavaria, because the tyrannical government knew that a secret society was dangerous to tyranny. Democratic leaders have often said the same thing.  This is confusing, for example the 33rd Degree Mason, Benjamin Franklin, and Freemason Voltaire are considered "good" masons.  But, Weishaupt is considered a "bad" mason.  At freemasonrywatch.org, an interesting tidbit is shown us. Andrew Johnson was plagued for the rest of his career by a letter left by John Wilkes Booth just hours before he assassinated Lincoln. "Don't wish to disturb you.  Are you at home?  J. Wilkes Booth."  Freemasonrywatch.com displays the similarities between the JFK and Lincoln assassinations.

*"1.   Both assassinations involved an elaborate conspiracy which implicates many prominent men, most of whom turn out to have met on the level and parted on the square.*
*2.  Both assassinated Presidents are not Freemasons.*
*3.   Both assassinated Presidents are replaced with Vice-Presidents who are Freemasons."*

Testimony from a Gen. Granger during President Andrew Johnson's subsequent impeachment trial states that he was present during a conversation between President Johnson and Albert Pike.   Gen. Granger is quoted as saying that Freemasonry was the gist of the lengthy conversation.  Also, the general believed that Pike was Johnson's superior in Freemasonry.   One of the men involved in assassinating Archduke Ferdinand admitted that his partner was a Freemason, and the group had passed the death sentence of Ferdinand. Also, Ronald Reagan had an assassination attempt made upon him. His VP, George H.W. Bush, is a Freemason, and knew the shooter's family very well.

Religiously speaking, there are many opinions forthcoming about the fraternal group.  One theory that seems to have some footing is that the Freemasons are actually descendents of the Johannites.  The Johannites worshiped St. John, but reviled Jesus Christ.  Both the Knights Templar and the Freemasons are accused of this.  In their rites, ample mention is made of John, but never of Jesus.  Much to do is made over quotes and facts showing that the Freemasons abhor Christianity.  It should be noticed by atheists, agnostics, and level-headed Christians that this was most likely in redress to the abhorrent, oppressive life leaders of Christianity had presented to the people in Europe up to that time.  Underneath, there is the charge of Luciferianism against Freemasons. Notable Freemasons, including Albert Pike, have stated that Christianity will be denounced and Lucifer will take his place as the ruler of the earth.  Pike claimed to be an atheist, but he wrote one of the most important treatises in Freemason literature, Morals and Dogma.13  That book clearly supports

Luciferian doctrines. Therefore, we must wonder if he meant that Lucifer, the deity, would reign; or, in context it seems he may have meant that humans would become gods. I am God, or Man is God is a common theme of the enlightenment and the New Age. This follows the philosophic lineage that started its modernity with Nietzsche and other intellectuals, reaching another apex with the writings of Ayn Rand. During Christmas, 2003, these secularists made an attempt to scourge Christianity and that religion's heritage by banning all Christian scenes from public places on its most important holiday.

It should be noted that Albert Pike helped form the Ku Klux Klan. He was rumored to be the leader of the Freemason group, Knights of the Golden Circle, who were the true instigators of the American Civil War. The House of Rothschild endorsed this war monetarily. Pike was a racist southerner, as were almost all white southerners at that time. What many Southern boys need to realize is that it is no accident that slavery and State's rights were fighting on the same side. Slavery would be defeated, as was evidenced by the growing consciousness of America. By defeating the South and slavery, the globalists were able to begin the long push toward the dictatorial central government that we have today. Pike painted his original KKK as a defender of State's rights. This made it easier to get the economically depressed white south to join. Men would hardly pay dues to uphold slavery when they couldn't afford slaves. They would, however, join and pay membership to rid the countryside of the oppressive Union military and odious carpetbaggers. Freemasons, without a doubt, are a group with many members believing in white supremacy. For that, they are wrong, as are millions of Caucasians in all walks of life.

Freemasonry has had a long, complicated life. Its lodges have been home to some of the world's greatest leaders, on the sides of both good and evil. There are many coincidences involving Freemasons that hint at shadowy dealings. It seems that most the criticism stems from Christians and patriots. Many have distorted what Freemasons have said and meant. Are some Freemasons atheists, and violently opposed to Christianity? Yes. In fact, Freemasonry membership is so high, and lodges are spread so far across the globe, it would be impossible not to have just about every denomination represented. Are many of the Freemasons elitists. Yes, and those elitists should be exposed. As an individualist, I could never join a club such as theirs. I do see the appeal, at least as it stood in the 18<sup>th</sup> and 19<sup>th</sup> Centuries. For Christians, there is ample fuel for a holy fire. Blasphemous the Freemasons are at times. In the end, it will be the reader that decides: are the Freemasons a positive or negative entity. In this author's opinion, the group's origination was a sort of workers' Union, and commendable. However, as with most groups that gain vast power, dishonorable men soon joined to wield some of that power. In the end, it was this that led to little semblance of good or fairness being left inside the Freemason organization.

## Shadows of Power - Chapter 13: The Illuminati

Although the actual secret society, The Ancient and Illuminated Seers of Bavaria (a.k.a. the Illuminati, the Order of the Illuminati, the Order, Illuminated Ones, etc.) no longer exists as a group, it is prudent to provide a biography of the society for several reasons. First and foremost, the term Illuminati has surfaced into the public consciousness. The word is used so widely and so often that a history of how the term began is needed. "Illuminati" has turned into a blanket term to define 'those in power that seek a one world government.' But, The Illuminati were truly a secret society, an offshoot of the Freemasons. Second, the Order of the Illuminati provides additional links and even more evidence to support the thesis that rich, influential members of the Order of the Illuminati have funded other groups and spawned offshoot societies to create chaos in the world. Finally, the Illuminati provides a looking glass into the minds of the elite and of the occult Freemasons who later evolved into groups such as Skull & Bones and the Bohemian Grove Club. The Illuminati may not have survived as a lodge, but the ideals of this group survives in the elitist attitudes and secret dealings of modern day secret society members.

The same year that America claimed independence from England, 1776, a German named Adam Weishaupt began a secret order with clandestine, and as we shall see, evil plans. The group has been known by many aliases and monikers, but it was officially dubbed the Ancient and Illuminated Seers of Bavaria. The lodge fused elements of occult Freemasonry, Sufism, Hatha Yogism, and many other mystical rites. The term 'illuminati' has always had a special place with the elite and also inside the secret societies, all the way back to Babylon. The upper echelon of Freemasons, aristocrats mostly, believed that they were enlightened - illuminated - and therefore needed to guide humanity in a paternal role. Humans were largely ignorant, the elite discussed, and therefore were like children needing a father figure, which is embodied in the idea of an elite government. The Illuminati, as they referred to themselves, would provide the light for which humanity could be led (herded) into a world super-state led by the said illuminated ones.1

The men who usurped the fledgling lodge of 'Illuminated Ones' were an inner circle of five, in accordance with the occult symbol, the pentagram. These men included Adam Weishaupt; his associate and confidant, Kollmer; Francis Dashwood (of the Satanic Hellfire Club); DeSade (a known sexual deviant and the man whose name is reportedly the origin of the term 'sadism;') and Meyer Rothschild (founder of the modern banking family.) They had one goal, but it was a large one: a goal they knew would not be achieved in their lifetimes.2

Ultimately, the Ancient Illuminated Seers of Bavaria wanted nothing less than to overthrow all national governments and world religions.

In writings of Myron Fagan entitled "A Satanic Plot for a One World Government - The World Conspirators: the Illuminati," the strategies utilized by these men are set forth. To attain the favor of leaders already in power, the use of bribery and sex were "arranged" by the Illuminati's agents. Members of the Order who were professors would seek students, preferably with wealthy families and internationalist leanings. They would cultivate these students for the next generation of 'illumination.' Also, complete control of the press was promoted as a means to sway public opinion and further the Order's viewpoints. Fagan states that because England and France were the superpowers of the 18th century, the Illuminati wanted to destroy them, making it easier to infiltrate the highest levels of their respective governments. Weishaupt brazenly laid plans for a French revolution to aid in this quest. He also wanted to pit America vs. England for as long as possible. In 1784, before the French Revolution and after the American one, the Bavarian government came across evidence to show that Weishaupt, Rothschild, and the gang were involved and were planning to overthrow governments. Because of this evidence, the Bavarian government outlawed the Order of the Illuminati and all of Weishaupt's Grand

Orient lodges. Even though the Bavarian government revealed the conspiracy, as did a Scottish rite member whom Weishaupt asked to join, the French Revolution started in 1789 as planned by Weishaupt and the Illuminati.3

The Illuminated Ones' quest to overthrow and infiltrate the French government was so successful that the Order decided to instigate more revolutions in Europe, so that they might enter into even more halls of power in a concerted effort. These became known as the Napoleonic Wars. An added benefit for the group was that the Rothschild financiers would finance both sides of the war, and thus would profit, no matter the outcome. This has always been the Illuminati's strategy. It is their modus operandi. Wars are begun by placing lower level Illuminati members into countries whereby they are able to foment a war, or at least internal dissent and disputes. International bankers make war loans ($160 billion has been financed to the U.S. for Iraq from 2002-2003. That bill will get much bigger, as rumors already suggest) to everyone involved. The end result is that all the surviving countries are bound to many years of debt and interest payments - for wars which need never have been started.

Adam Weishaupt died in 1830, but almost two hundred years after his death his dream is coming closer and closer to fruition. The Illuminati have infiltrated the halls of almost every government on Earth. The "rogue nations" who have not accepted central banks are being systematically traumatized by perpetual war and unjust sanctions, demanded by the IMF and World Bank to perpetuate welfare states that are always in debt.4 They, too, will join in the coming New World Order, simply to survive utter destruction. As to the destruction of religion, Illuminati agents have been successful in bringing about the beginning of the end of Christianity. For instance, Charles Taze Russell was a known occultist, pedophile, and high-level Free Mason. He started the Kingdom Hall of the Jehovah's Witnesses.5 Jehovah's Witness Lodges have served a twofold purpose against Christianity. One, the nefarious indoctrination and recruitment processes of the Jehovah's Witnesses has created a myth. The myth is this. Jehovah's Witnesses proclaim to be Christians.

Therefore, all Christians must be somewhat akin to Jehovah's Witnesses. This is patently false. Over time, the perception is that Christians are tainted. Two, the Jehovah's Witnesses were and are one of the largest growing creeds of Christianity in the World.6 One dogma is nonviolence, even is defense of one's country. This has led to thousands of the cult's followers opting to stand aside when and if their nation comes under attack, either by an outside enemy or a revolutionary entity within. Think about that. To think that Americans, through Jehovah's Witness brainwashing, will not fight to protect the very freedom that we afford them to worship as they please is astounding. I agree with not serving in an immoral war. But saying that you will not fight for your country no matter what is something else entirely. Only with the death of God, and religion of all forms, can the Illuminati herd the majority of the world's population to throw off the yoke of state sovereignty in favor of an even larger yoke, the one world government.

One of the more profound accusations that have been levied against the global elite and specifically the Order of the Illuminati, is that of Satanism. The conspiracy begins by claims that the Order's highest ranking members were descendants of the Merovingians, reported to be the 13th Satanic bloodline.7 It should be noted that David Icke reports this same bloodline as not the ancestors of Satan, but children of the Reptilians. Whether they are reptile/human/alien hybrids, or directly spawned by Satan, the evidence clearly lies in the fact that the Illuminati either believes in Satan, or that they want us to believe that they believe in Satan. The Illuminati actually derive their name from Satan, the Illuminated One. They believe that it was he, Lucifer, that opposed God with his knowledge of the light, and that Satan is the one true God of Earth. In "Satan's Method of World Dominion," written by G. Albert Darst, the author defines Satan's use of man to further his plans. "The word is conspiracy. And that is exactly what is happening in the events of our world today - a satanic conspiracy. As Christians, we believe that nothing happens by chance. God proposes all that is good. All that is evil is allowed by God, but used by Satan to further his plans. How diabolical that

Satan uses the evil in man to physically and spiritually destroy man." Darst and a plethora of other writers believe that Adam Weishaupt and Meyer Rothschild were agents of Satan. The goal of a one-world government is prophesied in Revelations, many claim. Singular world dominance by the elite Europeans was the admitted goal of the Ancient Illuminated Seers of Bavaria.8

Before conceiving the Order, Weishaupt trained as a Jesuit, the Catholic order that brought about the European Inquisition. The Illuminati used the pyramid with an eye at the apex as their logo, or symbol. It was the representation of initiates in the dark at the bottom of the pyramid, denoting the majority of humanity. Members eventually worked their way toward the apex and total illumination, wherein they would 'see' and know all. The pyramid with the all-seeing eye was imprinted on Federal Reserve currency for years. Even the Ministry of Information Awareness, started by George W. Bush, bore the symbol. Some say that Skull & Bones is the actual direct descendant of the Order of the Illuminati. Also, the Illuminati has direct ties back to the Knights Templar and the Moslem Assassins (Assassins means "hash smokers," roughly. The "illumination" was actually just pure THC-induced hallucinations.)

Texe Marrs has written a book called <u>Mystery Mark of the New Age</u>. Inside, he lays out what he believes is Satan's plot to bring about global domination through the subversion of world religions and the installation of a one world government, a.k.a. the design of the Illuminati. He believes that the Illuminati are going to use their new technology such as microchip, data base, and tracking devices to implant biochips into our bloodstream (the in-the-dark humans at the bottom of the pyramid, anyway,) and will eventually be able to keep tabs on us fully and completely. Marrs believes that these devices may be the mark of the beast as written in Revelations, the Bible.9

The final piece of damning evidence that supports the Satanic theory is the Illuminati's own "Bible," if you will. The tome's name is "The Protocols of the Elders of Zion."10 It was written by a man named Barruel, who became close to

Weishaupt, and eventually joined the Order. Inside this book are espoused the ideas that have been pursued by the Illuminati since the time of Nimrod in Babylon. Again, these philosophies include the destruction of religions, states, and even the family unit. The slogan of the United Nations Education, Scientific, and Cultural Organization is "Every Child Is Our Child." The "Protocols of the Elders of Zion" was also a fundamental basis for Communism, which seeks to impose unsurpassed collectivism at the expense of the individual. Today, even as we speak, we can see these ideas coming to 'light.' Christianity, Judaism, Islam and other, more fundamental, religions are being attacked on all sides, and we will soon be forced to refute God publicly on pain of persecution. Just look to the Judge Roy Moore incident and the debate over "under God" in schools for evidence. The battle is blatantly obvious. It should also be noted that the "Protocols" are not affiliated with Hebrews. European aristocrats, Illuminati, and a few elite Jews wrote them. Both groups were Freemasons.

The second step for the Illuminati, creation of a New World Order, is also plodding along its path. The once great and unique countries of Europe are being eaten and digested inside the acidic belly of the European Union. The African Union has been instituted. And, believe it or not, an American Union has been proposed and proceeds to take place. In this, the American Union will become one country, containing the provinces of America, Mexico, Brazil, etc. NAFTA was the beginning of the American Union, and the Free Trade Area of the Americas (FTAA) will be another giant step. Global leaders are forming us into "blocks" and creating increasingly larger international trade lines. Even the blocks will soon be erased until we all simply call ourselves 'Earthlings.' No other affiliation will be necessary - or allowed. The United Nations continues its assent to power. The weaker Christianity and the family unit become in America, the closer we are to joining the chorus for a benevolent world governing body. Even now, the Democrats clamor about the wonders of the United Nations, while Bush keeps inviting them into Iraq after he went against them in the first place. Whether or not the Illuminati truly believe in Satan is still not completely clear. The elites' use of Luciferianism and occultism is irrefutable, though, whether or not they actually believe in it. And, strategically calculated, their methods have been successful. I propose 20 to 50 years for the completion of their goals or a revolt by the 80% of poor people in the World, which in the lifeline of humanity, is a very short time from now. Others, however, are giving things maybe a decade or less. Still others say that the world is too disparate to ever be united under one central government.

The Illuminati, started by Weishaupt and Rothschild, has branched out into several other, distinct societies weaving a web across the globe. These societies include the Council on Foreign Relations, the Trilateral Commission, Skull & Bones, and other secret groups that guide the shaping of the world. They have all the money, power, and influence. Their aims are very close to becoming successful. However, it is now, as they make their final plans, that we, we in the dark are becoming 'illuminated' to their evil plots and devices. It should be every Americans' duty to study these plots, to learn of the Illuminati's methods so that, consequently, we can defeat them at the end game of humanity's enslavement.

## Shadows of Power - Chapter 14: The Zionists

Zionism. Simply the name evokes esoteric thoughts of smoky incantations, the Nothingness of the Torah. To many Americans, Zionists are a Jewish lobby, reportedly using their vast wealth to sway the economies, and therefore the fates, of nations. This is false. The Protocols of the Elders of Zion, the manifesto released by the order, has been proven to have been released by Freemasons, both European and Jewish. It is therefore pertinent to define the Zionist Movement, and also to categorize the two distinct races of Jewish People. Upon quantifying and qualifying our subject matter, a labyrinthine conundrum presents itself. Who was responsible for the concept of Zionism? What has been gained by the German-Jewish holocaust, and what benefits and detriments has the State of Israel brought to the World? This author will present a case that the Zionist Movement is another feint by the Elite, another diversion, another violent instability by which the international bankers, oilmen, slave traders, and drug traffickers are able to increase their wealth and power.

Zionism has been a quintessential - perhaps the most successful - example of the Hegelian Dialectic in a global petri dish. The Freemasons that overtook the highest Masonic orders in the 19th Century were responsible for many instances of social disorder. These chaotic events include an attempt to re-colonize America during the War of 1812; the manipulative instigation of the American Civil War through the Knights of the Golden Circle, consisting of high-level Masons; the assassinations of Lincoln, JFK, RFK, and MLK, Jr., the two non-Mason Presidents having had Freemason Vice Presidents.1 Zionism was constructed by the Globalists and has taken on a life all its own. Israel/Palestine is the center of the Earth, in terms of the strife, death, and geopolitical animosity emanating from around the country's borders. It is a source of intense fear and trauma.

Zionism, as defined by the Jewish Virtual Library, is "the national movement for the return of the Jewish people to their homeland." There's more, but that is the gist of it. It is quite possible that this obviously true statement of intent automatically takes Zionism out of the realm of secret societies, categorizing it as a quasi-religious/racial nationalist movement. Webster's Dictionary defines "Zion" as a "temple in Palestine which was the nucleus of Jerusalem," and refers to an "ism" as "a distinctive doctrine, cause, or theory." By this definition, the true definition of Zionism is the theory or doctrine of a Palestinian temple. So, as always we are slapped in the face with not only the absurd theory that an area around Jerusalem should be renamed Israel, with the Palestinians being expelled from the region; but that even the name itself, Zionism, is defined as "Palestinian Temple Theory." There most definitely exists a plethora of views concerning the Zionist Movement. What is evident is that while the cause has a name - Zionism - and a blatant definition, the methods and strategies of the Zionists are quite subtle, even malevolently clandestine. Thus, the term "secret society" does apply to the lobby.

Before I write further, we must explore the two histories of the Jews. The one group is the Israelites, the Children of God, the Killers of Jesus, the Chosen Ones. These are the people coming from the Middle East, possibly as far back as 6,000 B.C. The descendents of Israel are the only people that can call themselves "Blood Jews." Being of Jewish ancestry, they are Jews regardless of whether or not they believe in the Jewish Faith. An atheist of Israeli descent is still a Jew. Unfortunately, an early civilization located in Khazakstan has stolen the birthright of the Israelites, and by proxy become the mouthpiece of the Jewish people. Henry Makow, Ph.D. is an authority on the subject. Dr. Makow has written numerous articles on the Zionist movement and the true history of the Jews. He is Jewish himself, which lends him extra authority on the subject. He writes in an essay entitled "Do Jews Suffer From False Consciousness" that "Eastern European or Ashkanazi Jews (90% of Jews) were descendent of Khazars, a Turko-Finnish people who converted to Judaism in the 8th Century." The government of this region adopted Judaism to detach its peoples from the Christian/Muslim wars, crusades, and persecutions. Over time, they became known as Jewish people; however, they have no DNA-affiliation with Israel.2 So, as we go forward, we must remain aware of the two separate subcategories of Jews whose only common denominator is Judaism, the religion, and not Israel, the country. When the Khazar Jews were able to make themselves synonymous with Israelites, they soon thereafter began to push for a Jewish migration back to Israel. This is Zionism. So, the first Zionists were not even truly Jewish, or not wholly so. That is why we must look at the motives for creating the Jewish State.

Certainly, as most Jews are unaware of their history, (how a blonde-haired, blue-eyed person thinks he is of Middle Eastern descent is beyond me), so, too, are Zionists confused about their beginnings. The Jewish Virtual Library sponsors a website that is completely written from the Zionist perspective. They credit Nathan Birnbaum (he was so proud of his philosophy/ideology that he used the pseudonym Mathias Ascher. Freemasons used the pseudonym-technique extensively during this era) with "coining" the term Zionism.3 Birnbaum was an Austrian Jew, and therefore probably not of Israeli blood. It should be noted that the first Zionist movement was actually in Ancient times, and the Hebrews' tale of exile is documented in the Bible. The Jewish Diaspora began around the 6th Century B.C.4 The first official global pronouncement of Zionism was Herzl's World Zionist Congress, held in Switzerland in 1897.5 Interestingly, Herzl's movement was painted as a religious movement. Yet Herzl was agnostic, as are most Freemasons. Baron Edmond de Rothschild has been linked to land investments in the region of Palestine at the time Herzl called for the world to accept Jewish migration back to Israel.6 It behooved the Europeans of the late 18th century to find a place for the Jews. Many Jews had migrated from Israel to Europe, and the Europeans, most notably the Germans, had great animosity toward them. But, ousting blood Jews from the Fatherland was only a secondary concern. At that time, the Elite - i.e. Fabians, Knights Templar descendants, and bankers - were setting the stage for global chaos. Freemasons were almost certainly involved in creating the Zionist Lobby as one of the puzzle pieces in their construction of global domination and the enslavement of mankind.

Radio Free Islam, Centre for Monitoring the Impact of Peace, and the Jeff Rense archives are only three of the several dozen sources that have uncovered the connection between the Freemasons and the Zionists. The correlation between European Freemasonry and Zionism are obvious. The tract that has been used for decades to demean the common Jewish folk has been indisputably connected to Rothschild minions. Freemasons were supremely instrumental in espousing the racist views of Zion. The Rothschilds, a Jewish family of the Khazar order, used wealth and contacts to infiltrate the Freemasons and used the Lodges' ignorant members to recruit the weak with promises of wealth to further their New World Order. A mere 50 years after its modern inception in 1897, the Zionist movement came to fruition with the expelling of the Palestinians from their homeland and the transmigration of the Jews to Israel. The world has been a more dangerous, frenzied, and stressful place ever since.

Power is almost always formulated into the structure of a pyramid, with the few at the top giving orders to the generals directly under them. The generals, in turn, move the directions to another level in the chain of command until it reaches the bottom, where it out-sources by recruiting unsuspecting and unaware low-level members. Near the apex of the Zionist pyramid are the Rothschilds and several other elite, aristocratic families. The Rothschild generals directed their personal attaches to enter and infiltrate, or to begin "orders" that would cause social upheaval and civil unrest. The Zionist movement is simply one of those "orders." In addition, Meyer Rothschild's descendants could follow their father's format when sending generals to start new secret societies, gaining knowledge from Meyer's experience starting the Order of the Illuminati. It must be noted that many Jews did not want to move to Palestine. Many believed America to be the new "Zion." It was not until Rothschild money began funding a propaganda campaign that the Zionism of Israel became known as a valid world philosophy and a political reality. Still, most people knew that returning Israel to the

Jews after hundreds of years of absence was illogical, impractical, and possibly insane. Rounding up Palestinian families for removal was a large, moral hurdle. America itself was anti-Semitic, and didn't really care what the Jews did, as long as they didn't enter into their white, Protestant, social circles. That all changed, albeit begrudgingly, with the Nazi Holocaust. Hitler's Jewish extermination was the straw that broke the proverbial camel's back. Leaders of the Western Nations were able to show the atrocious gas chambers and mass graves and sell Zionism to the American and European publics. It is interesting that a hater of Jews, Hitler, was instrumental in reviving that race's global power. Ironic? Perhaps not.

Many sources have reported that Hitler may have been Jewish. That would explain his contempt, which stemmed from a self-hatred (much like J. Edgar Hoover's hatred for blacks, when he himself had clear links to a slave family.) But the largest conspiratorial jump is that Hitler was none other than a Rothschild himself. David Icke is the best selling author of books exposing the Illuminati. He has dedicated fifteen years of research to the material. Admittedly, some of his suppositions are fantastical. However, he documents his sources, and many of his pronouncements have subsequently been proven true. In his article, "Was Hitler a Rothschild," Icke attributes the discovery of the Hitler/Rothschild connection to author Walter Langer.7 The claim is that Adolph's grandmother became pregnant while working for the Baron Rothschild, who reportedly had a lascivious nature toward young women. Hitler's grandmother worked inside the Rothschild estate, where she became pregnant out of wedlock. Shortly after, her family had her married, and less than nine months later she had a bouncing baby boy, Hitler's father, Alois. The 1917 Balfour Declaration stated Lord Balfour and his English government's approval of a Jewish State on Palestinian soil. David Icke writes, "the Balfour Declaration was a letter from Lord Balfour to...Lionel Walter Rothschild." Admittedly, Hitler's grandfather is unknown to us. But, if Hitler were a Rothschild...it would explain much.

100

Today, America, the main supporter of Israel, has many ties to Zionism. I.G. Farben was THE company that supplied Germany's war effort.8 Besides English, German, and Rothschild backing, Prescott Bush, the current President's grandfather, made a mint funding the Nazis through I.G. Farben. The Nazi's killed Jews. The Jews were moved to Israel. It seems it took American money and a Rothschild heir to see Zionism's fruition. It is no wonder that George W. Bush unequivocally supports Israel. That is where much of his family wealth comes from. Very, very simple. Young, conscripted Jews who are indoctrinated into the philosophy of Zionism are used to create chaos in the world. The defense for this is Israel's protection...from the people originally inhabiting the area.

In the end, perhaps the most lamentable victims have been the Palestinians. Most don't condone terrorism or suicide bombings. Even the late Dr. Said, arguably the most outspoken scholar for the rights of Palestinians, decried the tactic.9 Yet, if land were stripped from the ancestors of Americans, we would most likely fight until death until we either won our family's land back, or until we were massacred. Are the Palestinians really that much different than you or me? Regardless of the answer to that question, we must view Israel in a different light. Nothing the world's leaders have done seems to bring about peace. In fact, it is evident that they have been laboring to keep the region in a state of destabilization. Freemason's Zionism has been the primary factor in this destruction and terror.

## Shadows of Power - Chapter 15: The Round Table

The Round Table is the nexus for a group of highly influential, semi-secret societies transplanted into powerful countries throughout the world. The American branch of the Round Table is the Council on Foreign Relations, which will be discussed in depth later on in this book. The Round Table is located in England. Their main goal is global imperialism for the English-speaking races, and more specifically the Anglo-Saxon Germanics that came to live on the British Isles. As we shall see, this group was concocted by racial-elitists who have successfully subjugated the Democratic Party in America and helps lead our foreign policy through the Council on Foreign Relations.

As with many of the secret societies of the 1800's, the Round Table was initially begun with the support of a Rothschild. Nathaniel Mayer Rothschild bankrolled the English industrialist and politico, Cecil Rhodes, to gain control of the African diamond (DeBeers) and gold mining industries. This in the 1880s. Cecil Rhodes and his ideological partner, Alfred Milner, believed in England's world dominance. Rhodes died a rich man, and left several legally binding wills upon his death. One called for the formation of a "secret society with but one object...the bringing of the whole uncivilized world under British rule." Another will established the Rhodes scholarship that gave university grants to like-minded students from England, America, and Germany. Still another legal will gave the power of attorney for the entire estate to the Rothschilds.1

Rhodes Scholars have gone on to become some of the most influential people in all of History. Rhodes Graduates have been instrumental in pushing forward the establishment of a one world government, and have themselves become Illuminati luminaries. David Allan Rivera, in his essays, "The Final Warning: A History of the New World Order," tells us that "the Rhodes fortune, through the Rhodes Scholarship

Fund, has been used to promote the concept of globalism and one world government...of 1,372 American Rhodes Scholars, 431 had positions in teaching and educational administrations, 31 were college presidents, 113 had government positions, 70 held positions in the media, and 14 were executives of foundations."2 These numbers are out of proportion with any other scholarship foundation, and may only be on equal footings with Skull & Bones members who go on to positions of power.

The Round Table was deliberately set up utilizing the best tactics and strategies of English Freemasonry.  Cecil Rhodes was made a Master Mason in 1877.  However, he believed that the English Masons were not doing enough to promote the Anglo-Saxon race throughout the world.  Rhodes also thought that the conspiracies surrounding Freemasonry made it a defunct institution.3  Ironically, all the members of the Round Table inner circle were high-ranking Masons. Watch Unto Prayer is a religious group who opposes the American "religious right" in America as a harbinger of secularism.  Watch Unto Prayer, Jim Marrs, and others have exposed Masonic-links in powerful organizations.  Pertaining to the true motive of the Round Table, they write, "What Cecil Rhodes and Alfred Milner had in mind was the formation of a master/slave society based on the principles of eugenics as derived from Plato's Republic. After Rhodes's death, Alfred Milner, Rothschild, and a group of Oxford Freemason graduates - called 'Milner's Kindergarten' - formed the first Round Table in 1909.3  The overarching theme could be summed up in a statement Milner once made.  'My patriotism knows no geographical but only race limits.'"

There are many separate extensions of the Round Table besides the Council on Foreign Relations.  These include the Bilderberg Group, Club of Rome, the Trilateral Commission, and others.  David Icke declares the following about the Round Table and its subsidiaries. "The network was created to advance through the 20th Century and beyond the Illuminati agenda for the centralized control of Planet Earth," and "as is provable with documentation, they (the Round Table groups) worked together to engineer that (WWI) global

conflict."4   The outcome? Consolidation of wealth and power
into far fewer hands than before the War.  Follow the money.
The prime recipient?   The house that funded it from the
beginning: the House of Rothschild.

This creation of conflict, or constructive chaos as it is
sometimes referred to as, is a continuing strategy of the Round
Table.   In America's recent past, we have seen one
culmination of the Round Table's plot to board America onto
the New World Order bandwagon.   Two-term President
William Jefferson Clinton was a Bilderberger.5   It is no
wonder that his eight-year reign as President saw a blending of
American and United Nation policies.   American soldiers
fought under NATO leadership in the Balkans.  Wesley Clark
was a General in that army, and later became a candidate for
the Democratic Party, a party with clear ties to the Round
Table.  America entered into the Kyoto Treaty under Clinton,
but later exited the agreement under G.W. Bush (one of the
only good things Bush has done in office.)  The explosion of
third-world welfare was directed under Clinton's guidance.
One journalist, J.R. Nyquist, reported in World Net Daily,
1982, that Clinton was already chosen to be a Marxist
American President, bringing about an age of world
socialism.6   In hindsight, we can see that this came to pass.
After only eight years of propagandized socialism, even the
Republican rank and file is willing to accept socialized
medicine in America.  Republicans are also oddly silent on 3$^{rd}$
World welfare, which continues along its failed path.  What is
even more interesting is the Clinton/Rockefeller connection.

The Rockefellers are leaders in the American branch
of the Round Table.  In fact, the Rockefellers are often called
the motivating force of the New World Order, and second in
command only to the Rothschilds.  Today, the Rockefellers are
still one of America's most powerful and influential families.
They own much of our wealth, control many of our industries,
and even help write our children's public (government) school
textbooks through their tax-exempt foundations.   There are
Rockefellers in the Senate and in the Council on Foreign
Relations.  Much like the House of Rothschild's experiments
with eugenics, or selective breeding, to form new bloodlines, a

test that may have begat Hitler; so, too, have the Rockefellers experimented with selective breeding. Is Bill Clinton actually a Rockefeller descendant? It would explain much of his rise to power, his pre-selection for the Presidency, and his one-world views. The writer, Sherman H. Skolnick, reports the chronology of this assertion. The Rockefellers have long run Arkansas, and Winthrop Rockefeller was once the State's governor. Clinton's maternal grandmother reportedly had a long affair with Winthrop. Skolnick writes, "Clinton is apparently the illegitimate great-grandson of old John D. Rockefeller." Rockefeller media went out of its way to portray Clinton as a man from meager beginnings who stumbled to the top. This mimics the propaganda by the Rothschilds of their bloodline descendant, Hitler, another man from a peasant background. Also, most of Clinton's large financial backers had vested interests in Rockefeller securities. These backers included Stephens & Co. and the Jacobs family.7

As we can see, the Round Table is so powerful, they have been able to inaugurate Presidents, sway public opinion, and subvert our political system. It is no wonder, then, that the Round Table seems to be involved in the September 11th terrorist attack on America. In the January 25, 2002 issue of the Executive Intelligence Review (EIR) magazine is an article entitled "Open Conspirators Behind September 11 Coup Plot."8 It informs that H.G. Wells was a leading member of the Round Table in charge of strategy and propaganda. Wells wrote a book back in 1928 called The Open Conspiracy: Blue Prints for a World Revolution. In this book, Wells points to a new religion, which must be spread worldwide. He sums up this new religion, and the Executive Intelligence Review lists the last bullet point of his summation. "(It is) the supreme duty of subordinating the personal life to the creation of a world directorate capable of...the general advancement of human knowledge, capacity, and power." EIR states that another famous leader of the Round Table, socialist Bertrand Russell, agreed fully with Wells' assertions. The magazine also states, "Wells set out to recruit a worldwide network of Open Conspirators, who would operate, within their national settings, on behalf of the global subversion of all nation-states, the 'scientific' depopulating of all darker-skinned races of the planet, and the establishment of one-world oligarchic leadership, under Anglo-American rule." EIR asserts that it is our modern Open Conspirators that were actually behind the 9-11 attacks.   This has allowed the English and American militaries to further their race-based philosophy by killing the dark-skinned peoples in Iraq and Afghanistan, and by the interbreeding of military personnel with those same darker-skinned races which inevitably happens when one sends young men into a foreign country.9

The Round Table, created by a few English elites, funded with Rothschild money, and supported by Rockefeller influence, now has extremely powerful hubs around the globe. The Council on Foreign Relations has been directing American foreign policy for almost a full century. In that time, we have been involved in several wars, which seem to have been lied about. Vietnam was partially about the rubber and oil industries, not Communism. Iraq has a lot, though not wholly, to do with oil, not terrorism. What does the Round Table have planned next? They are most likely at least two or three or twenty chess moves ahead. Why do we (Americans) continue to go along with their policies? Have we not learned that it is a sure path to hell and misery? Are we (the American people) immoral? Or is it simply that our standard of living is so high, we know and just don't care? The Round Table must be stopped. Unfortunately, with the power, wealth, and influence they wield, the Round Table will most certainly remain for a second century. We are witnessing the ascendancy of the New World Order.

## Shadows of Power - Chapter 16: Skull & Bones

Skull & Bones is now, 2004, acclaimed the most powerful secret order in the United States. Not only is the Bush Administration a Skull & Bones Cabinet, but the 2004 Presidential Election is a first. George W. Bush and John Kerry are both Skull & Bones members. Paul Goldstein and Jeffery Steinberg wrote an essay in 1991 entitled "George Bush, Skull & Bones and the New World Order." At the beginning of their article, they propose this thesis. "The reader will learn the President George Herbert Walker Bush's concept of a New World Order is a new idea, one which has its origins in the philosophy of the secret Skull & Bones fraternity...The Order, as it is referred to by its members, is a bastion of White Anglo Saxon Protestant (WASP) culture, which is at the core of the American 20th Century outlook."[1] In 2003, as the son takes the scepter of power, Skull & Bones has again risen to unsurpassed prominence. This elite group running the Bush Administration has proven over and over again that it has only one goal in mind: complete American hegemony.

Skull & Bones' modus operandi is termed 'constructive chaos' or the Hegelian Dialectic. This consists of three phases; problem, reaction, and solution. The Order was founded at Yale in 1832, and it is reported that the initial funds used to beget Skull & Bones were accumulated through the opium trade via the Russell Trust Company.[2] This is telling, as it was the Bush CIA that has been charged with several counts of cocaine trafficking and aiding and abetting the heroin trade.[3] Skull & Bones has only had 2,500 members ever, and only approximately 600-800 are alive at any one time. Their alma mater reads like a who's who of aggressive American politicians. Famous associates include several Tafts, including the former President Taft; most of President Taft's cabinet; Howard Stanley, founder of Morgan Stanley; Prescott Bush and his son and grandson, the Georges, and their cabinets. Goldstein and Steinberg also write, "it must be that the membership of the society has tended over the generations to converge upon a small group of New England families who have intermarried and then sponsored their sons or nephews into the order...It can be documented by comparing the family charts of the early Bonesman that there is today a core group of no more than 20 to 30 families who form the nucleus of the order."1

The Order of Skull & Bones is a truly American twist on Freemasonry and German nationalist societies. In fact, the Order came to be dominated by Brown Brothers Harriman, and specifically Averell Harriman, who was Prescott Bush's mentor.   These two, with John Foster Dulles, practically cornered the market on Nazi business enterprises.   Clear financial ties link the Bush family fortune to profits from one of the most vile businesses to support the Nazi war machine, I.G. Farben.4   All of these men and many of their family members became influential ambassadors and politicians after World War II, even though their fortunes had been largely gained by business arrangements with Hitler and his regime. Anthony Sutton has written extensively on these affairs and is probably Skull & Bones' most acclaimed critic.   His books show that these American elite bankrolled Communist and other fascist regimes in an effort to instigate wars.   These families, including the Rockefellers, made vast profits by choreographing constructive chaos.6

President Taft administration was loaded with Skull & Bones members. Skull & Bones members seem to dominate in the world of politics, finance, and education.   What is interesting is that also in the club is the leader of the militant Gay Activist Alliance, several heads of religious groups, and an owner of child day care facilities.   If there is an agenda, what is it?  Do these people have a part in the overall plan?  If so, what?  Has the Order infiltrated our sexual and religious institutions, too?  Many believe this to be so.

So just how influential have Skull & Bones members been? Alexandra Robbins recently published a novel exposing the Bones' society called "Secrets of the Tomb: Skull & Bones, the Ivy League, and the Hidden Paths of Power", and was recently interviewed by Guerilla News Network.6  She was asked if there was any relevance to the rumors that the fraternity's member were more than just college chums. "...There was a lot more basis to these theories than I had expected. For example, members of Skull & Bones did indeed oversee the deployment of the atomic bomb. They did choreograph the Bay of Pigs invasion. They did fund Hitler when they could." Ms. Robbins claims that it is not so much the group itself, but the individual members that exert power. They propel each other into enviable positions of power to better influence foreign policy. She says this is precisely what President George W. Bush did. "As soon as he (Bush Jr.) got into the White House, one of the first social gatherings he had was a reunion of his Skull & Bones' members. Then almost immediately he started appointing other members of Skull & Bones into positions into the Justice Department and later the Office of Homeland Security."7

There is also an air of morbidity and voyeurism inside Skull & Bones. One of their initiation rites is for new members to tell brothers their complete sex lives, and some say they must do this while masturbating. This is logical, as it would allow all members to have 'dirt' on each other, thereby allowing leverage if a member were to get unruly. It is also claimed that members must steal certain items. George Herbert Walker Bush was reportedly involved in stealing the skull of the famous Native American, Geronimo, from a sacred site, and the Order still will not return it to this day. Why these things were stolen, no one is certain. Some say it's simply college pranks. Others, that it is a means to ensure confidentiality. To add to the myth, the Skull & Bones lodge in Yale is called "The Tomb." It is inside this meeting place that members are initiated by lying in a coffin and being reborn into the brotherhood. Real bones and various body parts from famous people are kept in their inner vaults. Ritual sacrifice in effigy is a part of the initiation ritual. Each "neophyte," as initiates are called, must kiss a skull, one after the other. President Bush, in his biography, "A Charge to Keep", says only this about group. "My Senior year, I joined Skull and Bones, a secret society, so secret that I can't say anything more." John Kerry, after securing the Democratic Party nomination for President in 2004 said this about Skull &

Bones. "It is a group so secret, I can't talk about it." Almost verbatim, he mimics Bush's former comment.

Lyndon LaRouche did extensive research into the Bush family and Skull & Bones. For LaRouche, beyond a shadow of a doubt, Skull & Bones wields world power. As stated in my introduction, the clandestine part of a secret society is its intentions. LaRouche gives the following as S&B's ulterior motives. "It (Skull & Bones) is a very serious, very dedicated cult-conspiracy against the U.S. Constitution."8 Today, with the passage of the Patriot Act, which in essence suspends portions of the Bill of Rights, especially the 4th Amendment, it is easy to see the Order's policy has changed little, if at all. It seems that LaRouche is correct. Skull & Bones does want to take away our God-given rights granted to us by our most important legal document.

Another motif of the fraternity is war. Members must serve in the military at some point in their lives. They fancy themselves modern Vikings. By using constructive chaos, they have effectively learned to steer nations into war for their own profit, and to institute more laws in violation of the Constitution. This was done to great success during both Bush presidencies, despite public criticism. A conglomeration of Skull & Bones members was placed into the Kennedy and Johnson Cabinets. From them, we received Vietnam.

The final outcome, the ultimate goal, the perfect aim is no longer being kept secret. Bush Sr. first made the general public aware of a contemporary concept. Today, elite blue bloods no longer hide what they want. It is simply this: the final implementation of the New World Order. But, how does one define the new world order? In Sutton's famous expose, he states that the N.W.O. has a very specific meaning. Certainly, American domination of the world's natural resources, including humans, with the use of military might is one effect the Bonesman would like to have with a super government. Henry Stimpson was a leading Bonesman. It is reported that while Bush told the U.N. Security Council he was contemplating whether or not to invade Iraq, he was in fact reading Henry Stimpson's biography. Stimpson espouses that America must go to war once every generation or so, for spiritual cleansing. Many facts show that "Operation Iraqi Freedom" was one of these "cleansings." In 1990, then President G.H.W. Bush said, "The year 2000 will be a turning point for the New World Order." Henry Kissinger, criticized for presently being America's shadow government's Secretary of State, said the following prior to 9-11. While Jews were not allowed into the Order, the statement appears to be the prescription being filled by the Bush Administration's current Skull & Bones led war cabinet. Kissinger: "Today, Americans would be outraged if U.N. troops entered Los Angeles to restore order; tomorrow, they will be grateful! This is especially true if they were told there was an outside threat from beyond, whether real or promulgated, that threatened our very existence. It is then that all peoples of the world will pledge with world leaders to deliver from this evil. When presented with this scenario, individual rights will be willingly relinquished for the guarantee of their well being granted to them by their world government."

One last facet of the Skull & Bones society that I would like to discuss is their obvious near-monopoly on the C.I.A. Bush Sr. was the Director for a year, and had a C.I.A. building named after him...by Clinton. If we were to ask ourselves whom does the Patriot Act help most, we can easily see that it has been our intelligence agencies, and specifically the CIA. The FBI has long been a bane to the CIA, or at least an ornery little brother. Now, with the new Homeland Security Department, the FBI will meld with other groups to become a super intelligence agency. Yet, the CIA, under the gun in 2004 for failed intelligence in Iraq and for flubbing 9-11 prior knowledge, was not incorporated into Homeland Security. The CIA, the intelligence agency that has made the most paramount mistakes the last three or four years, is still operating with near autonomy. Tenet, a long time Bush family friend, was not terminated. Instead, he was allowed to resign. This, even though the 9-11 Whitewash Commission admits he was completely inept. Once again, it is Skull & Bones that is behind the intelligence sector's power grab.

I've often wondered about the association between Skull & Bones and other secret societies. The Bonesmen are

affiliated with the CIA and the Republican Party. The Council
on Foreign Relations is definitely more aligned with the FBI
and the Democrats. It often seems that these two groups are
more at odds with each other than many conspiracy theorists
want to admit. However, looking at what laws eventually get
passed, and how the country is trending toward socialism and
secularism, I believe the seeming battle is just a fine rendition
of 'good cop, bad cop.' Also, many members cross the divide
to meet at different annual meetings. Colin Powell is
reportedly a Bilderberg, yet he is a leader inside the Bones-
dominated Bush cabinet. Secretary of Defense Donald
Rumsfeld's links to the Council on Foreign Relations lends
even more credence to the belief that these groups seem at
odds, but are actually working in conjunction. Whatever is
going on in those murky, high places, it is definitely not in our
best interest.

   For now, I am saddened that our fellow Americans
cheer for the death of Iraqis, turn their back on our newest war
veterans, and squirm with a simple picture of bin Laden, or
whomever the evil villain is for any given year. But, it is the
loss of liberty at home, here in the States, which wrenches my
heart the most. The great men of the Great War gave up some
freedom to fight fascist foes. The confused men and women of
the '60's and Viet Nam forfeited a little more freedom in the
name of the War on Drugs and the ridiculous concept of a
Communist 'domino effect.' Now, the Skull & Bones
administration is asking for more than just a little more liberty.
The elite want a big chunk of freedom, and this time it is the
incomprehensible 'terrorist' that they need this freedom from
us to help fight. Terrorists they admit could be me or you or
the next-door neighbor. We are a country of suspects, and a
nation of the suspicious. We live in fear of drugs, pedophiles,
terrorists, cancer, and a multitude of other things. This is not
an accident. They have been feeding us fear for years and
years. Americans have much more to be concerned about with
the American Federal Government than they have ever had to
be with Arabs or drugs. At the end of the day, we must ask
ourselves this question: how will young adults of 2020 view
this generation's men and women? Will we have let pass

another incremental step toward American Tyranny?

## Shadows of Power - Chapter 17: Council on Foreign Relations

The Council on Foreign Relations (CFR) was created in 1919. This was during the period that America's money supply and economic future was handed over to the international bankers a.k.a. the Federal Reserve Act. As will be shown, the Council on Foreign Relations can trace its heritage back to Fabian and, later, Cecil Rhodes. Rhodes created the CFR to be the American satellite for the Round Table secret society of upper class, white supremacists. The 'secret' intent of the CFR is to install a one world government using an incremental, slow, and determined process.1 The Rockefellers, Morgans, and Carnegies have been familial cornerstones of this organization.2 Together with other mostly white, all wealthy men, they have manipulated and infiltrated the American government. Many methods and techniques have been created to aid in their effort, which includes mass mind control and the rewriting of American History. While many countries have followed suit and created their own foreign relations councils, the CFR was originally created as the instrument guiding the machinations of United States foreign policy.

There seems to be some confusion as to the relationship between Skull & Bones and the Council on Foreign Relations. I have researched extensively, and there seems to be no general consensus. One theory is that the elite power-families do not always agree on what the impending New World Order should be used for. The CFR seems to want to implement a liberal utopian society that will be perfect, with everyone making a nice living, no hunger, little disease, complete disarmament, with themselves as cultural saviors. Skull & Bones are more intent on military domination of the world through war and fascist governments so that they can continue to feed the international banking coffers with riches from the exploitation of natural resources. There are a few flaws in this theory, the most important being that George

Bush Sr. was a member of both Skull & Bones and the Council on Foreign Relations. The former President Bush seemed intent on the military and oppressive aspects of the New World Order. Perhaps, as the Skulls are a slightly more exclusive society - not to mention that the leaders of the Skulls gave Prescott his larger wealth with drug and Nazi money - perhaps the Skulls had more influence on Bush.

Another espoused view is that the Council on Foreign Relations was created to make the war plans for aggressive campaigns, and then the Skull and Bones' administrations would carry out the policies. Using this for a model, I predict there is a 50% chance that America will invade Iran or Syria or some other "rogue" nation if Bush Jr. is reelected. Probably Iran. The blood was not even dry in Iraq when Rumsfeld and company began sounding the war horn against Syria and Iran. "So what?" you say. Rumsfeld calls for war with everyone. He probably wants to go to war with Brussels to get rid of the war crimes court in that country that could potentially try U.S. military personnel for human rights atrocities. The correlating factor is that presently the CFR is laying down a groundwork for war with Iran, too. On the Council's official website, the question is theoretically asked, "Does Iran have a nuclear weapons program?" Answer: "Many U.S. officials and weapons experts believe it does." Are these the same officials and experts that told us Iraq had Weapons of Mass Destruction? If so, then the intelligence is highly suspect. The CFR subtly yet persistently lays the groundwork for action in another query about the issue. "Does the report (from the Internal Atomic Energy Agency) contain definitive evidence that Iran has a nuclear weapons program." Admission: "No." They quickly add, "But its (the IAEA report's) findings, combined with other information (no specifics given) about the scale and nature of Iran's nuclear program, have increased suspicion that Iran intends to produce weapons." Subsequently, the Council on Foreign Relations admits that Iran is allowed to have a nuclear energy program, which is the only thing Iran is actually known to have. The Council states that "it's not clear" whether or not Iran has broken any laws as to their public release of information. Many media sources have reported that Rumsfeld was instrumental in easing sanctions for Iraq, North Korea and other disreputable countries in the 80's so that they might easier acquire materials to create nuclear weapons. Rumsfeld then helped certain companies make a mint selling instruments "solely for use in creating energy."3

Why would anyone use nuclear power? The Europeans are proving that with a little money - money America could get by redirecting capital from the failed CIA - renewable energy is now becoming practical. American businessmen, like Rumsfeld, should not allow North Korea and Iraq nuclear energy. America should not use nuclear energy, for that matter. Tim Reid of the London Times wrote, "Donald Rumsfeld, the U.S. Defense Secretary and one of the most strident critics of Saddam Hussein, met the Iraqi President in 1983 to ease the way for U.S. companies to sell Baghdad chemical and biological weapons components, including anthrax and bubonic plague cultures, according to newly declassified U.S. government documents."4 This is pertinent, as the CFR reports that the U.S. may trade "increased access to western civilian nuclear technology" in return for Iran's signing of an "optional protocol...requiring more intrusive inspections." Let us see if we have this straight. The Bush Administration has members known to have helped rogue nation's get access to materials for weapons of mass destruction. They are also known to have either been completely inept or outright deceitful concerning Iraq's WMDs. Now, the officials are saying that Iran might be able to manufacture a nuclear arsenal. And how are they proposing to solve this problem? They want to give Iran more access to our nuclear technology! This is our Federal Government's modus operandi. The last piece of their puzzle will be to attack Iran as they did after selling nuclear and biological components to Iraq. Council of Foreign Relation's spokespersons will say that we must go to war with Iran because they have weapons, after Western elites sell said weapons to Iran.

The Council on Foreign Relations' primary purpose is to present an intellectual groundwork for these very types of foreign campaigns designed to depopulate regions, subjugate the natives, and exploit their natural resources. It is not much different than Britain's Boers War, or any other imperialist junta. These intellectual presentations are published successively throughout each year.

Another important issue that the CFR takes on is the Iraq debacle and the complete absence of weapons of mass destruction. This, despite Bush, Powell, Blair, and other officials' insistence that the threat against our citizenry was imminent. The Council on Foreign Relations answers to whether or not Bush exaggerated the matter: "Yes, say skeptics." The CFR continues, "Administration officials fiercely disagree." The Council admits that there will be an investigation. What they don't tell us is that many of the individuals on the panel of the investigation are members of the Council on Foreign Relations. This is also true of the September 11th investigative council.5 "Why haven't weapons been found?" the Council asks. Then, an answer, "critics say there are probably few or none to be found. But Secretary of Defense Donald Rumsfeld, speaking on May 27 (2003) at a Council on Foreign Relations meeting" stated that Iraq is a large country. Therefore, they are probably just hidden really well. Or, possibly destroyed without showing up on our satellites and radars. Very, very convenient.

Charles Overbeck, editor of Matrix magazine and webzine, asks a very significant question. "Who gave these people the authority to decide the responsibilities and obligations of the United States, if that power was not granted to them by the Constitution." There is a simple answer. Money gave Rockefeller and his minions the power. Overbeck goes on to report that the CFR is actually part of a large network of organizations that are guiding the world toward the New World Order. Democrats and Republicans both have party members who are concurrently on the Council's board of members. Interestingly, every Secretary of State since 1940 except one has been a CFR member. Overbeck continues by writing that most Intelligence Directors have been members, and "Clinton, himself (is) a member of the CFR, the Trilateral Commission, and the Bilderberg Group." All of these are satellite Round Table societies. Is it any wonder that Bill Clinton is being touted as possibly being the next President of NATO?6 This hints at a reward for causing devastation in the Balkans. Pat Robertson, in his famous book The New World Order, corroborates the assertion that CFR members have infiltrated our government. "This august body of wise men has effectively dominated the making of foreign policy by the United States government since before World War II. The CFR has included virtually every key national security and foreign policy adviser of this nation for the past 70 years."7

    There is a smaller subgroup of conspiracy researchers that claim the Council on Foreign Relations has developed and implemented a campaign of psychological warfare against Americans. This seems to be true, as the facts about Iran and Iraq listed above are relatively unknown or disbelieved by the general public. The claim that the Council is leading a propaganda campaign against Americans is as yet not fully substantiated. The methods used by the CFR and the fact that members are the editors-in-chief and producers for most major print and television media outlets seems to support the allegations. And honestly, all one has to do is watch primetime television or any cable news network to see the ideas of Goebbels taken to fantastical heights of subtlety and deception.

    Simply put, the Council on Foreign Relations was funded by drug and slave money and created by elite white supremacists to bring about the New World Order. Are your federal representatives members?

## Shadows of Power - Chapter 18: Bohemian Grove Club

A group of insanely wealthy, perversely powerful men meet amongst the towering Red Woods, secluded in the heart of over 2,700 acres. In red and black robes, these older men worship a pagan god and simulate a ritual sacrifice. Crosses burn and fire dances across the enclave of the super-elite. The place is the Bohemian Grove, located in Sonoma, California. But, just who are these occultists, mocking Christianity and nature with their incantations and witchery. The group includes a number of very famous American politicians and megalomaniacal businessmen. World Newsstand and other reputable news services reports that every Republican President since Herbert Hoover, and some Democrats, have been members of this very exclusive, very dark secret society.1

The first meeting of the Bohemian Grove Club was in 1879. It was predominantly attended by the artists and writers of the San Francisco area. As time went on, the group was taken over by executives and politicos. Presently, reporters are not allowed onto the site during the annual festival held three consecutive weekends during the each summer. The media blackout is of concern to stalwart Americans.2

The famous author, speaker, and admitted United Nations sympathizer, Noam Chomsky, has otherwise made many revealing statements about the media, one of which I find extremely apt...and scary. Regardless of his political leanings, his disclosures concerning propaganda are enlightening. Chomsky writes that it seems as if we are the consumers of television and newspaper news. This is not the case, he reminds us. We, my fellow Americans, are the PRODUCT that the CEOs of the information media are selling to the advertiser, who is the CONSUMER. By following the money, it is clear who the customers actually are. They are the mega-companies that are the largest contributors to both halves of our one party system. It is not enough for these men to use bribery to have laws passed that benefit the polluting, price-gouging conglomerates. They must make a small majority of the population WANT the laws to be passed. They do this through media outlets which air programming sympathetic to the corporate cause. If we agree that we are the product of the news channels, then we can also agree that the news that emanates forth is written as the consumer - the big businesses - wants it written.3

Which brings me to the Bohemian Grove's obvious lack of coverage anywhere, anytime. One of the most popular and widely passed articles about the club is the Extra! Magazine's November/December article entitled, "Inside Bohemian Grove: The Story People Magazine Won't Let You Read."4 The article claims that a reputable reporter from People was able to bypass security at the Grove and got a great story. Unfortunately, bigwigs from Time Warner, People's owners, were also members of the Bohemian Grove and would not allow the story to run. Another reporter infiltrated the Grove in 1989. His story actually ran in Spy, a periodical.5 More recently, Alex Jones, a documentary director and political activist, was able to take actual video footage of the shadowy world from inside the compound.6 All three of these men have shocking stories to tell us about the men who rule the World. What these three journalists, and others, have reported happens inside the Bohemian Grove begins with the obvious, and ends with the occult. Sometimes, truth is stranger than fiction.

At the beginning of the festivities, the men - Kissinger, Bush, Sr., Reagan, Ted Turner, and William Casey, to name only a few of the past participants - fly in on their private luxury jets and meet at the entrance of the forest retreat. Many waiters, bartenders, and other staff are employed to serve them hand and foot. There is quite a bit of drinking. Women aren't allowed, but outsiders and members alike have admitted that prostitution is one of the facets of the celebration for some members. The members are separated into different encampments, showing the elites' penchant for a class system, even inside their own ranks. Bush Sr. was in a lower-ranking encampment than Kissinger, while Bush was President.7 After the former President helped further

Illuminati agendas such as Iran/Contra, tax increases, and Desert Storm, I thought G.H.W. Bush now rests his head with the crème de la crème. However, this is not the case.

The main purpose for the meeting in California, besides the rituals, is policy speeches, given by some of the most prestigious names in politics and business. So, what's the big deal? Why would the Bohemian Grove not want news coverage of these policy-guiding speeches by the world's most powerful men? Obviously, the content of the orations are not meant for the media products' (our) ears. The stories that currently run in their magazines and on their television channels are what they want us to hear. Grove members such as William Randolph Hearst, Jr. and Tom Johnson (CNN) make it obvious why the movers and shakers of the media world are releasing what they are releasing, and what they aren't. O.J., Michael Jackson, and other celebrity stories are run into the ground for weeks, months, and years. Real news doesn't cut it for our intake. We, as the product being sold to corporations, are hearing what the consumers, the advertisers, want us to hear. Think about it. Do you think fifty cents a newspaper pays the bills. No. It doesn't even cover the cost of the paper. We are not the purchaser of the news. When asked, the media tells us that they are just giving us the stories we want. Even the rabid conservative watchdog news station, National Public Radio, was able to record one of the speeches at the Bohemian Grove - Henry Kissinger's, no less - but didn't air it! Propaganda, from beginning to end.

Two speeches politically conscience Americans would have been riveted by were "Defining the New World Order," by former Attorney General, Elliot Richardson; and "America's Health Care Revolution: Who Lives, Who Dies, Who Pays," by the former secretary of HEW, Joseph Califano. Colin Powell was said to have given a speech shockingly entitled, "America's Promise: Leading Armies and Leading Kids". The Manhattan Project is unofficially noted as having been conceived by Bohemian Club members. Now we begin to see why there has been a media blackout. If the content of the speeches are even half as fantastical as the titles, we - the news products - would be very riveted, indeed.8

I wish that were it. I wish the whole story was that the people who rule the world meet once a year simply to give speeches that could ultimately decide humanity's fate and then were suppressing the information. But, that is not it. It gets much, much worse. The following may only be frightening to Christians and other religious people. It has been stated over and over that these powerful men are performing mock-ritual slayings, worshipping a Babylonian owl god, and performing all types of vile and occult practices.

At the beginning of the retreat, members watch and participate in a ritualistic ceremony called the "Cremation of Care." Hooded men perform human sacrifice of a body in effigy to release care from the festivities. The focus of this ritual is a 40-foot stone owl that the men worship in order to let go of what they call "Dull Care." The Bohemian Grove Action Network, a citizen Grove watch group, states, "this ceremony resembles the ancient Canaanite worship of the idol, Molech."9 The Bohemian Club also uses druidic and other pagan practices. Even more grotesque than worshipping pagan gods and performing occult rites are the allegations made by John De Camp in his book The Franklin Cover-up. He makes the link between a firsthand account of a snuff film being recorded of a child murder and the Grove. The site the snuff film was recorded at was eventually confirmed as being that of the Bohemian Grove, near their false idol, Molech. This would seem too outrageous for most Americans to comprehend or accept. However, recent government admissions - of the FBI's imprisonment of innocents and MK Ultra mind control experiments, but two - lend feasibility to the accusation. The Bohemian Club wants to give speeches implying our need for their paternal guidance. They partake in pagan and occult practices, hire prostitutes, and then expect us not to believe they could create snuff films or rape children? Maybe the movies are real murders, but made to look like a snuff film that is meant to look real. A true "cremation of care." Also, see information of FBI whistleblower Ted Gunderson, and FBI/CIA/Bush/Bohemian Grove sex-scandals.9

The Grove's membership is primarily conservative.

The club consists of some of America's leading Republicans. The media suppression of the occult practices of Bohemian Grovers becomes evident. True Christians could never, would never support men that worship false idols. It is the first commandment: "Thou shalt have no other gods before me." It is perhaps the only truly unforgivable sin. If video footage were ever released on FOX News of Bush or Cheney or Rumsfeld or Powell standing in red robes and worshipping a 40-foot statue of some owl, the ramifications would be monumental. Even if Republicans were portrayed as mere bystanders in a copse of trees, with burning crosses and robed figures swirling around them, and all the time ghoulish, unintelligible voices were emanating from the trees, it might spell the end of the Republican Party as we know it. This would completely make the Republican Party defunct by withdrawing its religious power base, which would thereafter be shocked into disbelief and probably anger.

I do not understand how Christian conservatives can follow a party that has allowed socialized everything - health care, retirement, schools, welfare, etc., etc. I fail to know how freedom lovers can support a President who let the Attorney General stomp on the Constitution with Secured Homeland boots. I fail to see how we can endorse a President that is willing to kowtow to foreign threats and continue down the path of a failed world trade policy. But, Christian conservatives do, albeit reluctantly, follow the "moral" Republicans, if for no other reason than to keep their mortal enemies, the Democrats, at bay. This support is often tenuous, and the elite media knows that mass realization of the black practices performed by the highest-ranking Republican members...this could mean implosion for the conservative movement, which holds a slim majority as of 2003. "Perfect!" Democrats should exclaim. Since many of the media executives are Democrats, we should be able to have the truth about the Bohemian Grove made available nationwide. Unfortunately, as we have seen, even rabid liberal outlets like NPR are keeping their mouths shut. That, my friends, is why it is called a conspiracy. Don't let the mind control of the mainstream media trick you into thinking conspiracy is a dirty word. The Bohemian Grove Action Network sums up. "This close-knit group determines whether prices rise or fall (by their control of the banking system, money supply, and markets), and they make money whichever way the market fluctuates. They determine what our rights are and which laws have effect, and then sell us their candidate via the media which they own."

# Shadows of Power - Chapter 19: Bilderberg Group

The Bilderberg Group is quite possibly the most clandestine secret society ever conceived. Once a year the elite family names of Europe and America gather in closed quarters to discuss the proper course of humanity. Few journalists have entered their hallowed halls; none has ever reported from inside them. There has never been a list of members disclosed. We have had to rely on dedicated activists for pictures of members as they enter the ever-changing annual meeting grounds. It seems that we have the usual suspects in Rockefeller, Carnegie, Morgan: all names of the oppressive monopolizers of the Industrial Revolution and their cohorts. Their hidden agenda must be researched and uncovered by journalists following leads, looking for correlations. It is a difficult task. The Bilderberg Group has taken the concept of the secret society to a new level. No longer do they play with archaic mystic rituals. Strictly modern techniques are utilized, yet there is a trail of facts supporting the following thesis: that the Bilderbergs are less concerned with our bodies than they are with our minds.1 They have taken over our schools with their monolithic nonprofit organizations and rewritten public schoolchildren's history books. They have purchased the vast majority of mainstream media outlets to pollute our brains after the state schools have dumbed us down enough to believe their propaganda.2 It is arguable whether or not the Bilderberg Group is in league with or a foe of Skull & Bones, the dominant U.S. political force of the Bush Administration. Regardless, their intentions are the same. They seek to implement a one world government that joins banking, media, politics, education, culture, and business into a fascist, Big Brother-style global union. This infinitesimally small percentage of the world's population works fervently to remain upon Olympia as the masters of our universe.

Defense Secretary Donald Rumsfeld and Defense

Policy Board Chairman Richard Perle are Bilderberg
members. Along with comrade and fellow Neo-Conservative
hawk, Paul Wolfowitz, it is evident that the Bilderbergs have
placed their operatives into the government. It matters little
what political party is in power. Clinton was a Bilderberg, too.
Therefore, the group keeps a continual grip around our federal
neck.

Infos News Service gives some precursory
information concerning a recent annual Bilderberg
Conference, held in Brussels, Belgium on June 1-3, 2003.3
Much like the Bohemian Club during their yearly meeting in
the Grove, the Bilderberg Group meets to discuss political,
economic, a philosophical affairs which concern them. Unlike
the Bohemian Club, which is predominantly conservative and
Republican, the Bilderberg group consists of mostly European
liberal-socialists. The 2003 Bilderberg press release claimed
U.S. elections, Globalization, European Union enlargement,
and the European far right as subjects for the conference. First
of all, what do leftist Europeans have to do with our electoral
process. A lot, they think. The topic of globalization is no
surprise, as the Bilderberg Group is a European branch of the
Round Table. As was proven in "Shadows of Power - Chapter
15: The Round Table", the Round Table was set up to achieve
Anglo-Saxon worldwide rule. Duly noted, and already known,
is that the European Union is going to make a power play to be
the predominant government in the world, hoping to surpass
America as the premier superpower. When France and
Germany, two supposedly pacifist nations, begin discussing
the creation of a united military force, something is amiss.4
We are talking about the nations that gave us Napoleon and
Hitler, respectively.

(A side note. As of the week before publishing this
book, the 2004 Bilderberg meeting transpired in Italy in June.
John Edwards, the popular Democratic populist, was invited
for the first time. I predict he will be President one day. Also,
President W. Bush just happened to be taking a rare trip to
Europe that very week, and stopped over in Italy.)

Colin Powell and Bill Clinton are both members of
the Bilderberg Group. However, 2003 saw a decrease in such

American political luminaries being involved. The two American big-name exceptions that year were David Rockefeller and Henry Kissinger, a pair of the most powerful Americans in the World today. Both men adore internationalism. What is interesting is that, of the two United States Senators that were involved in 2003, one was a Republican and one was a Democrat. They were Christopher Dodd, Democrat from Connecticut and Chuck Hagel, Republican from Nebraska.8  Where do these Americans' loyalties lie, I wonder. Is it with America, their respective parties, or with the Bilderbergs.

The first Bilderberg meeting was held in 1954, at the Bilderberg Hotel in Holland. Thus the name. They are possibly the youngest secret society in existence that can claim royalty, prime ministers, and Western Europe's richest business owners amongst their ranks. Inside the pages of the November 5, 1999 edition of *The Big Issue*, an independent newspaper in London, writer Gibby Zobel claimed to have wrangled a copy of the minutes of that year's Bilderberg Conference.5  The minutes are fantastical, and show the power of manipulation that the group has over the media. Zobel reports that European and American leaders, via the Bilderberg Group, gave permission to Russia to attack Chechnya. This was a return favor for Russia allowing NATO to invade the Balkans on behalf of the Muslims. Other revelations that the 64-page Bilderberg Papers reveal are listed in Zobel's article.

*"- After the Euro, a global currency dollarisation may be the next step.*
*- Post-Kosovo, NATO is in danger of mimicking a global empire*
*- It's easier to cut welfare benefits if you call yourself a Socialist"*

The Big Issue article answers to the purpose of Bilderberg meetings. "Observer editor-in-chief William Hutton attended Bilderberg in 1997. He believes it is the home of the high priest of globalization."

The first person to launch a groundbreaking expose about the Bilderbergs was Professor Carroll Quigley of Georgetown University.6    Quigley states what conspiracy theorists have known for years, because of his contributions. The professor is one of the few elite-academics who have exposed his brethren.  It should also be noted that Quigley has unequivocally said that he is not opposed to the Bilderberg's aims in general, and that he taught Bill Clinton in college. Even so, his book, <u>Tragedy and Hope</u>, makes an astounding summary of the group.  "Their aim is nothing less than to create a world system of financial control in private hands able to dominate the political system of each country and the economy of the world as a whole.  The system was to be controlled in a feudalistic fashion by the central banks of the world working in concert, by secret agreements arrived at in private meeting and conferences."7

Without a doubt, the Bildergergs are the pinnacle of Western Globalization and Socialization philosophy.  They are very selective, with only 80 to 100 people being involved every year.  Regularly, membership includes people who are, when imbedded in the politics of their own countries, diametrically opposed.  However, a consensus for how we should live is agreed upon, and the governments of Europe and America almost always carry out their secret agendas.

## Shadows of Power - Chapter 20: Trilateral Commission

The Trilateral Commission (TC) was established in 1973 as a think tank for the three sectors comprising Japan, North America, and Europe. Japan has been incorporated with other regional countries to make up the Pacific Asian Group, and Mexico has been accepted into the North American Group. Now, I live in Texas. I've visited Mexico several times. It's a beautiful country, but poor, and often dirty. As a businessman in Texas, I can assure you that Mexicans are coming over here by the thousands and thousands because of the poverty that their government seems unable to control. If the Mexican government can't take care of its own people, why should they have any voice in what happens in North America. Nevertheless, they do. The Trilateral Commission meets for three-year sessions, the current session running from 2003 to 2006. The Trilateralists seem to have the same, basic goal that other secret societies have. They seek to ring in the era of the New World Order.1, 2

The group admits that they are right on track to attaining global governance, and they are satisfied that "the growing interdependence that so impressed the founders of the Trilateral Commission in the early 1970's is deepening into globalization."3    Although the New World Order is the Trilateral Commision's founder's guiding force, David Rockefeller spawned his brainchild, the TC, with a secondary reason. Winston Lord, former Assistant Secretary of State to the State Department, reports that David Rockefeller started the Trilateral Commission as a way to overhaul the International Monetary Fund (IMF). The IMF reforms would help out his Chase Manhattan Bank, which had already lent out over $50 billion to less industrialized countries during the oil recession of the 1970's. The latter goal was a complete success, while the former - one world government - is still in the process of being formed. Through the IMF reforms, Rockefeller and Co. have succeeded in passing on the risk of lending money to third world countries to first world taxpayers.

In 1973, David Rockefeller needed to reestablish the IMF. He went to a young Marxist from Poland, Zbigniew Brzezinski. Also that year, Brzezinski and CFR chairman Rockefeller were interviewing other potential members. One of the applicants that the two founding Trilateralists interviewed was an obscure, Southern politician. That politician joined the group, and in 1976 became our 39th President. The man was Jimmy Carter.4 You may think the Trilateral Commission lost the White House a mere four years later with the inauguration of Ronald Reagan. They did not. George H.W. Bush was a member of TC. He went on to become Vice President for the next eight years and then President for four. Then, eight more years for Rockefeller's group, as Bill Clinton was a Trilateral Commission member, too.5

Some time and effort should be made to explain why Rockefeller decided on Brzezinski as his partner in crime. Of course, Brzezinski was highly intelligent. As mentioned, he was a Marxist leader. He had organizational qualities, and was familiar with activism. Brzezinski wrote a book called The Grand Chessboard.6 This book is where we can glean the most information about the prolific Polish Globalist and the views he brought to the Trilateral Commission. Brzezinski claims that America's global dominance should be used to perpetuate that dominance. His analysis is that America's dominance must be maintained and that Europe is America's "natural ally." Brzezinski lists four things America must "institutionalize."

"* A collective security system." In other words, share our info with Europe, even France, which Brzezinski says is our friend even if it doesn't seem like it.
"* regional economic cooperation (APEC, NAFTA) and specialized global cooperative institutions (the World Bank, IMF, WTO)." We now know the devastation of "free trade" as we gear up for the FTAA. The World Bank, IMF, and WTO...well, these "global institutions" are just that: global.

*They will eventually bring down the borders of nations.*
*"\* procedures that emphasize consensual decision making,*
*even if dominated by the United States...*
*"\*    a  rudimentary  global  constitutional  and  judicial*
*structure."*

Essentially, Brzezinski was able to put into words the format for globalization that Rockefeller has been so laboriously working on for at least 40 years. America will be the strong-arm, and Europe a pacifistic hanger-on, who will reap in the rewards without the shedding of much European blood. As can be seen in Operation Iraqi Freedom, this seems true. America went in with nominal help. Now, the U.N is being allowed back into that country to "help with the democratic elections." Of course, America told Shiite leaders that direct elections were "not feasible."

The actual product released for consumption by the intellectual internationalists coalesce into a yearly report called the *Triangle Papers*.7 These reports make it possible to glean the strategies the Trilateral Commission employs to destroy trade barriers and shake national borders. For instance, one Triangle report was brazenly entitled, "Prospects for East-West Relations: Strengthening Multilateral Peace Keeping." I'm not very old or wise yet, but my historical research shows that 'peace keeping' almost always means imperialism. And multi-lateral almost always means under the guidance of the New World Order. Peacekeepers are supposed to be law enforcers, not mercenaries. That specific Triangle Paper report was evidently grasping for ways to strengthen the United Nations' military apparatus as an answer to unchecked American strength. Now, I understand that we are powerful, and that our government uses that power in ways that are adverse to America. One day, though, the United Nations will rival us. And, when that happens we won't be able to just invade Iraq without impunity (which might be a good thing.) America will have to sign tyrannical, one world legislation, such as they Kyoto Treaty, or worse. The United Nations, acquiring supremacy through the suggestions of the Trilateral Commission, will one day ask Americans to hand in their guns

like they did in Australia. Australian crime rates have gone
through the roof since then.8 But, the Commission doesn't
care about crime. They live in castles, on the plantation, and
up in the posh hi-rises. Even if America had no military
whatsoever, right now we would be able to fend off a military
attack by an outside invader because over 70% of Americans
are armed with some form of firearm. One side note to
consider. If we don't want the United Nations confronting our
U.S. government with force to fend off American hegemonists
and their little wars...Well, someone has to answer for
atrocities in East Timor, Central America, South America, Viet
Nam, Iraq, Iran, and other places ravaged by America's own
forays into peace keeping. The reason globalists want to take
guns is that it will make it much easier to attack our country or
control us with our own police force.

The REASON for TAKING the GUNS is that it will
make it much EASIER to ATTACK our country or
CONTROL us WITH our OWN POLICE force.

In the essay, "Trilateral Commission: World Shadow
Government", the comparisons and contrasts between the TC
and the Bilderbergs is presented. "The Bilderberg Group is
similar to the Trilateral Commission in that it is funded and
heavily influenced by the Rockefeller empire, and composed
of international financiers, industrialists, media magnates,
union bosses, academics, and political figures...The Trilateral
Commission was unique, though, in that it brought the
Japanese ruling elite into the inner circle of the global power
brokers."9 As Japan began rapid ascension toward their peak
in the late eighties, Rockefeller saw the necessity of letting
them into the loop. I believe that this was a case of a
Rockefeller applying methods from Tzu's The Art of War, as
in "keep your friends close, and your enemies closer."

One of the most outspoken critics of the Trilateral
Commission was Republican Senator and Presidential
nominee, Barry Goldwater. Senator Goldwater wrote about
the beginning of America's cultural war, which began with the
Beatniks, flourished among the hippies, exploded briefly
during disco, and became a drug induced orgy during the Me-
generation of the 80's. We heard a generation of Generation

Xer's bemoan the society this cultural war had brought by the close of the Millennium, which has since been turned into horrifying satire by Generation Y. Since Goldwater's books were published thirty years ago, we are staring face to face at gay marriage, porn on television, and the stripping of God from society. Now, I am not necessarily against these things, nor am I necessarily for them. But, I'm sure the conservatives know that they have all but been defeated, culturally speaking. Barry Goldwater was aware of the shadow government that surrounded him in Washington. He spent much of his time speaking out against the secret groups, and trying to make citizens aware of the truth. About the Trilateral Commission, Goldwater wrote a famous quote in his book, <u>With No Apologies</u>, that the group was "David Rockefeller's international cabal," and that "it is intended to be the vehicle for multinational consolidation of the commercial and banking interests by seizing control of the government of the United States."10, 11

Populist political activist Lyndon LaRouche also has much to say about the Trilateral Commission, none of it positive. In a speech given at the Schiller Institute, LaRouche proclaims "they are a mercenary force which was first set into motion by policies adopted by a Trilateral Commission meeting in Kyoto in 1975: policies originally of Brzezinski...the policies that were continued by then-Trilateral Commission member, George Bush (Sr.)." One specific barrier that needed to be overcome for Rockefeller was gold backed currency. Back in 1913, when the Federal Reserve began printing our money, the Fed took us off the gold standard. However, because of the fierce opposition by Americans, they continued to back 25% the value of the currency they printed in gold reserves. This changed in 1971, when Nixon completed the Federal Reserve's economic coup on America. Our money is backed by nothing. Congressman Ron Paul has often spoken against the current status of our monetary system. In a speech given to Congress in 2002, he stated that "central bankers and politicians hate gold because it restrains spending and denies them the power to create money and credit out of thin air." What is telling is that David

Rockefeller decided to begin the Trilateral Commission a mere two years after we were completely disassociated with gold. It was only then that he could broker deals with governments and create expansive trade lines that would merge culturally diverse countries into hegemony. It was only then, that he could rebuild the IMF and the World Bank to new heights. These heights, most Americans would have gone to war to stop 100 years ago. Now, most Americans don't know what the International Monetary Fund is. Even if they did know, they would not care much. Sad...very sad.

Whatever may happen in the world of American and Global politics, you can rest assured that the Trilateral Commission will have a hand in it. A mere three years after the Commission was founded, they put member Jimmy Carter into the office of President. Since then, they have dominated the White House. Certainly, Trilateralists have been major players in European and Asian business and politics. Behind most every foreign and domestic policy in America there lies a Rockefeller. I leave you with a quote from Gene Berkman, Libertarian writer and political candidate concerning American politics and the Trilateral Commission.

"The Bipartisan Political Establishment has turned our government into a monster, which is eating our substance, but failing to deliver on the promises the politicians make. Through the Internal Revenue Service, every one of us, and every working American, is in the government files. Our economy is being crushed by a burden of debt, taxes, and regulations. The last vestiges of our privacy rights are being eliminated as part of the War on Drugs (and more recently, the war on terrorism. E.F.). And now, the Trilateralists seek to police the world in alliance with revived Japanese and German militarism."

# Part Three

# Legacies of Power

## Legacies of Power - Chapter 21: House of Rothschild

In the prior two sections of this book, I have taken individual government agencies and secret societies and dissected them.  Granted, I only named their major organs, limiting myself from minutia.  As I have previously stated, more able writers than myself have done any one of these chapters in depth in other complete volumes.  In "Legacies of Power," I will bring some of the true leaders of the shadow government into focus.  These families and men have more to do with global politics than any of our elected leaders.  Many in these families are or were elected leaders.  It is therefore pertinent that I should begin "Legacies of Power" with a history of the House of Rothschild.  It will be shown that this perverse dynasty has attacked, and been victorious in becoming the most powerful family on the planet Earth.  It will further be shown that the Rothschilds may have wanted nothing more than to be the richest clan in the beginning, but the aim soon coalesced into the idea of World Tyranny.  Through the use of money and manipulation, the Rothschilds are situated to checkmate the world.  All of Freedom's pawns have been destroyed.  Many of her bishops and knights have been captured.  Aye, many have joined the opposing side.  At stake, though, are the soul of America and the soul of the Individual.

There are many angry people that I talk to everyday.  Their anger is universal, but what varies is the object of their ire.  From the Catholic Church to the esoteric and elusive Illuminati, from Satan to Aliens - the face of oppression has these forms and more.  And, one of the primary beneficiaries of the angst is the (also vaguely defined) international bankers.  These bankers, I believe, are the definite source of modern chaos and dictatorship.  These bankers MAY be agents of Satan; or, at least they believe they are Satan's generals; or they want us to think they are Satanic; or, finally, they want us to think that they think they are evil.  Whatever, the point is they have definitely chosen many strategies employed by Satan. These global moneychangers MAY be alien descendents, which would lend credence to the belief that they are 'of the Devil.' What I do know is that the fountain of these bankers, the House of Rothschild, is the source from which much of the world's sorrow has flowed.

In Frankfurt, Germany, in 1743 was born Mayer Amschel Bauer. Mayer's father, Moses, was a Jewish moneylender who wandered Eastern Europe until coming to establish his business and his family on Juden Strasse in Frankfurt. Moses emblazoned a red shield over the door. A symbol over the door was the custom for businesses to differentiate themselves to the illiterate masses. After training at the famous German Oppenheimer bank, Mayer returned to the family business and changed his last name to his father's business logo, red shield, or Rothschild. Mayer Rothschild, while well to do, was far from the richest man in the world at that time. Through cunning, trickery, thievery, and criminality, he would soon make that insurmountable leap.[1, 2]

In the late 1700's, separate principalities, or fiefs ruled Europe, and especially Prussia. Mayer Amschel Rothschild began his rise to power by ingratiating himself to these aristocrats. He gave them expensive trinkets and complimented them with flowery language. More importantly, he lent them money for their incessant turf wars. Notably, Prince William of Hanau became close to Rothschild. From that friendship, Mayer Rothschild was able to embezzle the equivalent of three million dollars; money that had been previously stolen by Prince William from his conscripted mercenary troops. At this point, we might merely call Rothschild an unethical businessman, except it was with much of his ill-gotten gains that he funded Adam Weishaupt and the first modern Illuminati. The Illuminati's objective was to foment revolutions, especially in France. Mayer's sights were already reaching toward war between nations, instead of merely war between Prussian aristocratic warlords. This would create a monetary need for the put-upon monarchies. Also, it would allow Rothschild agents full access to the newly installed leaderships. This allowed for easier infiltration of cabinets. And, this inevitably led to subjugation of law, education, and finance. Mayer Amschel Rothschild is the Father of the modern Illuminati.

Of Mayer's five sons, it was Nathan who could be described as a prodigy. It was also he that was given control of the Rothschild headquarters located in London, England. Mayer Rothschild's last will and testament reveals his true character. He adhered to a strict code of oppressive patriarchy. Only male heirs could conduct family business. To keep things in the family, his offspring were only allowed to marry first or second cousins. This practice was later relaxed to allow some of the other Jewish families that had attained great wealth on the coattails of the House of Rothschilds to marry into the family. A non-disclosure agreement was mandatory. In other words, no family member was allowed to disclose any part of the family business. All of these rules are still followed on pain of losing that member's portion of the estate.

The first major instance of the Rothschilds funding both sides of a war was during the Napoleonic Wars. In conjunction, they funded Voltaire and other Freemasons to agitate revolution inside of France. It soon came to pass that the Battle of Waterloo would decide the fate of Europe: who would wield superior influence, England or France. The man that Nostradamus predicted as one of the three Antichrists, Napoleon, was highly favored to defeat Wellington's Brits and their allies, the Prussians. Now, the Rothschilds had invested into putting into place the most rapid and far-flung intelligence web the world had seen to that point. Most sources agree that Nathan came to work on the day of the Battle of Waterloo, just as he did every day. The market speculation was running rampant as to the outcome of Waterloo. Suddenly, Rothschild agents began selling off all holdings in British stock. The news spread. Rothschild knew! England had lost. A selling spree ensued that sent the Sterling Pound into a depreciation to under 10% of its original value that day. Then, with the sweep of severally well-placed men, Rothschild bought up every Pound on the market for less than 10 cents on the dollar, giving him complete financial control of the newest

138

superpower and the actual victor of Waterloo, Great Britain. On the resale of the suddenly coveted British stock, the Rothschilds were able to increase their fabulous wealth twenty-fold. Benjamin Disraeli, then Prime Minister of England, spoke out against the Rothschilds and their newest invention, the 'international banker.' In reality, Disraeli sought to divide America and give Rothschild half the spoils. For England, then, it was too late. They had already succumbed.3, 4

After their defeat to England and Prussia at Waterloo, France needed money. They did not seek assistance from the Rothschilds. Unfortunately, with the House of Rothschild's now limitless income, the clan was able to manipulate and undermine France's bond market. This created dismay and panic. The French government had no choice but to become indebted to the Rothchilds, borrowing from them instead of the previously chosen lenders. France succumbed to Rothschild power and wealth, just as England had. Now, the Rothschilds had the two largest powers in the world, France and Britain, in their pockets, so to speak.

It can be seen that the Rothschilds had an almost otherworldly drive for wealth and power. They sought complete control. This forced them to acknowledge the fact that America, and its curious 'self-government,' was becoming an economic powerhouse. America angered the House of Rothschild more than once in those early days of our history, back when we had principles, and dignity, and ingenuity; and a sense of self-reliance, destiny, and individualism. We angered them when we printed our own, debt-free Colonial Scrip.5 We angered them when we refused to allow banking monopolies within our borders.6 We angered them when we disallowed a powerful central government, which made it much more difficult for them to control us. This anger the Rothschilds honed into a series of strategic attacks on our country. They have killed our Presidents. They have built a coven of secret societies that use OUR militaries as protection AGAINST us. The Federalists were Illuminati plants that advocated a strong federal government by destroying the previously agreed upon Articles of Confederation. They succeeded in establishing America's potentially powerful federal government, but only with a concession to the Anti-Federalists: the Bill of Rights. Round one between America and the House of Rothschild - a draw.

Robert Gaylon Ross, Sr. tells in <u>The Elite Serial Killers of Lincoln, JFK, RFK, and MLK</u> that the Rothschild Clan became angered over President Jefferson's exile of his international banking agents and the dissolution of their banks. They were so angry, they sent the English army back into America for re-colonization. This was the War of 1812, in which we won, but were weakened. Round two - America.

Round three went to America in 1832 when President Andrew Jackson made illegal the establishment of a central bank in the United States and abolished the national debt. As I have quoted before, I will do so again, what in 1836 President Jackson said to the Rothschild cabal that wanted to take charge of America's wealth.

*"You are a den of vipers and snakes. I intend to rout you out, and by the Eternal God, I will rout you out. If the people only understood the rank injustice of our money and banking system, there would be a revolution before morning."*

The bankers made an assassination attempt on Jackson, but failed. The next time they attempted the murder of a President, the Rothschilds would be more fortunate. The Rothschild agent, Booth, killed Lincoln. The Freemason fomenters, the Knights of the Golden Circle, aided him.

Through the Masonic Lodge of The Knights of the Golden Circle, the Rothschilds were able to foment civil war in America. They funded both sides. When Lincoln refused to pay the outrageous interest rates to the bankers after the war, they had him assassinated. A stinging right hand from Rothschild in the fifth. America fell to her knees.

Finally, in 1913, it appears America may have been dealt the knockout punch. The Rothschilds were able to reestablish a permanent central bank inside America, the Federal Reserve. The Kuhns, Loebs, Rockefellers, Harrimans, Warburgs, Carnegies, and Morgans were their main agents. These representatives committed fraud by manipulating the money crisis of 1907. This strengthened the propaganda advocating a central bank, which was considered and eventually passed into law. At the time, Congressman Charles Lindbergh claimed, "When the President (Wilson) signs this bill the invisible government of the monetary power will be legalized...The greatest crime of the ages is perpetrated by this banking and currency bill."

David T. Freeman, in his expose "Economic Rape," gives evidence that the Rothschilds and their minions are the majority owner of the private banking corporation, the Federal Reserve. He writes that publisher R.E. McMaster became privy to inside information. McMaster was able to use his European banking contact to name the top five shareholders of the Federal Reserve.

*"1. The Rothschild Banks of London and Berlin*
*2. Lazard Brothers Bank of Paris*
*3. Israel Moses Sieff Banks of Italy*
*4. Warburg Banks of Hamburg and Amsterdam*
*5. Lehman Brothers Bank of New York"*7

Truly, this was an assemblage of The International Bankers.

In recent years, the Rothschilds have tended to stay behind the scenes. The House of Rothschild is established as the dominant dynasty of the world, yet we don't hear much about them. Notable media exposure is not looked upon with favor in the family. An exception to the this media blackout is the story and photo of the meeting between Warren Buffett, Jacob Rothschild, and Arnold Schwarzenagger - IN 2001!8 This, two years before Arnold was elected as governor of California. It wasn't long after Schwarzenagger announced his gubernatorial bid that both Democrats and Republicans began proposing to grandfather the clause allowing only U.S. citizens to be President.9 The son of a Nazi SS member born in the Nazi country of Austria is basically being endorsed for our Country's highest office.10 All this with links going back to Rothschild at least as far back as 2001. Money does buy power.

The New World Order is the creation of the House of Rothschild. They control the United Nations, America, Europe, Russia, and almost everyone and everything else. To be more honest, famous video documenter, Alex Jones, asserts that the House of Rothschild is the major stockholder in about half of all the World's central banks.11 All they need do is pick off the remaining countries that had heretofore been too fundamental to accept the dictatorship of a secular, possibly Satanist group of bankers. All the wealth is not enough for the Rothschild power-mongers. They will not stop until they control our bodies and minds, as well as our pocketbooks. They have used our CIA to conduct experiments in mind control on American military personnel, orphans, prisoners, and citizens. They are funding research into genetic cloning, and have long been proponents of eugenics. Biometrics is upon us, as is biochip implants. The matrix system is in every urban area. Soon, you will see cameras in rural and suburban regions. We must revolt, nonviolently. Demand that your Congressman repeal the debt and disassemble the Federal Reserve. Refuse to use credit to buy anything.. Buy from artisans and local sellers when possible. And most importantly, spread the message. Kevin Costner played District Attorney Jim Garrison in Oliver Stone's *JFK*.12 In the movie, Garrison reveals the proof of a conspiracy for our President's assassination by a shadowy cabal, implicating Lyndon Johnson, the CIA, and others inside the government. Jim Garrison beseeches that America's citizens not allow for such corruption. Costner looks sadly yet hopefully into the camera, leaving movie land to enter our homes, and to speak to the movie viewers as well as the jury in the film. "It's up to you."

# Legacies of Power - Chapter 22: The Rockefellers

One can't escape the truth. The Rockefeller family has influenced almost everything that is 'American'. Their legacy in U.S. and World politics, society, military, banking, and business is irrefutable. The Rockefellers have shaped the minds of at least five generations of American public school children. They have hammered at the good and moral forces that existed in America's free market, and beaten it into an unrecognizable lump of cold, calculated, globalist/corporate profit. Capitalism no longer resembles what it was meant to be. Now business is about war, and mind control, and everything the Communists proclaimed were 'evil' about us. Business and government have joined forces to turn America into a bloated bully for the United Nations, indebted to the foreign banks and Federal Reserve. At the heart of the abomination that America is becoming, behind the curtain of the wizard's chamber...there stands the House of Rockefeller.

The story really begins with the grandson of a German immigrant, John D. Rockefeller. Born in 1839, John D. would mature from the son of a snake-oil salesman into becoming one of the richest men in the world. His progeny would become the most influential personages inside the halls of power in American Life. It cannot be denied that John D. Rockefeller and his descendants would donate more money to our nation - schools, foundations, charities, scientific institutes - than possibly any other family. Today, though, the message emanating from the Wizard's Tower is nothing less than the complete removal of national boundaries and the incorporation of all modern religions. One world government and one globally accepted dogma are quickly becoming cultural norms.1, 2

John D. Rockefeller, Sr.'s grandfather emigrated from Germany to America around the turn of the 19th Century. John's father was William Avery Rockefeller. William, or 'Big Bill' as he was known, was by most accounts a grifter, a

143

thief, a philanderer, and a cheat. He sold vile mixtures with the promise that they could cure one's ills. Big Bill's area of expertise was cancer medicine. William Avery Rockefeller is reported to have come into trouble with the law and fled, later appearing in Illinois as Dr. William Levingston, where he continued to create a public menace by womanizing and selling his cure-alls.3

It was in this environment of low morals and get-rich quick schemes that young John's character was shaped. The son, John Davison Rockefeller, Sr., had bigger eyes and a bigger stomach than did his father, Big Bill. John's drive for success is commendable in one who uses ethics while tending to business. John D., however, had no problem using his dad's cons - and many he created on his own - to wrestle the oil industry into his hands, exclusively. By the time America caught up to his destructive scams with anti-trust and monopoly laws, the man referred to as "the most ruthless American" had already taken a large portion of America's hard-earned wealth. That wealth is lent to back to us from Rockefeller Banks. We are charged interest on that illegally gained money when we use Rockefeller credit cards or take out Rockefeller mortgages. The fortune that our father's father's sweat made for Rockefeller has created an America that is heading down a path to Socialism, and worse. This is not an accident. It is by Rockefeller design.

Like the patriarchs of many of America's ruling families, John D. made his first chunk of wealth in drug trafficking. Yes, drugs are bad, but we (Americans) can't seem to stop taking them. In Rockefeller's case, the entrepreneur saw the profit in selling moonshine to Union soldiers during the civil war. Soldiers gotta drink. Especially with all the death they are witness to. If there is no alcohol, soldiers will smoke cannabis and hashish. If the weed is taken away, they will use harder drugs. This is a fact, especially among draftees and the conscripted.4 Well, John wasn't stupid. He didn't want to have to run from the law and resurface in another town, with another alias, like his father had done. So, John D. Rockefeller took his whiskey return and invested it in oil.

By 1870 he and his brother William incorporated

their holdings into the legendary Standard Oil Company of Ohio. Historically accepted is the fact that the Rockefellers employed what would today be considered illegal and unethical tactics to monopolize the industry by 1881. John D. was also one of the stranglers of the steel industry (United States Steel Corporation), and the banking business (Chase Manhattan), second only to J.P. Morgan in the latter. (Check out Robert Lederman's 'Artists' Response To Illegal State Tactics,' for a wealth of Rockefeller info.)

In 1897 John D. Rockefeller turned his penchant toward philanthropy. Also, Rockefeller came into contact with Rothschild affiliates. These men - as has been shown with the creation of the Round Table, the Council on Foreign Relations, the Trilateral Commission, and other secret societies - hailed the beginnings of the modern New World Order. They wanted white, aristocratic supremacy everywhere. They advocate secularism as a religion unto itself. They would have the world and all Christians refute the divinity of Jesus. They believe in eugenics, first through selective breeding and, today, by gene manipulation. The creation of the Federal Reserve Bank of America was fathered by Rothschild, Rockefeller, and Morgan.

Philanthropically speaking, what first were gracious donations to the United Baptists Church, YMCA, and other charities soon became Rockefeller's most ingenious idea. He started his own institutions: the Rockefeller Foundation, Rockefeller University, and the General Education Board, to name only a few. These organizations have promoted ideas that are adverse to the American moral fiber, even in all the fiber's diversity. Rockefeller institutes and foundations are nothing more than fronts on the assault against the Constitution. They are mockeries of our belief in a free republic, which should be comprised of responsible citizens. The Rockefeller clan has continued to attack America, and John D.'s only child was no different. The obvious goal of Rockefeller's foundations, so influential in writing public school textbooks, is spreading the seeds of globalism and secularism. I already hear people thirty and under saying that a one world government would be a good thing! What will they say in two or three more generations? Let me guess. The N.W.O. will be hailed as a necessity for world peace. And, there will be a leader proposed who will aid in bringing the peace. Sounds like Revelations to me.

John Davison Rockefeller, Jr. was born in 1874. He was an exemplary student, and graduated from the prestigious Brown University in 1897. He worked in the family enterprises, after college. Like his father, he used his proceeds to fund major centers of globalist agendas. He created the Rockefeller Center, and donated the land in New York that is the home of the United Nations headquarters.6 The article, "Rockefeller Connection," reports that Edith Rockefeller, John Jr.'s daughter wrote in 1963, in her "Universal Theocratic State", that "curriculum is being drafted to indoctrinate our children in what John D. Rockefeller calls 'the church of all people.'" He is responsible for the U.N.'s Temple of Understanding, which incorporates the six major religions and beliefs into one homogenous religion. On the latter issue, The Christian Alert Network (TCAN) has compiled a great list of telling article pertaining to the Rockefellers, the U.N., and the coming one world religion.6, 7, 8

Perhaps John, Jr.'s most vile agency is the United Nation's Educational, Scientific, and Cultural Organization. UNESCO, at least on the surface, seems to be a grand and noble experiment in the education of every human on the planet. This education is necessary, UNESCO notes, for the dissemination of information.9 Literate people are more easily propagandized. Bert Kjos's book, Brave New Schools, is one of many heeding a warning against UNESCO.10 The evidence is all around you. Computers in the schools are linked to an international server, which gives our kids a more "global view" of life, culture, religion, the family. As many as 40%, 50%, even 60% of high school graduates are essentially illiterate. This illiteracy grows exponentially as we glimpse into the fields of Math and Science. Kids can't pray. Cameras watch their every move, as if they were sub-citizens. In fact, we do treat children as sub-citizens. As of 2003, the argument was raging about whether or not they can say "under God" during the pledge.11 Kids are punished for thinking individualistically and rewarded for displaying a collective mentality. The goal is not to educate, but to indoctrinate into a unilateral ideology, encompassing politics, religion, and culture. The United Nation's Education, Scientific, and Cultural Organization is brainwashing your children to throw off Christianity and Individualism. This is the offering of John D. Rockefeller, Jr.

\* To understand how the Communists and their banking backers infiltrated America through the United Nations, read the seminal work, G. Edward Griffin's <u>Fearful Master</u>.12

A Rockefeller report from Wake Up America tells us even more about the Rockefeller legacy's control over our country. "No one knows how many foundations and trusts the Rockefellers have. They have hidden trusts within secret trusts within secret trusts. It is estimated they have between 200 and several thousand trusts and foundations. The finances of the Rockefeller's are so well covered that Nelson Rockefeller did not pay one cent in income taxes in 1970, yet he was perhaps the richest man in the U.S."13

But, I digress. John D. Rockefeller, Jr. had a daughter and five sons. The third generation went even further than their father in condemning the United States to the role of vassal in a global fiefdom. John D. Rockefeller III served the family in several capacities. Notably, he founded the Population Council, which promotes global abortion. He is the father of the current West Virginian Senator Jay Rockefeller, or John Davison Rockefeller IV.14

Winthrop was Governor of Arkansas, and is rumored to be the biological father of William Jefferson Clinton.

Nelson Aldrich Rockefeller served in several family businesses, but eventually worked in high offices for the federal government. Barry Goldwater beat Nelson in the Republican presidential primaries. Nelson Rockefeller did make it to the White House, eventually. He was sworn in as Vice President of the United States under Ford, after Nixon's impeachment. Nelson also was a major architect of the United Nations. One only need read Nelson Rockefeller's writings to see that he was a staunch proponent of the "new world order," a term he referred to often.

147

Laurance Spelman Rockefeller was one of the first conservatives to spread the environmental message. This seems a worthy cause, but it was through his Human Ecology Fund, now called the Human Potential Foundation, that his scientists reportedly conducted mind control experiments in conjunction with, and independently of, the CIA. Laurance was also involved in UFO and paranormal research. In much of the study of UFOs, his scientists talk about alien abductions, specifically by the 'greens' and the 'grays.'15  This runs parallel to the research conducted by David Icke.16  Also, many people who for years believed they had been abducted by aliens have learned that they were actually unwitting test subjects for mind control experiments. Add another one to the coincidences list.

David Rockefeller, President of Chase Bank, created the Trilateral Commission and has been the ruler of the Council on Foreign Relations for many decades. The CFR and Trilateral Commission's one-world philosophies and communistic viewpoints are recorded in great detail by various researches.

Everybody has a theory concerning the Rockefellers. Christians believe that they are Satanists, and some even believe they have the devil's blood running through their veins, literally. Conspiracy theorists believe they rule the world in a shadow government so secret and so powerful, it is only a matter of time before they bring about world fascism. Icke proponents believe they are reptilian shape-shifters. The accusations run long. What we do know is that the Rockefellers come from con men that gained their money fraudulently, at least initially. They manipulated the oil, banking, and steel industries until they became the richest family in America. They spent the ever-increasing wealth to become influential in politics, science, art, music, education, business, ecology, religion, and everything else of importance to individuals and cultures. Through this influence we see that they are most assuredly behind a diabolical plot. It is a plot so big, so grossly obvious, that our fellow countrymen have failed to see it thus far. Oh, many know that there is an attack on Christianity and the Bill of Rights and basic American values.

148

It is just that many fail to see that these attacks are NOT coming from random, various, unrelated sources. These molestations are coming from inside and outside the country. What we must come to understand is that certain elite families are behind these sources, coordinating them, guiding them toward complete collectivism and universality. The Chairmen of the Board for the global super-state is most assuredly the Rockefeller Family. They are a truly un-American legacy of power.

## Legacies of Power - Chapter 23: Clan Bush

For this particular family history, I will begin in the present. Our first subject for consideration is President George Walker Bush; son of the former President, George Herbert Walker Bush; brother to Jeb Bush, Governor of Florida; grandson of Prescott Bush, former Senator from Connecticut; great-grandson of George Herbert (Bert) Bush. The Bush Family is an elite legacy. The current President, Dubya, brings out strong emotion in almost everyone. Republicans love him to the point of worship. Democrats hate him with virulence. Libertarians run the gamut of emotions. He cuts taxes (good), then spends too much (bad.) He takes us out of the Kyoto Treaty (good), then keeps funding the United Nations to the tune of approximately $300 million plus per year (bad). A statement I used to believe was "Bush is better than Gore." Now even I wonder about that. Need I remind you of that evil document, the Patriot Act? Sick, sick, sick. The Bill of Rights is not to be compromised. Yet, Bush has already compromised the document, perhaps more harshly than any president before him. George W. Bush has forced us to make concessions on the Bill of Rights.

President Bush is the 43rd President of the United States. He has posed Socialist stances, such as passing the $400 billion expanded prescription drug handout for seniors,1 the $200 billion in farm subsidies,2 $150 million for state-sanctioned art and culture,3 and a host of other programs. All these subsidies sure 'feel' nice and warm and fuzzy, but they are still, essentially, socialist programs. He passed the Patriot Act. We all know how bad that could potentially be. President Bush supports the Clinton '95 gun ban.4 So much for the 2nd Amendment. He has taken us to Iraq despite the cries of many Americans, Iraqis, and a majority of the world. Besides England and Spain, who are our allies. Rwanda? The Ukraine? And, now Spain has jumped ship. I hope we don't have to depend on 'coalition forces' if Russian, Germany, China, France, and the U.N. decide on a military reprisal. Bush signed laws and executive orders lengthening the already long amount of time that government documents can be hidden from the public. I mean, I understand national security and all that. But, sealing records for forty, fifty, or seventy-five years and longer is plain ridiculous.

Before G. W. Bush was President, he was the Governor of Texas. While in office, he did sign a bill to allow Texans to carry concealed weapons (good.) The governor actually has little power in Texas. Our legislature only meets once every two years in this State. It is a weak government, which was a direct result of the fascism that oppressed the South after the Civil War, causing Texans to establish a very limited central State power. Bush didn't have much to do here while Governor, and he didn't. In Texas, we prefer our representatives squabbling over their districts. It gives them less time to pass laws. You know the story before that. Dubya barely got into Yale, barely graduated (C average),5 barely made it into the National Guard during Viet Nam, reportedly skipping over 150 candidates with better scores than he.6 Once in the Guard, he left for at least five months to help on a family friend's campaign. The army said that he was allowed to take the time off during a war, and that he was not AWOL. The story isn't totally clear, but I know my Dad wouldn't have been allowed to leave 'Nam to help on any campaign, or anything else for that matter. About the draft, the term Selective Service is apt, since the elite families' kids get to select whether or not to actively participate in our military service.

Nevertheless, after not being present for at least part of his military duty, Bush got a Masters in Business and was handed a multimillion-dollar oil company. He promptly ran it into the ground.7 Then, there was some strange dealings, and then more strange dealings with the Saudi Royal Family who were close to his daddy through the Carlyle Group.8 It seems that unless things are handed to Bush, he just can't pass the muster as a businessman. Bush has been involved with several of the criminals from Enron.9 Whatever happened to Enron? Weren't they going to put everyone involved behind bars. It appears to have passed out of the spotlight. Fox News Channel reported that Kenneth Lay will probably not be convicted for ripping off millions of customers. Yet, what is on the propaganda box? Martha Stewart and a simple insider trading deal that should only result in a heavy fine. And then there's Halliburton and their multibillion-dollar no-bid contract. Conservatives says that Halliburton is the only company that can do the job. I guess they don't think Americans other than Cheney and his cronies have the ingenuity and where-with-all to do a good job. Oh yeah, now it has come out that Halliburton overcharged the government $70 million for fuel, and even charged taxpayers for soldiers' meals that were never served. And to top it all off, now Halliburton says that the government violated their rights by checking their accounting book and finding the fraud!

You are right, President Bush. Most other Americans couldn't do a job like that. Most Americans were raised better.

To sum up Bush's business career, the online journal Bush Watch printed the following example of his stealthy rise to power at the taxpayers' expense. "Wealthy family friends and others invested millions with him, but with poor results. A 1985 disclosure shows Bush's track record: Investors got back 45 cents on the dollar, but few complained. The reason for accepting such losses was that investors got tax deductions averaging more than 80 cents on the dollar."10

President Bush's brother is Governor Jeb Bush of Florida. As we all know, Bush lost the popular vote in 2000 but won the electoral college. The deciding State was Florida. I don't know what really happened, but it is interesting that it was Jeb's State that allowed Bush to storm the White House. Jeb has been involved in the same shenanigans as his brother. He signed $150 million in corporate welfare, while Florida struggles during a poor economy.11 Jeb Bush has been claiming that crime fell while he was governor. Statistics show this is a half-truth. While some crime is down, sexual assaults and murder have risen under his rule.12 Look for Jebby Bush to be appointed a high post in successive Republican administrations. If Bush Jr. gets reelected in 2004, the Republicans will need to run someone in 2008 (Cheney couldn't win the highest office.) Is it possible that we could see sixteen straight years of the Bush Dynasty? And don't forget, I'm predicting an extension of the Clinton line with the eventual rise of Chelsea Clinton. Her main opponent will most likely be Jeb's son, George P. Bush. Both Chelsea and George P. have decided on the career of politicians. Proof? They are both receiving a higher education as lawyers. Lawyers make up a majority of our federal politicians. In twenty years, we will see another clash between these two clans. This doesn't even go into when (not if, when) Hillary is going to run for President.

Who were the Vice-President and then President during a time when our Bill of Rights were slashed and graffitied in the name of the War on Drugs? You guessed it: George Herbert Walker Bush, the 41st President of the United States. Oh, my. Where shall we begin with him. Let's see, the Wall Street Journal ran an expose proving that Daddy Bush was still working with the bin Laden family on September 28, 2001, even meeting with Osama's brother on September 11, 2001.13 Osama was just a bad seed, the Bushes say. The rest of the Saudi Arabian royal family is a great, almost Christian-like family. (Remember, President Bush Jr. gave a speech in England where he said that Christians and Muslims worship the same God.)14 Unlike his son, George Herbert Walker Bush raised taxes during office, going against his promise to not do so. "Read my lips." Bush Sr. took us to war with Saddam in '92, but left the tyrant and his terrorist regime in office. Now that I think of it, it may have been Bush that started the whole Iraq mess. First, with Bush's approval, Rumsfeld sold weapons to Hussein, to help us fight the Iranians. With Bush knowledge, Hussein gassed Iranians and Kurds with his American chemical purchases. Congressional records show that Bush was then involved in an act that was shady, and illegal. It was this. He, through Oliver North and Admiral Poindexter, sold arms to Iran. Now, first of all, America has a strict code of not making deals with terrorists. Bush broke that code, by trading arms for hostages with Iran. Second, when the dirty mess went public, Bush's actions caused Saddam to be reasonably angry with us, because we were arming both sides of the Iran/Iraq conflict. You know the rest. If Bush would have either not sold weapons to the dictator, Saddam, or if he would not have traded arms with the terrorists in Iran, we wouldn't have this f*%king (excuse my French) mess.15

There are implications that Vice President Bush was involved in Reagan's assassination. We do know that two previously assassinated Presidents had Freemason seconds-in-command.16 Reagan was not killed, but Bush Sr. is a Freemason. The would-be assassin was John Hinckley, Jr. What is interesting is that the Hinckleys are good family friends of the Bushes. Heck, the Bush family has done political favors for the Senior Hinckley's Vanderbilt Energy Corporation, even as recently as three weeks before the assassination attempt.17 The Bush-Hinckley link is further asserted in a North Star article entitled, "Hinckley: Hitman for the Shadow Government." I quote, "Although John Hinckley, Sr. was characterized repeatedly on the national news media as a strong supporter of President Reagan, no record has been found of contributions to Reagan...Hinckley raised funds for Bush's unsuccessful bid to wrest the nomination from Reagan. Furthermore, he (Bush Sr.) and Scott Hinckley separately contributed to John Connally in late 1979 when Connally was leading the campaign to stop Reagan from gaining the 1980 presidential nomination."18 The official government line on Reagan's assassination attempt is...you guessed it, a lone deranged gunman, John Hinckley, Jr. Bush Jr. later appointed the judge that presided over Hinckley's trial to a federal judgeship. Judy Woodruff, an NBC news correspondent, claimed that she saw shots fired from the top of the roof on that fateful date. This is starting to sound like JFK all over again. A patsy shooter, with other gunmen hidden to make the actual kill. The difference is that LBJ didn't know the shooter Lee Harvey Oswald, as far as we know. Bush Sr., however, personally knew John Hinckley, Jr.

Old Poppa Bush was involved in so many more crimes against America. He was implicated in Watergate, with the CIA. Iran/Contra. The attempted assassination of Reagan. Business dealings with the bin Ladens. Both Georges are members of Skull & Bones, Bohemian Grove Club, and other secret organizations. It is said that Bush, Sr. was on his way to give a speech to the Trilateral Commission when Reagan was shot. Reagan spoke out against the Trilateral Commission. Bush Sr. was an ambassador to the United Nations. He was director of the CIA and Vice President when Hussein bought biological weapons and nuclear components from America. Is he corrupt? I don't see where there is much debate. He is.19, 20

Bush Sr.'s father, Dubya's grandfather, was the patriarch responsible for the current position of power that the Bushes now enjoy. Prescott Bush was a Senator. He was a banker. He funded the Nazi Party and their genocide of Jews. Prescott Bush was not simply implicated in treason. With him, we do not have to rely on coincidences to prove our case. Under the Trading With the Enemy Act, Union Bank was confiscated. Prescott Bush was the director of the bank. Under the same act, the government seized Prescott's shares in the bank. Prescott Bush made millions supporting Hitler. That money has bought the White House for two - and possibly three, in 2004 - Bush terms. Also seized for trading with the enemy were several other businesses and banks of which Prescott Bush was a direct or indirect member. The story of I.G. Farben and the Prescott Bush affiliation has become legend. This legend is true. Prescott Bush supported the Nazis and through I.G. Farben committed genocide against the Jews.38 Money was only one reason Bush did this. He lost his first bid for Senator when his belief in eugenics was exposed. Prescott's father was George Herbert (Bert) Bush. He also funded the Nazis. Furthermore, he was a bedfellow of Rockefeller and Standard Oil.21, 22

The Bush Family is stained. Bert and Prescott traded with the Nazis. George traded with the Iraqis and Iranians - AT THE SAME TIME. George W. is openly trading with a favored China, and mark my words, China will come and bite us. The Bushes are not Americans, they are Illuminati. They have used their legacy of power over and over again to enrich their family and friends. Bill Maher disclosed on HBO that President Bush's wayward, nonpolitical brother, Neil Bush, has been busted accepting hookers

155

overseas.  Worse, he received a multimillion-dollar contract to head a software company for the son of the former leader of China!   Neil Bush admitted that he has no knowledge whatsoever about the software industry.  The Bush power has been used to defeat enemies - Bush enemies.  More truths will come out about Bush Jr., after he leaves office and there is no longer a vested interest.

Plus, let's face it.  The Illuminati are always a few (many) steps ahead of us in the grand chess game of civilization.  The Bushes are no different.  Yet, we must remain ever vigilant.  We must stay on guard.  We've had four generations of Bushes in American business and three generations in politics.  We have a few years to go with the third, and a fourth generation is already being preened and coddled for the offices of influence.  Will the Bush heirs be any different than their forefathers?  The answer, sadly, is probably not.

## Legacies of Power - Chapter 24: The Du Ponts

Du Pont, a name synonymous with wealth, power, and scandal. It is true, the Du Ponts are one of the wealthiest, most powerful, and scandalous clans ever to walk the land. They have not only reaped huge profits on the backs of American workers; not only have they polluted the Earth with their despicable environmental policies; not only have they influenced legislators with bribery and threats. The Du Ponts are one of the key families in the rise of the Illuminati. They are bringing about the death of America.

The Du Ponts come from a very old, very aristocratic French family, stemming back from Burgundy. Pierre Samuel du Pont was the first family member to become involved in the Illuminati. Pierre was purportedly a genius. His father misunderstood him because he was not as smart as his son. After Pierre's mother (reportedly from a long line of occultists) died, the 16 year old ran away to escape his father's beatings. He was taken in by an uncle, and became a watchmaker. Pierre Samuel du Pont endorsed Plato, became a Freemason, and eventually migrated to America. Jefferson asked him to help structure a public school system in the U.S. Later, he was instrumental in the Louisiana Purchase. Pertaining to the national public school system, it must be noted that this was one of the many strategies the Illuminati knew was essential for world control. Just look at our schools and our graduates to see the effects of mind control, collectivist ideas, and drug use. Pierre had two sons. One was a Freemason. The other, Eleuthere Irenee du Pont became a Jacobite.1

*A valuable resource to any study of the Illuminati bloodlines should be Fritz Spring Meier's <u>Bloodlines of the Illuminati</u>. See bibliography.*

Eleuthere made a ton of money as a defense contractor, and owned the largest gunpowder factory in the world. It was Eleuthere du Pont, Astor, and Biddle that helped create Hamilton's first central bank. Like most of the Illuminati tribes, the Du Pont's bloodline was selected, watched, and documented. Cousins often married each other.

Through the defense business, the Du Ponts were able to basically own the State of Delaware by the time of the Civil War. Since then, Delaware has seen numerous Freemasons, including two Du Ponts, as Senators. One of these Du Pont Senators was actually impeached and removed from office for vote fraud. Three Du Ponts eventually took over the gunpowder factory, bought up all the competition, and created a munitions monopoly. The Du Ponts have profited from every war since the inception of their first factory, through Gulf War II. The family is secretive in all its dealings. Family members are often unaware of the amount of wealth they have, and money is communal. The chosen family patriarch disperses, or has someone disperse, money to family members on an as needed basis.2, 3

The Society of Cincinnati was a group that the Du Ponts have been involved with for years. Yet, most people have not heard of it. The Massachusetts legislature deemed it dangerous. Fritz Springmeier writes in <u>The 13 Bloodlines of the Illuminati</u>, that "the Society of Cincinnati was the beginning of a hereditary aristocracy in the U.S. dedicated to subverting the Republic." They were successful and guided America away from republic government and into a democracy, which made it easier for them to pass laws in their favor. Springmeier reports, "The Society of Cincinnati favored a strong central government, a central bank, etc.," and that "every President of the United States has worn the Diamond Eagle Jewel of the Society of Cincinnati." The Society claims it is simply a group that brings together descendants of the Revolutionary War. Yet, its membership is strictly controlled and lists almost exclusively elite American families as members. I guess only aristocrats fought the English.

The affairs, murders, suicides, and in-fighting that dominate the Du Pont family history run rampant. The instances of corruption are too many to name, and add no relevance to the Du Pont's role in the New World Order, except by showing the family's shady character. It adds a preface as to the type of family it has become. The scandals that have riddled the dynasty's corporations are more telling.

As I have stated, the two goals of the New World Order are to destroy nations and religions. The Du Pont company training has been exposed as an indoctrination into New Age philosophy. In his article, "The Siren Call of Modern Pied Pipers," Lawrence A. Pile exposes that under the guise of increasing productivity, major companies (all the usual suspects: Du Pont, GE, Boeing, etc.) are suggesting - and sometimes forcing - employees to be exposed to secularist, New Age, and Scientologist philosophies. They call this 'advanced training.' The underlying subtle theme is that God is all, therefore I am God. This deduces to right and wrong, good and evil, are merely created concepts, and therefore relative. Du Pont training manuals suggest that meditation be used as a relaxation technique. The belief that the trainees' reality is true reality regardless of whether or not it is the true reality is subtly suggested. Pile admits that in some cases these techniques produce self-esteem and a sense of belonging in some employees. Pile's addendum is not reported by these training seminars and their proponents, however. As many as 15% of the trainees are affected with varying degrees of PTSD, paranoia, and confusion. My own observation is that this 15% of the population are either A) true monotheists, or B) individualists. I believe that these two belief systems, Christianity and patriotism, more often than not overlap. Patriots and Christians would feel an adverse reaction to group think and New Age ideals, the very ones that Du Pont espouses.4

When I was younger and deciding on a career, I worked for MCI. As I admitted, I was younger, and wasn't fully cognizant of politics yet. I was put through six weeks of intensive training before I was allowed to work on the floor as a computer tech. That training consisted of submitting journal entries (personal data retrieval,) as well as the aforementioned training. The atmosphere during the instruction was one against making any comment about race, gender, sexual orientation. I'm not saying we should use slang in the work place, but some things are just obvious and not meant as harm. It is often not the person you are talking to, but anyone who might overhear (eavesdrop) that we were forced to consider.

We were constantly whispering, and an air of suspicion reigned. Political correctness (thought control) at its worst. MCI's methods are evident in Du Pont training. In fact, Du Pont has been one of the leaders in perfecting these subversive methods. (By the way, I did suffer from mild depression and anxiety while employed for MCI, though at the time I thought it might be me who was going crazy.) The Du Ponts have gone so far as to put school children through this training. Sprimgmeier writes that school children of cities close to Du Pont plants (Du Pont employees' children) were taken to similar, albeit simpler, thought manipulation programs.

The Du Ponts perfected many mind control techniques while making large profits from the Drug War. "A Clockwork Straight: Rehabilitation, Thought Reform, and the Destruction of Young Minds" was a referenced and cited article by Wesley M. Fager. To preface, he states that former Drug Czar, Robert Du Pont, controlled two intensive in-patient drug rehabilitation facilities - Seed and Straight, Inc. Through physical and mental abuse, degradation, and isolation, these rehabs were able to emotionally scar hundreds, maybe thousands of misguided children. Fager writes, "From page 34 of Dr. Newton's first PhD thesis (on Straight, Inc.)...'It is a cult, plain and simple, of people who seize on parents' frustrations with their youngsters and then subject the kids to torture and brainwashing to make them obedient and drug free.'"5 Read it as 'obedience is patriotism' in Orwellian newspeak. In my opinion, this is just mind control with the parents' permission. Dan Baum confirms in his book Smoke and Mirrors. Referring to Straight, Inc., he writes, "Court papers and complaints to State health agencies document dozens of similar cases of food and sleep deprivation, beatings, forced confessions, and complete isolation from family and friends."6 Despicable. Shame on the parents who sent their children to this hell simply because the kids were experimenting with drugs or having sex. Shame on the facilities and Mr. Du Pont for overseeing this torture of American children. Shame on America for allowing a bogus drug war to cloud their logic and con their good sense. We don't even allow this kind of treatment to our worst serial killers and pedophiles. Shame on us all.

Another issue is Du Pont's grave abuse and subversion of American environmental policy. Shame on us all again. Many Libertarians basically believe that the only time the government has a right to interfere with the people is when one individual infringes on another individual's life, liberty, and/or pursuit of happiness. Well shame on Libertarians who don't endorse strict environmental policies. When Du Pont, or any other entity, (Du Pont is a corporation, which in the eyes of the law makes them an individual,) when these entities pollute, it damn well infringes on thousands of persons' right to life. Presented are several instances of this blatant disregard of humanitarian and environmental law, and of any sign of a soul being existent in the Du Pont family or businesses.

Du Pont has several water treatment facilities, and is implicated in injecting fluoride and other toxic substances into that water.7    Fluoride is put into approximately 2/3 of America's public water systems. We were and are told this is to protect children's teeth. But, in the time between now and the first use of fluoride, we have discovered that the substance is actually toxic and detrimental to the human body in hundreds of ways both known and unknown. This should be common knowledge. Joel Griffiths and Chris Bryson report in the article "Fluoride, Teeth, and the Atomic Bomb," that "the documentary trail begins at the height of WWII, in 1944, when a severe pollution incident occurred downwind of the E.I. DuPont de Nemours Company chemical factory in Deepwater, New Jersey." Apparently, fluoride is one of the necessary toxic elements used when making an atomic bomb. Du Pont has been master of the defense industry, and therefore was a primary atomic bomb builder. This fluoride leaked from a Du Pont plant and effected crops, livestock, and humans in adverse ways. So what did Du Pont do with that crucial health information. They were powerful and influential enough to not only force our governments to put it in our water supplies at the taxpayers' expense, they were able to make us BELIEVE it was for our own good. And we fell for it. But, the Du Pont companies have polluted our land with and

161

exposed our brothers and sisters to hazardous wastes without thought for generations. Groundup.org reports that "currently, over 7 million people in the U.S. are at risk from just 10 Du Pont plants."   In fact, our own government, despite its penchant for lenience in matters of pollution, has sued Du Pont for environmental damage. The United States Environmental Protection Agency (EPA) published a report entitled "EPA Sues DuPont For Hazardous Waste Monitoring Violations." The title says it all.  Donald Sutherland tells us of Du Pont discretions in the article, "Most of America's Liquid Toxic Waste Injected Undergroud."  He writes, "Du Pont alone injects 1.5 billion gallons of hazardous waster a year."8   I contend that we must actively campaign to stop this putrid practice.  We may not be able to get rid of the internal combustion engine.  We must, though, stop toxic materials from being flagrantly released into our land and bodies by companies that could introduce safeguards.

I know I can't make anti-drug supporters believe that cannabis is good.  Maybe I can give some readers information that has been suppressed by mainstream news.  For centuries cannabis (hemp, pot, weed, marijuana, etc.) was used by our forefathers. They used it for fuel, rope, wood, paper, and many other materials.  In the definitive cannabis tome, <u>The Emperor Wears No Clothes</u>, Jack Herer makes us privy to certain facts. "In 1619, America's first marijuana law was enacted at Jamestown Colony, Virginia, ordering all farmers to 'make tryal of' (grow) Indian hempseed."  Also, "clothing, tents, bed sheets and linens, rugs, drapes, quilts, towels, diapers, etc. - and even our flag, "Old Glory," were made from fibers of cannabis."  And, let us not forget that our own Bill of Rights was handwritten on hemp paper, which has added greatly to its durability against time.  At times, settlers were forced by law to grow it, mostly for war efforts.  Our founding fathers endorsed the growing of cannabis and thought all farmers should section off acreage for the plant.9  Medicinal uses for cannabis are becoming public knowledge.  What might not be known is that the hemp plant used to make most of these products is of a different strain than the plant used as a recreational drug.  There is no mental effect from industrial hemp when smoked or imbibed. A final note: recreational marijuana is now legally Canada's biggest cash crop and possibly their most profitable export. The primary target market is the United States. We could add anywhere from $6 to $60 billion to the annual GDP if we legalized marijuana, a drug that is safer than cigarettes, alcohol, prescription pills, many over-the-counter drugs, and possibly coffee. Finally, the billions of tax dollars spent on the "War on Drugs" could be redistributed to education or public health. Or, maybe even back to the taxpayers.

In the early 1930's, Du Pont began to use plastics and other manmade materials that were not equal in quality or price to hemp products. The free market wouldn't accept these plastic items, and that was BEFORE we knew what havoc the unnatural chemicals wreak on land and to body. With William Randolph Hearst as an implanted media manipulator, Du Pont was able to demonize the "evil marijuana," saying such things as it made white women sleep with black men, and that it corrupted the youth. No one even considered a thing like this up to that time. As stated earlier, industrial hemp that was used in the making of most cannabis products, the type that was a commercial bane to Du Pont, had so little of the active ingredient, THC, it couldn't make a person "high." Unfortunately, after months and years of propaganda, Americans made the plant illegal, whether it was used for recreational, industrial, or medicinal purposes. Shame on us all. This has allowed only gangs and governments to reap profits from the drug trade. If it were legal, it might be American farmers and entrepreneurs that receive the benefits. One thing is certain, demand for the recreational variety of cannabis will never be squelched.10

While the Rockefellers control much of the culture of American life, the Du Pont family makes many (most) of the products that are needed for such a society. Their record on pollution is abhorrent. Their scandals are infinite. But, it is the Du Pont's power and secrecy that should be the focused upon. They have been involved with Weishaupt's Illuminati almost since that subversive branch of philosophy was first espoused. Given Du Pont's power and role in the New World

Order, I would advocate not buying Du Pont products. Unfortunately, the Du Ponts produce so many of the things we purchase, to boycott them would be well nigh impossible. To offset the seemingly impracticable task, please research Du Pont policies and connections and report them to any American you can get to listen. Our ultimate (though, naïve) goal should be to change policy through Congressional and economic pressure. Spread the word.

# Legacies of Power - Chapter 25: The Morgan Family

To find evidence that the House of Morgan is one of the primary enemies of the state and the individual, one only need read the typical biography headline from most encyclopedias or textbooks about the family's patriarch, J.P Morgan. The bio usually reads something like this: "The world's most-famous banker, John Pierpont Morgan, acted as America's Central Bank when none existed. He helped save America during several depressions. He also founded the giant U.S. Steel." What the encyclopedias don't tell you is that Morgan helped take America off the gold standard and under the control of the Federal Reserve. J.P. Morgan wasn't really an agent of Rothschild, he was a contemporary. As we shall understand once we study the Morgan family and J.P. Morgan, this clan is just another globalist legacy seeking to install the New World Order.

John Pierpont's father, Junius Spencer Morgan, seems to have gotten rich the old fashioned way, which is commendable to a point. He did work his way up from a grocery clerk to one of the most successful of the new breed of elite in the 1800's, becoming one of the first international bankers. Like Rothschild, Junius funded both sides of wars. Most notably for the elder Morgan, he made a mint off the Franco-Prussian War.1 Junius's son, John Pierpont Morgan, was able to take his father's fortune and expand it exponentially. Also, J.P. Morgan had a son, also named John Pierpont Morgan. They resembled each other in much more than name. The elder was forced to testify in front of Congress over money trust issues. Many of both men's business tactics would today be considered illegal. It is because of the anti-trust laws created to stop the Morgans and their ilk that America is able to flourish with small businesses today. Conversely, it is the ongoing fight with corporate welfare and favoritism toward the Morgans and others that makes opening and maintaining a small business such a difficult, bureaucratically-stifled task.2

John P. Morgan, Jr. is accredited with "saving" America by providing outrageous loans because it was "necessary" for America to enter World War One. I'm sure Morgan funded a few of our enemies, too. I exposed in "Legacies of Power - Part 1: The House of Rothschild" that Rothschild, Rockefeller, and Morgan were three of the five largest shareholders in America's Federal Reserve Corporation. If the reader gleans nothing else from this book, I hope it is this. The Federal Reserve and their strong-arm, the Internal Revenue Service, are our enemies whom we must press our Congressman to remove from the American political and economic system. The Morgans helped create the Federal Reserve at the infamous meeting on the posh Jekyll Island.3. After establishing the Federal Reserve to loan money to our government in 1913, the Morgans advocated entering World War I. Who did American taxpayers pay the crushing debt that the loan accrued to? Yep. The Federal Reserve and J.P Morgan.4

Unfortunately, the only way to legally fight the Morgans and their kind is through a little pain. Americans must throw away their credit cards. It is only if we, the citizenry, act with fiscal responsibility that we can demand our government to do so. The trillions that the elite banking houses of Morgan, Rockefeller, and others would lose with a halt in credit card use could deal a crushing blow to the helm of the New World Order. Some say that it is impossible to live without credit. How do I buy a house, they ask. A house is the only thing that should be bought on credit, as land almost always appreciates. Everything else should be bought when you have the money. This author is not chastising. I, too, have fallen for the temptation of credit cards, financed loans, and the like. The hurt that they left on my life taught me a giant lesson. If a majority of Americans threw away the credit for all but the most important items, we could ask the Federal Government to do the same. If the government refuses, THEN we might have a right to undertake a tax revolt. But, if we are as out on loan as the Fed is, we have no right to protest.

Unfortunately, the Federal Reserve, IRS, and credit cards don't seem to be set for a sweeping "out."

As recently as July 28, 2003, The Federal Reserve admitted that J.P. Morgan Chase & Co. was implicitly involved in the Enron financial scandal.5  In fact, the banking giant was found guilty by the Securities and Exchange Commission of maliciously helping to mislead Enron investors.  What did the Fed dole out as punishment to the Morgans and Rockefellers?  Small fines, and they had the bank sign a written agreement.  The agreement stated that bankers would watch their accounting practices more closely.  Wow.  Big friggin' deal.  They rip off America, her stock investors, and her energy supplies.  They then sign a written contract saying they'll make sure and try not to let it happen again.  I guess it doesn't hurt that Donald P. Morgan is affiliated with the Federal Reserve Bank of New York, writing much of its policy.

The Freedom From Fiats Foundation (FFFF) published a news release entitled, "It's Time To Indict The Fed".6  The FFFF are devoted to ending the grip of the Federal Reserve on America, and made me privy to some information I was unaware of.  For instance, they say that "the fifth plank of the Communist Manifesto calls for: Centralization of credit in the hands of the state, by means of a national bank with state capital and an exclusive monopoly."  Add that to all the continuous expansion of social and corporate welfare, and America is looking more and more like the Soviet Union every decade.  The Freedom From Fiats Foundation links this socialist trend with the Morgans.

The main argument in favor of the Federal Reserve being created in 1913 was the economic depression of 1907.  What we know in retrospect is that Morgan and Rockefeller manipulated the 1907 downturn after they practically monopolized America's banks through Mafioso-like methods.  Specifically stated by FFFF is that "J.P. Morgan intentionally started it (Panic of 1907) by spreading rumors that the Knickerbocker Bank and the Trust Company of America were insolvent.  Believing the rumor, the public began a run on the banks - and the rumors came true."  In response to the panic,

Congress set up a committee, with a Rockefeller on the panel, to study centralized banks. What resulted was the secretive Jekyll Island meeting where the bankers wrote their own legislation for a central bank, which was accepted and passed by Congress. To help elect as President a Federal Reserve proponent, Woodrow Wilson, Morgan funded Teddy Roosevelt and his Bullmoose Party. This siphoned off enough votes from Taft for Wilson to attain victory.

After solidifying the Federal Reserve, the Morgans needed a way to collect their debts. Nelson Aldrich, known Communist, was often considered the mouthpiece of J.P. Morgan. He helped with the creation of the Federal Reserve. He also helped invent our tax system. The Supreme Court had ruled an income tax unconstitutional in 1895. It is no wonder that Morgan's agent, Senator Aldrich, was a key player in amending our Constitution so that the government could beget the Internal Revenue Service. The IRS allows the Federal Reserve to forcibly collect its yearly debts from the Federal Government, which is we the people only when it comes time to pay bills. In my opinion, the Federal Reserve is nothing but a loan shark syndicate and the IRS is their muscle.

Another area we have looked at is the elites' creation of foundations. Heretofore we have only seen them using these organizations to guide public policy, education, etc. "The Council on Foreign Relations and the New World Order" is a detailed essay by William Blase. He shows us the original and primary reason for these foundations. Foundations are a means by which the rich can write off huge sums of money so that they themselves can escape the tax collector's noose. Blase ties it all together. "With the means to loan enormous sums to the government (Federal Reserve), a method to repay the debt (income tax), and an escape from taxation for the wealthy (foundations), all that remained was an excuse to borrow money...In 1914 WWI began, and after American participation debt rose from $1 billion to $25 billion."7 Wow, just one year after the Federal Reserve came into existence we raised our spending and debt levels twenty-five times over. Still, Americans think we entered the War for some altruistic reason. WAKE UP, PEOPLE. We are being manipulated.

One of the goals of the Federal Reserve was to take America off the gold standard, thereby forcing Americans to buy gold with cash. On the gold standard, money was actually redeemable with gold. That had been the case prior to the Federal Reserve. After we were taken off that standard, our money became worth whatever the Fed says it's worth. So, is it no wonder that J.P. Morgan has been sued for manipulating the gold and silver markets? Of course not. Not only has Morgan illegally rigged Wall Street and been found complicit in accounting scandals via Enron and others, they are also fixing the gold game.8 They take us off the gold standard, and then control the gold market. Is our government going to do anything about this? President Bush says that they are, but news on corporate scandal is light and arrests are lighter. Looks like the Morgan Family is still allowed to have monopolies in America. Considering that our federal government is infested with CFR and S&B members, I suspect this will continue to be the case until we vote them out. Why did I mention the CFR? Because of great note is that John W. Davis was a founding member of the Council on Foreign Relations. Davis was the personal attorney of J.P. Morgan. Remember that the CFR's primary, clandestine goal is to destroy American sovereignty. The House of Morgan's influence in the New World Order is irrefutable, even today.

## Legacies of Power - Chapter 26: Henry Kissinger

I felt it prudent to add a chapter dedicated to Henry Kissinger. Is he a Savior, or is he Satan? He was awarded the Nobel Peace Prize, yet many people and groups claim him to be a partner in the House of Rothschild/Rockefeller. He does claim to be Jewish, but whether that is through Kazakhstan or Israel, I'm not sure. Because he is from Germany, I suspect he is of the former bloodline. I did read a great letter written by Dr. Horowitz in response to a typical Jewish conspiracy article (See Chapter 39.) He points out that most of the New World Order is white European descendents of royalty. Blue bloods. Germans, English, French. I believe that when patriots get off on an anti-Semitic track, they have let the powers above manipulate their minds. It is just as ridiculous to think Jews rule the World as it is to believe the Democrats and Republicans are two radically different parties. We are going to have to band together, if it ever comes to a military strike against us. With chemical trails, bio-engineered foods, genetic cloning, and toxic waste: humans are bound to become completely 'domesticated' very soon. It will be that much easier to round us up, group by group, dissident by dissident. If humans stand together, despite our differences, tyranny can be defeated.

So, Kissinger is Jewish, so what. Bush is German. That doesn't mean Germans are the enemy. It is Henry Kissinger, the man, we are to research. What were his policies? He was the adviser to kings. What did he advise our Country's rulers do? These are the types of things one should ask when researching political figures.

To the common layperson, a typical Kissinger biography reads like the man is some sort of political godsend. He migrated from Germany. He received his PhD from Harvard, where he was a member of the faculty for almost 20 years. He served as Secretary of State from 1973-1977. He also started Kissinger Associates and became a political advisor. Dr. Kissinger has written many award-winning books. He was awarded the Nobel Peace Price, the

170

Guggenheim Fellowship Award, and the Rockefeller Brothers Prize, among others. Kissinger has also served on the board of the Council on Foreign Relations, J.P. Morgan Bank, the Joint Chiefs of Staff, and as a National Security Adviser. As I said, to John Q. Public, Dr. Kissinger seems to have lived a charmed life. For patriots, this bio has Illuminati written all over it. The same names keep popping up, such as Morgan and Rockefeller. It should also be noted that Henry Kissinger is barred from entering several countries on pain of being tried for war crimes. Chris Hitchen's The Trial of Henry Kissinger is one of the best sources for this information.1, 2

We know the truth about the Nixon Administration, of which Kissinger was a part. We know the truth about the internationalist Council on Foreign Relations and Bilderberg Group, both of which Kissinger is a high-ranking member of. We know the truth about J.P. Morgan, and Kissinger's collusion to keep the Federal Reserve in place. We don't even have to go into details about Kissinger. Because of the men he works for, we are positive that he is a golden boy of the New World Order. If we give his life more than a precursory glance, we can see his anti-American stances in stark detail.

Let's start with Vietnam conflict. Kissinger received a Nobel Peace Prize in 1977 for his role in ending the conflict. This is a complete joke, as Kissinger was one of Nixon's cronies who helped keep America at war for far too long. In reality, Kissinger diabolically staved off an end to the conflict during the Democrats' reign with a promise that the Republicans would give the Vietnamese a better deal if the Communists would only prolong the war. Of course, several years later, the Republicans offered Vietnam the exact same deal, allowing Nixon to take credit. Nixon and Kissinger are therefore responsible for thousands of American deaths and billions in tax dollars. An even darker side exists to Kissinger and Vietnam that makes his Nobel Prize a slap in the face to every American who fought in that war. Mark A. Sauter, Jim Sanders, and James D. Sanders wrote a book in 1993 that reveals some of the worst acts ever perpetrated by our government. The book, The Men We Left Behind: Henry Kissinger, the Politics of Deceit and the Tragic Fate of POW's

171

After the Viet Nam War, should bring about the automatic forfeiture of Kissinger's Nobel Peace Prize. The authors use military and government documents, as well as first hand testimony to prove that our government, and specifically Henry Kissinger, lied to the public and left thousands of veteran POWs to rot in prison camps, like lambs to the slaughter. This is UNACCEPTABLE. He should be taken to court. He should be tried. If found guilty, he should be hung from the nearest tree. How can we call him an American elder statesman? If we do not hold him accountable for soldiers lost, then no one will.3, 4

Kissinger proponents often point to his opening of trade with China as a highlight of his resume. However, as we watch countless manufacturing jobs migrate to the Communist country, and the ever-widening trade gap with China, we know that it was not beneficial to the United States. It bestowed on China's vast growing market access to the hugest corporations and banks; namely, Rothschild, Rockefeller, Morgan. By now, we all know who "They" are. In fact, as more Americans are becoming aware of Kissinger's role in world politics, he is more and more often being referred to as a war criminal and enemy of the United States.

Long ago, writers like Hitchens and Isaacson exposed Henry Kissinger's role in the secret bombings of Cambodian civilians during Viet Nam. They have openly documented his war crimes in Chile, wherein he "advised" for the assassination of an elected President and the mass slaughter of innocents. While experts disagree whether or not Kissinger is a war criminal (Hitchens says yea, Isaacson says nay,) even conservative intellectuals know that it is entirely possible that Kissinger could be brought to trial at some point in the future.

The race issue played big in the 1970's. African-Americans were forced to take up arms to defend their civil rights against a bigoted America and a racist American police force.5 Martin Luther King, Jr. was different than Malcolm X, the Nation of Islam, or the Black Panthers in that he advocated peaceful revolution as a means for change. Yet, Kissinger was a key ally of J. Edgar Hoover in painting Dr. King as anti-America. By propagandizing the civil rights leader as

Communist, Kissinger and Hoover were telling us that revolution against totalitarianism is anti-American! Was Kissinger involved in MLK's assassination? We know Kissinger has been involved in hiring government hit men in the past. The Reverend King elimination was endorsed by the Illuminati, because they wanted the war in Viet Nam to continue. Martin Luther King, Jr. opposed that war. The corporations and elite families of America were reaping huge profits from defense contracts, slave trading, the rubber industry, and drug trafficking. While our fathers, brothers, and sons were dying on the other side of the globe in the name of freedom, Kissinger brokered deals to keep the conflict ongoing. While our fathers, brothers, and sons were maimed to give Vietnamese citizens liberty, Kissinger helped defile the good name of Martin Luther King, Jr., who was trying to promote liberty right here at home.

As a member of the CFR and other Illuminati organizations, it is evident to whom Kissinger is beholden. Viggo Mortensen, the actor that played Aragorn in the "Lord of the Rings" trilogy, summed up a truth about the former and current Secretaries of State. "Kissinger and Ashcroft are servants of Sauron," Mortensen was quoted as saying. While Republicans and the Illuminati may disagree with that, it is becoming an ever-increasing prevailing wisdom the Dr. Kissinger is nothing more than a Rothschild/Rockefeller Nazgul. He gives the orders for his masters, thereby protecting them from public scrutiny. So what if much of the world thinks he is a war criminal. He gets bestowed with the highest honors and accolades, which go down in all of our "official" History books. One hundred years from now, after they have purged the internet and all free speech, no one will be the wiser to the truth about Henry Kissinger.

Kissinger has other affiliations, including leadership roles in the Bilderberg Group, Bohemian Grove, and most of the other insidious, occult-laden secret societies previously exposed in this compendium. There are a plethora of books that prove his guilt in several global and regional conflicts.6, 7 It may be far-sighted to glean the true character of the man by what he has written and said, himself. I leave you with these

Kissinger quotes.

> *"Power is the ultimate aphrodisiac."*
> *"The illegal we do immediately. The unconstitutional takes a little longer."*
> *"Corrupt politicians make the other 10% look bad."*
> *"Even a paranoid has some real enemies."*
> *"I can think of no faster way to unite the American people than a terrorist attack..."*
> *"The issues are much too important for the Chileans voters to decide for themselves."*

Let it be heard, loud and clear. Whenever Kissinger is involved in brokering any deal, in any country, and with any leader, he works to further the agenda of the New World Order, not the United States of America.

# Legacies of Power - Chapter 27: The Dulles Brothers

The Dulles brothers were instrumental in the formation of the modern New World Order. It was under a Dulles CIA Director that Project Paperclip and MK Ultra found wings. These were programs that used unsuspecting American citizens as human guinea pigs in the research of mind control techniques. A Dulles Secretary of State for Eisenhower helped create the coalition for war against Viet Nam, sparking America's newfound interest in entangling treaties and global empire. Both brothers were active in recruiting, funding, and running the Council on Foreign Relations. Both were primary concocters of the United Nations. With leaders like these, who needs enemies.1, 2, 3

John Foster and Allen Welsh Dulles were brothers. John Foster was the eldest. His Union Bank was involved with Prescott Bush and Averell Harriman. These elite men funded the Nazis and the Communists and then pitted them against each other for monetary gain. John Foster Dulles was awarded the Secretary of State position partly in thanks for his treasonous actions in setting up this global conflict. The brothers are aligned all the way back with the English traitor, Aaron Burr, through Yale. Their father, J.H. Dulles was reported by Tarpley and Chaitkin in <u>George Bush: The Unauthorized Biography</u> as being in a Yale secret club, similar to Skull & Bones, called the "Society of Brothers in Unity."4 John Foster, though, became a leading member of the CFR. Again, I could stop here, as we all know that the Council on Foreign Relations is an anti-American group. John F. Dulles was prone to expounding on the advantages of Communism. "The United States should take immediate steps toward the abridgement of its own sovereignty," Dulles said to a Committee for a Just and Durable Peace.

The second prong to the New World Order approach, as we have seen, is the destruction of religion. John Foster Dulles was on the executive committee of the Federal Council

Webs of Power                                Erik Fortman

of Churches. The Council is known to have corrupted the churches of America, introducing New Age and other dogmas that are adverse to Christianity.5 "The Greatest Hoax," printed at sweetliberty.org, adds the following transgressions to the John Foster Dulles list.

*"Helped formulate Wilson's '14 Point Peace Plan'...the forerunner of the United Nations Organization.*
*Founding member of Council on Foreign Relations, 1921.*
*U.S. delegate to the U.N.'s founding."6*

As chairman of the Carnegie Foundation, J.F. Dulles hired the Communist Alger Hiss. Finally, successive J.F. Dulles heirs are intermingled with Rockefeller blood. John Foster Dulles was chairman of the Rockefeller Foundation and married into that Illuminati family.

Allen Welsh Dulles was John Foster's younger brother. He served in many capacities for the White House, including diplomatically and later in the Office of Strategic Services. From 1953 to 1961 he was the Director of the Central Intelligence Agency. It was during his reign as master of America's foreign intelligence that Allen Dulles approved Project Paperclip, MK Ultra, and their many subprojects. Project Paperclip was a 'procurement' phase. The CIA and the KGB had a race to see who could procure the services of the best Nazi scientists after Allied Forces demolished Germany. Allen was able to gather many of the Nazi doctors and made them American citizens when he could. These scientists then began their experimentation in earnest. During MK Ultra, American citizens were used as test subjects for various mind control projects. The CIA admits that this is so. A dangerous and flawed aspect of these projects was that the scientific method was not used or even understood by many agents. For instance, in public places CIA agents would "slip a mickey" to an unsuspecting American, using perilous drugs like LSD (which the government invented,) a powerful hallucinogen, and placed the substances into the "patients" drinks. Many times, the crazed test subject would leave the premises and could not be followed. So, the actual effect

176

could not be recorded. Ultimately, much of the evidence was destroyed by the CIA concerning these projects, due to "paper inundation."7

One of MK Ultra's subprojects under Dulles was dubbed MK 78. Freedom Magazine was able to obtain documents pertaining to MK 78 under the Freedom of Information Act. It was during this operation that the CIA spooks tested biological and chemical weapons on American citizens without their knowledge. These tests continued for three years after they were made illegal. Remember, the CIA is an organization strictly to be used for foreign intelligence. I fail to see how any of these projects are Constitutional. The CIA, during the "Joint Hearing Before the Select Committee on Intelligence on Health and Scientific Research of the Committee on Human Resources, United States Senate, Ninety-fifth Congress, First Session, August 3, 1977", admitted to all of the above and more.

Racism has long been a component of the Illuminati's ideology. The North Eastern blue bloods despise blacks and other people of color. African-Americans aren't still mad about slavery. They are angry about the physical and psychological warfare conducted against them in the century and a half AFTER slavery was made illegal. Freedom Magazine broke two stories that demonstrate Allen Dulles and the Central Intelligence Agency's attacks against black folk. In 1956, swarms of mosquitoes were infected with strains of yellow and dengue fever. These mosquitoes were released on the predominantly black city of Savannah, Georgia. Many African-Americans were adversely affected, as you might expect. In a separate operation, a fungus was released in certain Eastern cities specifically because it seemed to affect blacks more than whites. Was this the beginning of race-based diseases, a precursor to SARS? Is it now more believable that AIDS was released by the government, or that it has its genesis in some nefarious human/animal relationship?8

Like his brother, and similar to other CIA directors, Allen Dulles was a leading member of the Council on Foreign Relations. He was also a Trilateralist. This is enough to prove his globalist leanings. Remember, the two aims of these

177

groups is the destruction of national and religious borders to bring about world government. In the end, Allen Dulles was forced to resign his post due to the unraveling of his morally destitute clandestine projects. Specifically, it was Allen W. Dulles who was behind the Bay of Pigs debacle and the manipulation of Kennedy into accepting the operation. After decades of service to the N.W.O., seen by Americans as service to America, Allen Dulles was fired by Kennedy. He left Washington in disgrace.

The Dulles brothers were lavished with great wealth and power by the Illuminati. We even have the famous Dulles International Airport, named after a family who was an enemy of free America. Influential marriage arrangements were bestowed upon them. They are given a high place in our nation's History. Your country - your America - is telling you that if you believe in disentangling from intricate foreign affairs, you are a radical. If, like the Dulles Brothers, you are a proponent of destroying American sovereignty, you will be given influence, power, and a place in American History.

# Legacies of Power - Chapter 28: Richard "Dick" Cheney

Here is the multibillion-dollar question. How do you get a multibillion dollar contract from the Federal Government for your business cronies without having to bid, then overcharge the American people for millions more, and eventually declare that those who exposed your illegality are acting illegally? Easy. All you have to do is become Dick Cheney. Vice President Cheney is one of the most dastardly personas in American politics today. His legacy is interwoven with war, oil, and energy. He has reaped the rewards of following orders and covering up scandals.

In 1999, I became a Libertarian, although I still felt some affiliation with to Republican Party, my being from the South and all. My new libertarian friends promised me that Bush would be a megalomaniac. Conversely, my father begged me to vote for Bush so that Gore wouldn't win. I voted for Harry Browne, but Bush expectedly won Texas. Three years later and my father has become angered by the Republican Party and the Bush/Cheney Socialist programs. Yet, even with all the abuses of power, Dick Cheney is only an assassination or accident away from becoming the leader of the free world. Now, that's a scary thought.

Born in Nebraska in 1941, Richard B. Cheney grew up in Wyoming and graduated with a Masters of the Arts from that State's university. He served in several appointed positions during the Nixon/Ford years. Cheney then returned to Wyoming and served six terms as that State's only Congressman. During his time spent as Wyoming's delegate, he served in several other capacities, including House Minority Whip. Cheney returned to appointed office as Secretary of Defense under Bush I. Dick Cheney is now our country's second in command under Bush II. The Vice President's only role is to cast a tie-breaking vote in the Senate, and to assume the Presidency if the President were to be unable to fill that position.1

179

It should be no surprise that Dick Cheney started his political career as a staffer for Richard Nixon. Tricky Dick Cheney was schooled by Tricky Dick Nixon. Under Nixon, Cheney supported the Vietnam Conflict. So did most Republicans. The obvious correlations can be made to the "war" and offshore oil drilling off the expansive coastlines of Vietnam, and "war" for oil in Iraq. That was one of the ultimate goals of the conflict, not stopping the 'Communist domino effect.' Can't you just imagine Cheney as a young man, taking orders, making coffee, and meeting the people that would ultimately use him as a Pentagon liaison, hire him as Halliburton's CEO, and eventually vault him into the Vice Presidency? How high do you think he is on the Illuminati Pyramid? Fifth level? Fourth? Or do Cheney and the Bushes have a second order, the oilmen against the international bankers? Skull & Bones versus the Round Table? Whether or not the Rothschilds and the Bushes are in collusion, they are both seeking the same prize - to be the highest master of humankind. Also, an issue for Cheney is the level of guilt in Watergate. Maybe he was involved, either with Nixon or the plumbers, and maybe he was not. He did retain power under President Ford. What Dick Cheney definitely learned during the stint with Nixon was how to use scandal and war as a smoke screen for malignant industrialization.

Similar to Viet Nam, Watergate was definitely about more than only Nixon and his Cabinet's transgressions. Watchdog reporter Sherman Skolnick began his career in the 1950's, reforming the American court system and then writing about his experiences. He has been barred from several higher federal courts because his exposes have lifted the veil from several high-profile cases involving government/corporate backroom deals. In "The Enron Black Magic, Part Five: Big Oil and Big Electricity," Skolnick's research provides invaluable information on Watergate. It was a standard "wag the dog." In the 1950's, the CIA installed the Shah in Iran, aiding and abetting the bloody coup against the democratically elected government. During the '70's, the Shah helped reduce oil supplies which fraudulently inflated gas prices. Even in oil-rich America, fuel prices skyrocketed. Of course, most

Americans would want to know why this insane rise in fuel prices happened. Media to the rescue. Well, the media saved the oil barons and sheiks. The plumbers exposed Nixon's illegal activities, and Watergate completely consumed the country's thoughts for weeks and months and years. It was all a ruse. Behind the scenes, Middle Eastern and American businessmen had struck a deal to scratch each other's backs. By the time the citizenry realized what had happened, the damage had been done. Skolnick sums up. "Thus, the Watergate Affair was used by the oil-soaked, energy-grabbing, spy riddled monopoly press to divert public attention from the oil rip-off and what it was all about." Nixon was pardoned and given a posh condo directly adjacent to "major oil crook, David Rockefeller." Those last words are Skolnick's, also, and quite fitting. Twelve of the "plumbers," it should be noted, died in a tragic plane crash soon afterward.2

I must state that Cheney was probably not implicitly involved in all this. He was young and unproven. But, this is the backdrop that adorned the stage as an eager Dick Cheney entered for the first time into the political fray. Ol' Cheney must not have learned his lesson. The Republicans were swept out of office after Nixon and Ford, and replaced with Carter, because of the scandals and the unsuccessful war in 'Nam. But, that didn't last long, and the Republicans came back to power through Reagan. Cheney became Secretary of Defense under George H.W. Bush. The Vietnam tragedy didn't stop Poppa Bush and Cheney from starting another war, this time with Iran's neighbor, Iraq, during Operation Desert Storm. It was during the elder Bush's eleven year reign as President (beginning after Bush family friend, Hinckley, attempted an assassination on a CFR opponent, Ronald Reagan. After the attempt, Bush ran the White House,) that Cheney played his part in making money with Saddam Hussein. Even as Rumsfeld and Cheney were doing business deals with Hussein in the 1980's, they knew all along that they were actually setting the Iraqi dictator up. When Bush finally had the driver's seat, officially, he declared war on his associate, Saddam in Iraq. Cheney completed the war plans.

It was during the '80's that Dick Cheney took a

primary role in the creation and control of the tax-thieving Enron. Everyone should be aware by now of the Enron story. Most apathetic Americans are not. Even less are they aware of what is actually going on with Halliburton. Robert Scheer tells us in his article, "Cheney's Grimy Trail in Business" that in 2002, Securities and Exchange Commission Chairman, Harvey Pitt, launched an investigation into the Enron-style accounting practices and into the tax dodging done by Halliburton and the company's CEO, Cheney. The truth is, Halliburton's theft under Cheney was so totally fraudulent, Pitt had no choice but to investigate. It's OK, though. Cheney and Pitt are pals, and Cheney actually was a backer of Pitt for the SEC post. Scheer darkly jokes, "And why are we not surprised that Halliburton's accounting firm was Arthur Anderson, earlier this year (back in 2002) convicted of obstruction of justice for shredding documents in connection with Enron." That brilliant debacle has hurt Halliburton. Well, it's hurt laid-off workers and shareholders. Cheney's inner circle made off with possibly billions.3

Which brings us to the no-bid contracts. Not only has Halliburton been given these preferential contracts, Cheney handed out a similar lucrative contract to Kellogg Brown & Root, which lasted years. I don't know what George Washington and Thomas Jefferson would think, but I'm pretty sure they would compare no-bid contracts with English oppression. The practice of not bidding for contracts is blatantly un-American, yet our leaders have practiced this for two centuries and counting. Cheney says he was completely oblivious to the wrongdoings of his former employer. Yet, CBS News, Associated Press, and a report by the Congressional Research Service refute Cheney's feigning of innocence. As Vice President, he still has financial ties to Halliburton and receives payments, which is a blatant conflict of interest, not to mention illegal. And just when we thought it couldn't get any worse, the Institute for International Studies revealed recently uncovered Bechtel (another Cheney war-for-oil company) and governmental internal documents. Counterpunch journalist, David Lindorf, concurs with these findings in an article about Bechtel.4 These documents prove without a doubt that a primary motive for war was oil all along, even though Cheney and Rumsfeld have refuted the claim. Vote Republican, so you can be raped by the oil companies, raped by government corporate welfare, and then let your political heroes make off with the nation's wealth. This is America today.5

A very chilling item that must be scrutinized is Cheney's involvement in sex slavery and mind control slaves. He has been implicated, and the more I read about it, the more I believe it. For the reader to get a bearing on this issue, I recommend starting with the book, <u>Trance: Formation of America</u>. One author, Cathy O'Brien, claims she was Cheney's sexual toy. She gives first hand accounts of torture and rape by many popular politicians, including Dick Cheney.

Dick Cheney's treacherous, illegal career is well documented. From Nixon to the current Bush, he learned the ropes inside the military/industrial/corporate complex. He won't be put in jail. If you steal a loaf of bread because you are starving, you would definitely see the inside of a jail cell. Dick Cheney rips off millions and billions from the government and from third world countries and from American citizens, just because he can. He gets to be the Vice President despite his theft. He'll probably win a Peace Prize or some such thing, so that eventually History will look favorably on him, like it does for other Illuminati servants. This is a disgusting display of democracy gone wrong. Dick Cheney's legacy will live on, as he will be promoted within the ranks of the Illuminati's internal hierarchy for his treason against America. In the end, it was simply a matter of him becoming one of the wealthiest men in the world, and then utilizing and using American soldiers to enslave foreign natives, thus acquiring their resources.

## Legacies of Power: Chapter 29 - John Kerry

As I write this, John Kerry has won 14 out of 16 States in his bid to be Democratic Presidential candidate. This is a special time in United States politics. This election is so unique, even the mainstream media has had to give a blurb to the Skull & Bones connection. I've been consistently battering the Neo-Conservative Republicans lately, so now it's time to assert my animosity for yellow-dog Democrats. You know, I thought the Democratic Party may have had some honor. But, alas, they won't choose a truly radical anti-Iraqi War activist, Howard Dean, or a populist with a squeaky clean record pertaining to lobbyists, John Edwards. Instead of these men, the Democrats choose a ultra-rich elitist who supported Operation Iraqi Freedom and the Patriot Act. That would be Senator Kerry.

John Kerry's first and most important link to the Illuminati is his affiliation with the secret, life-long fraternity, Skull & Bones. The inception, initiation rights, and methods of S&B have been well documented. I have dedicated a chapter to the group, as well as interjecting several tidbits when talking about the Bushes. Because we know that Skull & Bones is the globalists' war council, we must decide what ramifications are posed by:

1. The first Skull & Bones vs. Skull & Bones Presidential election
2. What does it mean that Kerry, a Democrat, is a member of the historically conservative club.

I have several friends who will attest to the fact that I said John Kerry would win the nomination the week that he announced his bid. Skull & Bones' power has not been so full since the Vietnam era. I believe that higher forces, people who own the media outlets and polling institutions, staged the Howard Dean phenomenon. These people are almost exclusively members of S&B, CFR, Bohemian Grove Club, etc. They inflated Dean's status, thus causing the other eight

184

Democratic candidates to attack Dr. Dean during every single debate. Then, one week before Iowa, when no more debates were scheduled, the polls all of sudden miraculously showed Kerry ahead. He swept New Hampshire and Iowa, both states located in the region he is indigenous to. Those wins basically angled him for the nomination. Dean never had a chance, with no major secret society behind him.

Unfortunately, I can't claim being first in predicting the Bush/Kerry match-up. Alex Jones may be able to claim the title as prophet. And, it is here that I will relay who the activist/patriot/documentary filmmaker, Alex Jones, is. When I began to write articles, many papers said they liked the writing, but that they couldn't possibly run such exposes, true or not. Alex Jones, ran them. Jones is from the same town I am from, Austin, Texas. Being the home of the University of Texas, and being the most liberal city in Texas, Austin has wonderful community television access programming. Alex Jones began broadcasting, attacking oppressive government, and especially the coming police state. He then used this platform to direct documentaries, and has since become a leading activist against the New World Order. His website, infowars.com, gets millions of hits a month. In the last week of May, the New York Post wrote an article claiming that Michael Moore's new movie, *Fahrenheit 911*, was just a rip-off of Jones's film, *9-11: The Road to* Tyranny. On top of all this, Jones finds time to broadcast his radio talk show for three hours a day. His base is growing. He may not know it, but he has a virtual army of men and women who are as angry as he is. His movies are great tools in helping others understand the level of depravity the rulers of the world are stooping to. He urges that you show his films to your communities, churches, and family. To top all this off, it was Alex Jones who crafted the legislation, passed by the Austin City Council, refusing to participate in any unconstitutional action brought about by the Patriot Act.

Bringing this all back to John Kerry, Alex saw the Skull & Bones connection early on. He reported as far back as April 1, 2003 that the Senator was a member of the elite secret society.1 What does this mean? Does this mean that the "blue

185

states," liberal strongholds, prefer a Northeastern, aristocratic, blue-blood, Skull & Bones member as their nominee more than John Edwards, a man with integrity? (After writing this, Edwards showed up at the annual Bilderberg conference. He was soon thereafter proclaimed Kerry's running mate. This is similar to "red states" choosing a Northeastern, aristocratic, blue-blood, Skull & Bones member in Bush over the war hero John McCain. Either this is what our country wants, or the media manipulation of most our countrymen's minds has been successful.

So, what does it mean to America that John Kerry is in Skull & Bones? We may never know. Perhaps he is a patsy, so that Bush will be reelected. Already, rumors are swirling about a possible affair between Kerry and an intern, as reported on rense.com and at the Drudge Report.2, 3 Kerry refuted this buzz on IMUS, on February 13, 2004, but time will tell. The true test will be when and if Kerry defeats Bush and becomes the President. Will he extend the occupation of Iraq indefinitely, in line with Skull & Bones' directives, and against his liberal constituency? I believe he will. Will John Kerry, if elected, let the tyrannical Patriot Act expire in 2005? These two issues will tell the tale. We must also consider the United Nations. Bush seems to be against the organization, yet he continues to fund them, went to them for permission to invade Iraq, and has let them into the country to "help with elections" even though they opposed him. So, does Skull & Bones secretly work in conjunction with the United Nations? If so, watch for Kerry, with his Socialist tendencies, to invite that world body into more and more of our business. If the two groups, S&B and the U.N., are aligned, watch for Bush to be stabbed in the back so that Kerry can more ably bring the United Nations back into the global discussion.

One of the hot button issues in 2004, as always, is campaign finance reform, lobbyist agendas, ungodly sums of money being passed for favors, and corporate scandals. The far left has raucously tried to let us know that Bush is in up to his eyeballs in all of the above. So, then why did the Democrats choose John Kerry as their savior? CNN, Fox News, and MSNBC have all been reporting that Kerry has received more money from lobbyists than any of the other Democratic candidates. On the flip side, John Edwards has claimed, and I have heard no refutation, that he has not accepted one cent from lobbyists. This author has a decidedly libertarian ideology, leaning toward anarchy. But, damn it, I would have voted for John Edwards. I'll go down on record as saying I would be willing to vote for a populist, and exchange some taxes for true campaign finance reform. They will never allow this, and therefore John Edwards will never be President or even the Democratic nominee. This is because Edward's campaign finance plan would allow all truly viable third parties to have a shot at some form of federal representation.4 Can't you just imagine a Congress that was truly representative of the United States of America. If we had true equal representation in the Senate, we would have thirteen or fourteen African-American Senators. Their ideology would definitely run more populist, but there would be, and are, several conservative black representatives. We would have fourteen or fifteen Hispanics, about half liberal, half moderately conservative. There would probably be three or four Green Party members, and three or four Libertarian Party members. There could possibly be about ten or twelve Constitution Party members, which is the Party that many who vote Republican are more aligned with. Of course, you'd have one or two Communists. Only three or four Jews would be Senators, as that is the percentage of Jewish in our country. Right now, over 80% of the Senate is lawyers! That number would drop to maybe five to ten. Half or more of the Senators in Erik's fictional House would be women. That should keep warring to a minimum. There'd be mechanics, and farmers, and waiters. Maybe even a subversive or two. Yeah. Now, that would be a Senate. Then the little people could get those lifetime $100,000 dollar retirement checks with automatic pay-raises yearly, like all those retired, elite Senators who never needed the money in the first place get. The attorney/representatives would have to cede some power. That idea probably disgusts most of those maggot lawyer politicians. Of course, with a Senate that diverse, only the most important things would get done. Like my Dad always

187

said, "I'd rather they do absolutely nothing. Whenever they finally get around to it, they f*#k it all up." Bottom line is, nothing would get passed unless almost all Americans wanted it too, under true representation on the Hill. That's what representative government is about. Protecting the minority from the majority.

Wow. That was a tangent. Back to John Kerry. How is he going to run against George W. Bush on a platform of fighting special interests. Bernardo Issel of Free Republic reports some not-so-shocking facts in his article, "Extended Discussion of John Kerry's Enron Hypocrisy." He claims that Kenneth Lay was trustee for and close friend to Teresa Heinz and her businesses. Issel writes, "Oddly, Mr. Lay served as a trustee even after Enron's demise - a pamphlet obtained from the Heinz Center in the Spring of 2003 listed him as a trustee affiliated with Lay Interests LLC. This seems odd in light of Kerry's highly critical comments of Enron."5   Even mainstream news can't suppress Kerry's vast campaign coffer filled with special interest money. CNN reported on the issue. Howard Dean called John Kerry a "special interest clone." Kerry's rebuttal? "Those guys (special interest groups) have never, ever, ever gotten anything" as a return favor for all that money. OK, Kerry. That convinces us. Sure.

Of course, one of the central themes of Kerry's campaign is his Vietnam service. I commend his service. Then he came home and became an activist against the war. I commend him on this, too. He saw the shit. He deserves to protest if anyone does. Of course, he did throw his medals off a bridge. Then, he admitted they weren't his, because his are hung on the walls of his office. So, what is it, John? Are you proud of Viet Nam are appalled by it? This medal fiasco will probably be enough to keep most military votes with Bush. That isn't even the worst of it. Mackubin Thomas Owen is the contributing editor to the National Review Online.6   He reports an event that can be defined as a debacle. After 'Nam, John Kerry became part of the pseudo-subversive group Viet Nam Veterans Against the War (VVAW).   They were affiliated with agitators such as Jane Fonda and Dick Gregory. The VVAW "Dewey Canyon III" event, which saw over 150

Vietnam Veterans give testimony about American atrocities in Vietnam, seems commendable at first glance. The United States doesn't want to be involved in human atrocities. Of course, this helped re-channel the hippie's anger at the war toward returning veterans. The truth of the matter, as Owen writes, was much worse than simply calling out his fellow veterans. Owens writes about Kerry and the incident. "He said in essence that his fellow veterans had committed unparalleled war crimes in Viet Nam as a matter of course, that it was American policy to commit such atrocities. In fact, the entire Winter Soldiers Investigation was a lie." It was eventually revealed that the men testifying to Congress about their war crimes "either had not served in the Viet Nam or had not done so in the capacity that they claimed." Now, that's true Washington Activism.

Some information that may or may not be relevant is John Kerry's true heritage. Somehow, when he was first elected to office, his constituents got the crazy idea that he was Irish. Several newspapers reported this as fact, but John Kerry insists that he has never said he was Irish. What Kerry has discovered is that he is at least one quarter Jewish.7 There have also been rumors that Bush and Kerry are distantly related. Finally, rumors are that Kerry is a descendent of the Visigoth leader, King Harald. Is or is this not relevant to today's politics? I'll let you decide.

Finally, what of John Kerry's sex life? Not that I care, but it will be and already has been a campaign issue. He's on his second marriage with a wife worth half a billion dollars. Democrats definitely don't want some perverted sleaze to represent them again. Clinton II would not be pretty for the party. At least Clinton was a genius. I don't think Kerry can match the former President in political prowess or sheer intellect. A Drudge Report posted on February 13, 2004, states that there are allegation of Kerry and a 22-year old intern having been physically attached. The intern has left the country according to the Drudge Report. The Wall Street Journal and Rush Limbaugh have taken Drudge's cue, and there is reportedly a Time Magazine article in the works on the subject. His nose, and other extremities, better be clean.

When it comes right down to it, Kerry is not much different than Bush. They both supported Operation Iraqi Freedom and the Patriot Act. Both of their military histories are swirling with innuendo and questions. Both men graduated Yale and are members of the elite secret society, Skull & Bones. They both have financial ties to Ken Lay and Enron. In 2004, the elite have decided not to even pretend and give us a semblance of choice for our most prestigious office, leader of the supposed free world. Never vote Democrat or Republican again, I say.

## Legacies of Power - Chapter 30: The Merovingians

I write the last chapter in the "Legacies of Power" series not so much as a brief account of the Merovingians, but as a wake up call for those who are still not aware about the elites' attack on Christianity. The Merovingian lineage, as Fritz Springmeier points out, is so interwoven with the other aristocratic bloodlines of Europe that it would take a lifetime to unravel.1 This chapter will give my opinion on the religious revolution that is going on throughout America. This revolution is the death of Jesus. This has been happening for one hundred years, beginning publicly with Nietzsche's cry that "God is Dead." The New World Order carefully constructs this revolution, for their eventual aim is a one world religion, to "promote peace." Once the seeds were planted, it was only a matter of time until a snowball effect started. The snowball is getting larger. The latest written culmination in the agenda to destroy Christianity is the fiction novel by Dan Brown, The Da Vinci Code.

I have tried to discover where the idea that Jesus was not the Son of God was first espoused. Of course, sects and factions began doing this even before Jesus died. However, in my search I came across the book that seems to have brought the concept to modern America. It is the nonfiction tome, Holy Blood, Holy Grail. I am going to look at this book from a (hopefully) agnostic viewpoint. In other words, I don't assume that Jesus was or was not divine. That is for the religious to decide. Texe Marrs, a Central Texas pastor, writer, and lecturer would say that I have succumbed to Satan's lies by even being agnostic. And, he may be right. The reason I am no longer sure of spirituality is the collectivist religious concepts of which my generation (child of the '70's and '80's or Gen X) has been totally inundated with. Marrs's tome, Dark Secrets of the New Age: Satan's Plan for a One World Religion is very telling, and made me rethink what side of this fence I want to be on. Marrs and other religious leaders

believe that the concept and instigation of a One World
Government and the One World Religion issues from the same
source, Lucifer. His research proves that there is a movement
of elite and academics that are emanating forth the universal
religion.

Let's take a chapter to go over the spiritual
ramifications, and then I can get to my great discovery while
reading Holy Blood, Holy Grail. Here are four possibilities.

1. Jesus is the God purported in the Bible, the only way to
heaven. If this is so, then the installation of the New World
Order, encompassing every facet of human life including
religion, is all foretold in the Bible, most notably Revelations.
If the Bible is true, the New World Order WILL come,
eventually ordaining the Antichrist as the World's sole ruler.
The Antichrist will need to be seen as THE Christ. Now, what
Holy Blood tries to get the reader to realize is that Jesus' death
was merely symbolic. The important thing is that Jesus had a
child. This child was taken to France, then known as Gaul,
and protected. Jesus' line became rulers known as the
Merovingians. Supposing that the Bible is true, this would
make the Jesus' son theory very devious. If the world believed
that Jesus had an ancestor, some person presented
today…well, that is a person that could be heralded as Christ,
when it is really the Antichrist.

2. Our second theory is premised with the assumption that
Jesus was not divine, but that there is a spiritual battle between
good and evil. This follows the Babylonian/Freemasonic/New
Age doctrines, loosely. If this is the case, we need to believe
that man is an evolving God. Not only that, but man can
spontaneously create spiritual evolution which is the
predecessor for civilization's evolution. If this is the case, and
each man is a God, why would we need any religion
whatsoever. If morals are relative, then why do we need to be
watched by the growing global world super state as if we are
always doing something wrong? If man is a god, and can find
the answers alone or with a guru, why must all things be
controlled by a "Council of Twelve" or whatever group will

subjugate the new man-gods? If one believes this, then one must believe that each person can have his own religion, *regardless of whether or not it is an inclusive religion.*

3. Again, I will mention David Icke's reptilian theory. He believes that reptilian aliens have taken over the minds of many of the world's powerful elite. These reptilians are manipulating the powerful into installing the New World Order. Sounds like Icke just got his reptilians mixed up with Marrs's demons, or vice-versa. However, both Icke and Marrs believe that other beings have entered human bodies and are using them as a physical form to further a plan for a global totalitarian state.

4. Finally, I will write about what I know for sure. No one can prove that God exists or does not exist. So he may or may not. The Christians acknowledges this fact, and reminds us that it is faith that must be present for salvation, in lieu of proof. Atheists, however, are much more rigid and intellectually unbending. They know God doesn't exist, whether or not they can prove it mathematically or scientifically as yet. But, it's the same, there is no proof. Therefore, there's no absolute proof that Jesus was the Son. What is a fact is that the Illuminati and those seeking global domination are doing one of two things. Either, THEY believe in the Ancient Mysteries and are using them to wield ultimate control, OR they are just manipulating us with OUR belief in spirituality, which I might add was all handed down by elders, the 'elite' of ancient days. Regardless, a one world religion is supplanting all others.

Whatever the answer to life's questions, I believe that <u>Holy Blood, Holy Grail</u> is an invaluable reference source for one glaring reason. While Dan Brown wrote <u>Da Vinci Code</u> because of the growing popularity of disbelieving in Jesus, <u>Holy Blood</u> was written by, or with the guiding hand of, our world's true Illuminati. So, while the religious end of the book is irrelevant, the Historical accounting is possibly more accurate than anything else ever written.

Holy Blood, Holy Grail should be on everybody's bookshelf. It is the Illuminati's inside view on the History of the Knights Templar, the Merovingians, and Middle Ages of European History. I firmly believe that the book was written by the true Order of Zion, a secret society which turned into the Freemasons, and I believe is mutating into something else during this era.

Why would I say that the Order of Zion actually wrote the book? Several reasons. One must remember that Jews did not write the "Protocols of the Learned Elders of Zion". It was, in fact, written by European elite to demonize the Jew, and thus take fomenting anger away from them. Henry Lincoln claims that simple curiosity brought him to document what became the book. He was rewarded with the help of two experts in the fields he was covering. How often does an author receive such experts, especially on a book that was sure to remain somewhat anonymous. While the writers wrote, they were rewarded again with the good fortune of having people claiming to be the Order of Zion depositing fresh tracts into the French National Library. This information was verified as historically accurate, therefore the suppositions were taken seriously. How very convenient. Too, the writers were granted exclusive interviews with very elite royal personages of Europe. All of this smacks of the guiding hand of some segment of the New World Order.

Much of this book is interpretation, or connecting the dots. Much of it is proposed substantiation for the book's claims. I had a very imposing question after reading this book. Where are - who are the Merovingians now? For that we must look to Jewish, Egyptian, and Babylonian Histories. Hislop's classic, The Two Babylons, begins to make the connection.4

Hislop and others claim that the Illuminati have been in power and can trace their heritage back to Ancient Babylon and Egypt. This is where many of the occult practices of the secret societies are derived. To mock the twelve Jewish tribes, the Illuminati formed thirteen tribes, which are described in Springmeier's 13 Bloodlines of the Illuminati. The thirteenth bloodline was to be the seed of Satan and of Christ, combined.

When these two bloodlines meet in perfect conjunction…well, supposedly the heir will be the Antichrist as reported in Revelations and by Nostradamus.

I believe that Holy Blood, Holy Grail was written by the Illuminati. Its main purpose is to break its reader from believing in Jesus Christ. Why would they want that? To usher in the One World Religion. The European History that the book issues makes much more sense than anything I've read before. It tells us that a group of families have been conspiring to rule the planet since at least Jesus' time. It tells how they infiltrated the Church, the Temple of Jerusalem, and virtually every monarchy. It makes us aware that the Freemasons were, indeed, a group set up to further the ends of the family, by destroying the Old Order. Nostradamus was listed as one of the grand masters of the Order of Zion. This would explain his powers of prophecy. The Illuminati has a grand plan that has been set for ages. Nostradamus, a former grandmaster the Order of Zion, would have been privy to the Order's long-term objectives and strategies. His texts are not spiritual prescience. Neither are they guesses or extraneous poetics. His writing constitutes a documentation of what the elites have in store for us. That's why he was right about 50% of the time: their plans do not always come to fruition as desired.

But, the biggest plan is near completion. Because I despise what the New World Order represent (the State's power over the individual,) I hope and pray that Christians will let me fight beside them. The Grand Plan, well, that is something I could never accept. Mainstream Christians had better wake up to the coming dark time. Whether or not there is a God, the One World Government and Religion is coming. And Christianity, with its exclusivity, will be targeted for extinction. How long will you wait? Until ALL the cameras are in place, tracking your every move? Should citizens wait until we are set up on a totally cashless, universal monetary supply? Should Christians wait until the government dictates to the churches what or with whom they are allowed to worship? Should Christians keep quiet until AFTER they are no longer permitted to worship Jesus Christ as the Lord and

Savior?  The time is upon those very Christians to make that decision.

The Merovingians, in one sense, have never left us. They are the elite that rule from the ivory tower.  They are the men behind the curtain.  They are those who would seek to control humanity.  The Merovingians are our masters, and they must be stopped before we are all forcibly attached to a Central Consciousness and our thoughts are never, never again our own.  It would be the Death of God and the Death of Individuality in one fell swoop.

# Part Four

# Politics in G Minor

## G Minor - Chapter 31: Mass Media Mind Control and the World of Illusion

By Randy Lavello

An enormous false world has been constructed by the globalists with the intent to trap us in a prison of illusion. This deception has penetrated so deeply into our consciousness that it has grown difficult to discern fact from fiction...this, of course, was the goal of the mind manipulation. Upon the corruption of our minds lies the trail of globalist fingerprints.

The wealthiest men of our nation are in control of our education system. Our schools teach curriculums created by the Ford Foundation, Carnegie Endowment, the Rockefeller Foundation, and the Guggenheim Foundation. While President of the Ford Foundation in 1954, Rowan Gaither, explained the Foundation's mandate: "...we operate in response to directives, the substance of which is that we shall use our grant making power to alter life in the United States so that it can be comfortably merged with the Soviet Union." Openly admitted, for the record, the tax-exempt foundations that determine what and how American children learn have tried to manipulate attitudes toward a socialist model - specifically the Soviet Union. What are some alterations that would favor this change in attitude? In the Soviet Union there were no guaranteed rights, freedom of political expression was outlawed, the government regimented all aspects of life, and religion was systematically abolished in favor of the belief in atheism.

Upon examination of my own U.S. history book from school, I realized the Bill of Rights was excluded from the book - the only mention of our Bill of Rights was in implied meanings, reworded by the authors. This is a blatant attempt to undermine the original meaning of the Constitution! It is only justifiable to interpret the meanings of each right after reading the actual words written by the Founding Fathers. Couple this with the passage of the Patriot Act and Homeland

198

Security Act, which negate major portions of the Bill of Rights, and we begin to see a pattern: our inherent rights from God are being destroyed!

When one knows whom their readers will be they can then attempt to alter their opinions through their writings. As Nietzsche says, "He who knows the reader, does nothing further for the reader. Another century of readers - and spirit itself will sink. That everyone can learn to read will ruin in the long run not only writing, but thinking too." Because those who mandate our education have set a goal for themselves - the destruction of our Republic and a merger with world government. They have written textbooks accordingly. Through these means, they manage the thinking processes of the readers - the children attending school to be 'educated.' Our children's minds are being manipulated to turn away from Individualism, in favor of Collectivism.

Because the Homeland Security Act and Patriot Act allow for indefinite detainment, it is now legal for U.S. citizens to be held as political prisoners. The Federal Government is not required to give any reason for detaining a person. Why isn't this analyzed in the media? Why is this important turn of events being swept under the rug? Furthermore, federal agents may enter homes without warrant or the homeowner's knowledge; this provides the perfect opportunity to frame their adversaries: those in favor of Constitutional Government. With the DNA database being constructed, it will likely be possible to grow human hairs in a laboratory that could conceivably be planted as evidence in a crime.

The physical shackles of oppression are much more sloppy than the restraints which can be placed on the mind. The tragedy of our situation is that we first must win a spiritual war - then, likely a physical one. Nietzsche observed, "We believe in reason: this, however, is the philosophy of gray concepts. Language depends on the most naïve prejudices. Now we read disharmonies and problems into things because we think only in the form of language and thus believe in the 'eternal truth' of 'reason.' (e.g., subject, attribute, etc.) We cease to think when we refuse to do so under the constraint of language; we barely reach the doubt that sees this limitation as a limitation. Rational thought is interpretation according to a scheme that we cannot throw off." Nietzsche knew well the restrictions language places on thought. Another genius, George Orwell, explained in his book 1984, how a corrupt totalitarian government called Oceania (U.S.A. merged with Britain) reduced the language to restrict its subject's range of thought. In this new language, Newspeak, a person was unable to form concepts to disagree with the government. This becomes important as the illiteracy rate in our nation increases every year.

The main concept of mind control, in the book 1984, was to cause a person to 'doublethink.' Orwell explains 'doublethink' as a willingness "to forget any fact that has become inconvenient, and then, when it becomes necessary again, to draw it back from oblivion for just so long as it is needed." For example, the U.S. places Saddam Hussein in power, arms him to the teeth, then declares him a menace to the world and attacks him. We are supposed to forget that Donald Rumsfeld handed Saddam a briefcase - the Weapons of Mass Destruction kit! If I hand a person a gun, then shoot him, does that make me a hero? We are supposed to 'doublethink' and not care how many times the Federal Government lies to us, yet still believe every word they say at present. When our nation blows something up it is called an 'operation.' When anyone else blows something up it is called 'terrorism.' By this interpretation, terrorism is defined as using a bomb without dropping it from a plane or delivering it by missile! Because they don't spend the money on the high-tech gear, they're terrorists!

There was a War on Illiteracy - more people are illiterate. There was a War on Drugs - more drugs hit the street. Now there's a War on Terror - a war on a concept, which will, of course, bring us more terrorism. We see the results of these so-called 'wars,' yet we 'doublethink' and ignore the facts.

Perhaps the most enormous lie perpetuated upon us today by the schools and media is the idea of Macroevolution: the notion that we somehow evolved from apes. Of course, Microevolution is proper and evident - for example, giraffes with longer necks survive during times of drought, while the shorter necked giraffes starve because they can't reach the leaves to eat. But Macroevolution, the idea that we coincidentally, just happened to evolve from nothingness, is absurd to the point of lunacy!

First of all, Macroevolution defies the very laws of physics which it is supposed to enforce. Those who believe in this theory consider themselves "students of reason," yet reason itself denies this theory. Mathematicians have studied the odds of this theory taking place and the odds are so miniscule, they are not even calculable... in other words, there is not even a chance this actually took place. The Theory of Macroevolution relies on an assumption that we evolved from simplicity into something much more complex - this defies the Second Law of Thermodynamics which states that simplification of structure is the natural state of all things. The idea that genetic mutations might occur, every time, to add complexity to simple genes is absurd and reckless. The scientific evidence proves the course of genetic degeneration: Bacillus Circulans was analyzed after 300 million years of suspended animation in rack salt; it was found to be more genetically complex than its current forms. We are in a state of degeneration, not 'evolution.'

Nietzsche, who lived and wrote during the birth of Darwinism, wrote, "Anti-Darwin. - What surprises me most when I survey the broad destinies of man is that I always see before me the opposite of that which Darwin and his school see or want to see today: selection in favor of the stronger, better-constituted, and the progress of the species. Precisely the opposite is palpable: the elimination of the lucky strokes, the uselessness of the more highly developed types, the inevitable dominion of the average even the sub-average types. If we are not shown why man should be an exception among creatures, I incline to the prejudices that the school of Darwin has been deluded everywhere."

"That species represent any progress is the most unreasonable assertion in the world: so far they represent one level. That the higher organisms have evolved from the lower has not been demonstrated in a single case. I see how the lower preponderate through their numbers, their shrewdness, their cunning - I do not see how an accidental variation gives an advantage, at least not for so long a period; why an accidental change should grow so strong would be something else needing explanation."

"In summa: growth in the power of a species is perhaps guaranteed less by a preponderance of its children of fortune, of strong members, than by a preponderance of average and lower types- The latter possess great fruitfulness and duration; with the former comes an increase in danger, rapid wastage, speedy reduction in numbers."

The great farce of Darwinian macroevolution has been insinuated upon mankind...but why would this be beneficial to globalists?  Those who believe in atheism and evolution, which is just as much a blind leap-of-faith as any other religious belief, usually have the attitude "life is mere chance - who cares about anything?" and "nothing is sacred, we are just monkeys ourselves, let's defile the world." Those who believe in nothingness are more easily led to their demise. Those who stand up for a code of ethics, and believe in God and goodness, are more likely to stand up against tyranny.  A belief in Macroevolution supports the materialist philosophy of purchasing happiness at the local Galleria and teaches nothing of discovering spiritual happiness.

Our "education" system is not the poorest in the world by coincidence; neither is it because Americans are of sub-normal intelligence.  The school system is designed to dumb students down - to teach them to memorize and obey, instead of teaching them to think for themselves.  Add to the equation the intelligence-insulting media, which couldn't say a three syllable word if this were desired, and we have a system of idiocy manufacturing cattle.  All this is no accident.  This has been perpetuated upon us with the intent of degrading our mental attributes for the purpose of exploitation.  The veil hiding these wealthy puppet-masters with their tax-exempt 'educational' foundations and mass media must be lifted if we are to win this spiritual battle.

## G Minor - Chapter 32: Non-Violent Alternatives to Combat the New World Order

"What can you do about it?" This is often the final judgment I hear, after weeks or months of debate, which, if I am fortunate and the contester is open-minded, sometimes ends with a persuasion to reason. Once one has realized that our government is, has always been, and will be for the foreseeable future, an illusion, one must always ask this question. "What can you do about it?" As David Icke says, we are living in a "prison without bars." It therefore needs to be answered by those of us who are prepared to take the next logical step after enlightenment. That is, the desire to disseminate information and educate the public. Only the marriage of a diminutive, localized collectivism to a responsible individualism will bring about human equality. It is a brotherhood of compatriots, the ilk that risk public persecution and the hauntingly empty FEMA internment camps. We write; about the inherent dangers in a New World Order; the fraudulent proclamation of some (most) (all?!) American Wars; the strategic, nearly decisive rewriting of History; and our secret society power structure.

"So, what CAN we do?" First, I would like to define to whom I am speaking. It must be assumed that the question asked was queried because of elucidation. We are lovers of freedom, privacy, defense, family, and justice. Despite or because of this "New Freedom Philosophy," there is one urgent quandary. I have opined on several occasions that individuals whose highest principle is responsible individual sovereignty are an intelligent, unique, creative lot. This conglomeration of ideas and stories, lives, and cultures, inevitably becomes enmeshed in differences of opinions about almost everything. Liberals, Libertarians, Anarchists, and other groups from both sides of the intentionally coined and purposefully divisive term "aisle" have somehow found themselves fighting on the same team. A dictate, or common stance, must be proposed and adopted unanimously if we are to be victorious.  In fact, our own survival may depend on it.

There is one thing that must be agreed upon by all in order to keep alive the spirit and mandates of liberty.  The tyrannical New World Order must be stopped from ripening to fruition.

The first thing one can do once one decides to oppose the globalists' agenda is to join the ranks of the exponentially growing number of information warriors.  This begins by becoming extremely knowledgeable about conspiracy facts, government organizations, leaders of as many countries as possible, and especially one's own State and Federal politicians.  It is unwise to ever speak from emotion: logic is the better choice.  Propaganda may be more effective than truth, but only for the short term.  Truth has a way of rising from it's own supposed ashes, a phoenix that must soar afire in it's certainty.

A good place to begin practicing speaking skills is with anyone who seems interested in debating.  This serves a twofold purpose.  First, debate techniques are honed and mistakes are minimized due to the smaller audience.  Because neo-con "news" that permeates our society is stated as logic, it is sometimes difficult to force a point.  The Elite are not stupid.  In fact, they are highly educated.  How does one prove, without a computer or library handy, that the Iraq debacle is a Skull & Bones operation funded by the Council on Foreign Relation's select membership and guided by 'darkened' CIA agents?  How does one prove that to a person who is brainwashed by Rush-speak?  Lies are reinforced by the 24-hour disinformation distributed by the corporate cable news programs.  Letters to the editors of journals will help to apply and gauge writing proficiency.  Once the Truth is known, it is almost impossible to NOT speak and write out against the War on the Individual and all who support it.  Always suggest the reading of websites like infowars.com, propagandamatrix.com, and other fact-based pages.

It may be grandiose, but I liken Prison Planet writers and other scholars of freedom to Samuel Adams in the early days, before official "revolution" was declared.  Samuel was able to do what he wanted and work in the print media industry. Still, taxation was keeping him in servitude to King George's oligarchical monarchy. This is similar to what America and Europe still have as government today. The British military had the authority to search any person or place without discretion, as does our police force. Of course, they did not do this to very many people, so most of the population didn't care. Ditto, presently. Adams knew that the mere ability to impose fascism would inevitably lead to a domineering, centralized government imposing military rule with evermore-oppressive tones.

It was fifty years before the Constitution was penned (1740's) that Samuel Adams wrote essays based on his newly formed ideology centering on the themes and writings of John Locke, Voltaire, and other aristocrats. Yes, they were wealthy, distant cousins of aristocracy - and many were Freemasons. Taken in a social context, these men, too, were lovers of freedom. They sought to break free from the crushing power of the Catholic Church and the whimsical nature of their kings and queens. Of course, the British Empire had no desire to see Samuel's words and ideas reach the public. Their tenuous hold on other colonies was very disconcerting. It was therefore necessary for Samuel Adams to take his pamphlets and his oratories to the pubs, and the mercantile unions, and especially to the agricultural co-ops. Farmers have long been supporters of freedom. Taxation used to mean "give us a portion of your food," not money. I believe that this is why our government has allowed gargantuan conglomerates to take over agriculture, imposing strict regulations and heavy taxes on independents. Their one hundred year attempt to end the family farm has all but succeeded. So, Samuel Adams made friends with people of all types of religions and ideologies, philosophies and industries. That is what we must do, if we are to overthrow the current regime by nonviolent means.

There are things that should be despised about the Elite and their methods. Outright lying to defraud a person or entity is never acceptable, no matter your race, religion (or lack thereof), gender, etc., etc. However, there are certain strategies we would be wise to embrace. The upper echelon braying the NWO battle call - I have seen numbers purporting they are as few as ten families ruling the globe; but, they probably number approximately 2,000 - are so effective because of their extremely centralized power.  Can we agree that the  ultimate goal is the dismantling of all organizations, by peaceful means, which would implement a one world government?  If we can agree to take this as our guiding principle, we will have effectively created a common ground that streamlines our efficiency. At this point, getting enmeshed in bickering over environmental issues, abortion, race, and religion will only play into the hands of our opponents.

Another technique being implemented increasingly in our society and throughout the world is video monitoring and recording.   We have tried to combat this by opposing legislation that allows for it. Ultimately, the lobbying strategy has failed.  I suggest this: use available, legal technology AGAINST them.  CBS Evening News reported, "From intense scrutiny at airports to expanded government authority to track internet use, federal agents now watch American citizens more closely than ever."  This is our reality.  Therefore, we might combat fascism by reversing this surveillance.  Alex Jones has stated that his program now has 2 million listeners.  Might we all go out and buy a $500 dollar digital video recorder and begin monitoring misdeeds against our clans and other American citizens.  Imagine if every local, state, and federal officer knew that it was possible they were being monitored and recorded.  The next home they entered without a warrant, which is legal though controversial, they would have to wonder if microchip-sized recording devices, easily acquired at the local "spy" shop, were making duplicate copies of the agents' actions and words; every important nuance.  Might then things start to change, even a little?  A good example of what may be incidentally acquired is the "Secret Police" scene recorded by Mr. Jones, himself.  He was able to bring the reality of a police state to TV screens, which is a much more powerful medium than mere oration.   Monitoring the thousands of searches performed at airports "to protect us from terrorists" would bring corruption into focus, thus staunching its ugly wound.   Keeping the skies safe by frisking, embarrassing, and harassing American citizens, including the obviously handicapped and the very aged, must be halted. We must record tens of thousands of official arrests to make sure all parties follow all laws. This might also be our reality.

Another advantage would be to show certain groups that the ones they follow are not of their own ilk. Many Christians hope that George W. Bush is a devout man (I hope so, too;) but there is a gnawing in their gut that screams something is wrong. Would printed documentation proving that certain leaders are members of pagan and Satanist societies lead these Christian victims to a 'search for answers,' also? A formal list of members of the Bohemian Grove and proof of their "harmless" ritual sacrifice of a human, purported to be in effigy, might make them raise an eyebrow. Their robed worship of Molech may also begin the process. Membership lists and the true ideologies of Freemasons, Skull & Bones, and other secret societies would speak volumes concisely and honestly. In the First Commandment, God says "You shall have no other gods before me." True Christians will have no option but to discontinue being led by one who goes against God's primary law.

There are other organizations that might be brought to our side. Minorities already mistrust government. This is most understandable as they have historically been lied to, abused, raped and slaughtered by those in power (white, European elites) for centuries. Will a new cleansing of America be any different for them. Even now, Asians, Arabs, Latinos, and Blacks, both immigrants and legal citizens, are quietly being subjected to authoritarian rule. It would behoove us to make this clearly evident, not only to individual members of these groups, but to their leaders and the boards of their organizations.

The most influencing media in information dissemination is the Television. The Elite have an extreme advantage over us, for they own the news channels that the majority of the population watches. Someday soon it may be necessary to start a true Freedom Channel. First and foremost, this channel would have to be entertaining. This network would be primarily a news source, but we are dealing with the general public. How many people out there jump from Fox to

CNN to MSNBC trying to find a unique and relevant documentary? Most times, the major news channels are playing the same stories...all day...ALL WEEK...until the next news story miraculously explodes on the screen and scene only to be covered simultaneously and with no end by all the stations once again. Like Bush's wish for American hegemony worldwide, the television news landscape is unexciting and similar. A different story would give a Freedom Network a definite entrepreneurial advantage.

When Fox News really achieved success, with shows like O'Reilly and Hannity and Colms, they were rewarded with monetary and critical acclaim. Truth be told, practically the only 24-hour news source prior to 2000 was CNN. CNN had become very leftist, and Fox used the smokescreen of our two-party system to gain control of the news media. This forced CNN to assimilate conservative rhetoric even as Fox became more liberal. It also allowed the Nixon/Reagan/Bush/Bush Jr. regime currently in office an advantageous disinformation outlet. Just by being the first pro-Constitution, anti-Establishment channel, we can be assured that the major media will have to take notice, even if they abhor doing so. I can't wait to hear all the screaming about anti-Americanism from a channel that is more for freedom than any other. A unique, TRUTHFUL program could not help but to attract viewers. And advertisers, as a whole, will put their dollars where the most eyes can see their ads. Rerunning syndications of shows like "That 70's show", or the epitome of social satire, "The Simpsons" could not fail but to attract viewers. Of course, the advertisement breaks would be filled with pertinent public items, such as hemp products and information, gun advertisements, and other legal marketing. This will make the channel money, sell products we believe in by providing an outlet for retailers that are currently shunned, and sensitize the public to the advantages of owning a gun, using industrial hemp, and living in a truly free America and World.

For Generation X and Y, there could be network features akin to HBO's "Buffy the Vampire Slayer" and "Six Feet Under." A diverse group of individualists will naturally have a diverse palate for entertainment, both its creation and viewing. Music groups with Libertarian-leanings and political commentary, such as The Dixie Chics and Audio Slave, should have segments for promotion. This will attract the MTV generations, (plural.) This would get out the truth, providing jobs in a failing economy, creating outlets for other industries, and promoting political agendas and politicians adhering to the policies of Freedom. While this idea is certainly not feasible currently, it is an idea to ponder and bandy about.

There is one reason why a nonviolent victory against the Super State and police enforced collectivism needs to be pacifistic in nature. Speaking from a strictly theoretical standpoint, the opportunity to win freedom though armed resistance has all but past. As of now, the best weapons a militia can utilize are some descent rifles and small handguns. In a metaphoric sense, it is akin to a social David and Goliath. Goliath was huge and fierce, and had the highest reputation amongst warriors, though even soldiers were aghast at some of his methods. David had only a sling and a dagger in which to take on his mighty foe's awesome spear and deadly broadsword, Goliath's superior strength and experience. Unfortunately, the fable ends better than real life usually does. In reality, David would have most likely died in armed combat with Goliath. David and his people found a much better way to defeat the enemy. They rewrote history and vaulted their kinsmen into positions of power across the globe. They were ingenious, and in so being were able to become arguably the most powerful people - and most persecuted - on the planet. And that is how it must be with us. We must use their method, only the history we are leaving behind, in books and on the Internet, is honest and real. Through this can we be successful. Musicians must sing about freedom and the fight against oppression. Artists must create pieces that reflect their philosophy and, too, the times as they are now so that they can be documented from one of the truest perspectives: an artist's. Writers must write and speakers must speak. We are turning the tide. Because Goliath was a military force, the Jews were at war even before they picked up a weapon in retaliation. Once Goliath had admonished David with servitude or extermination via the use of force, it became a military war.

Yet, many of the most important triumphs have been accomplished using guile, the pen, and diplomacy. Let us not forget that presently a majority of our brother-peasants in Europe agree with the minority in the U.S., and are against war. Many are against social regulations, which is some common ground we can stand on, together . And, if there is a God, I hope he is on freedom's side.

In my largest leap, I propose the term Neo-Activist and its definition for consideration. When the revolutions of the late 17 and early 1800s occurred, the writers and leaders were still members of the aristocracy. To gain freedom for themselves, they had to at least appear to want it for everyone (well, all white upper-class males, anyway.) A very small percentage of the population, namely said aristocracy, was literate. As the succeeding generations of elites were born, they gained power and thus, because power breeds corruption, have become just as or more dictatorial than the preceding monarchies. It is time for the new breed, the new revolutionaries, to use every nonviolent mean at their disposal to tear away the reigns of power. These numbers will not have many from Yale or Harvard in them. The ranks of this new organization will not be bloodlines dating back to some aristocracy or other. Our schools were public, or the School of Hard Knocks, and that brings more real life experience to the table than the Bushes, Clintons, Rockefellers, or the others will ever have. The majority of our country are working class, making $24,000 - $100,000 per year. We are told that the middle-class has risen to power. That is false propaganda. We are, or can be, equally intellectual. We are already harder working and much more creative. My next proposal seems like an insurmountable task, but I believe that it is the only way to preserve our true culture.

First, we must not waiver when faced with the choices of our predecessors. We must devote ourselves to 100% equality. Any and all who love freedom must be accepted. Brilliant men and women must come together to form a global society of believers in freedom, responsibility, and tolerance. It is understandable that many are afraid of societies, as individualists. That is why our true intent must never be

210

hidden. We must scream it to the mountaintops. The ultimate goal is to place members into positions of power in business, politics, media, and education. Everywhere that there is a Skull & Bones or CFR or Bilderberg member, there must be a greater number of this new group of diverse individualists. We must own the nonprofit groups that rewrite the public school history books. We must own all of the news channels. Disinformation must be abolished. We must brainwash the people back into Truth. It seems hypocritical, yet because we are not ready to take up arms, in which case we would win in an extended guerrilla warfare campaign, we must form a Federation of Neo-Activists. This must be done by recruiting a centralized group of men and women, with an outer circle of generals, and on and on. Yes, it is the same method employed by Freemasons and other groups. But it works, and that can't be disputed. It would be prudent to have a council of x number of people, x representing the number of leaders, one each from any viable group that opposes oppressiveness wherever it rears its ugly head. Voluntary donations and private savings will be needed to fund this project. Private schools should be formed, home schooling promoted, and scholarships given to motivated individuals who believe in liberty and the Rule of Law. Eventually, these men and women will become lawyers, and doctors, and politicians. We are fighting to save not only the bodies of our children's children: we strive to defend their minds. The only true possibility of achieving our unifying goal is to begin a nonviolent hostile takeover of the world's power structure.

From the easily performed person-to-person debate to the materialization of a dominantly middle class, nonviolent (except in defense) unconcealed society legislating and enforcing the rule of law, we must stop the onslaught of the Global Elite. We are in the midst of war. If everyone does his or her part, we may be able to start the pendulum on its opposite path. We must all become Information Warriors.

## G Minor - Chapter 33: Rothschilds Conduct 'Red Symphony' - The 20th Century Unveiled

By Henry Makow, PhD

Incredible and bizarre as it sounds, humanity is indeed the victim of a diabolical conspiracy.

War, depression and genocide in the past century were not accidental or inevitable but the result of a malevolent design.

Shocking evidence is a 1938 Stalinist police (NKVD) interrogation of a founder of the Communist International, Christian G. Rakovsky, 65, who was facing the firing squad for plotting to overthrow Stalin.

The 50-page transcript of his interrogation, dubbed "The Red Symphony," was not meant to become public. It confirms that the Rothschild-Illuminati planned to use Communism to establish a world dictatorship of the super rich.

This is perhaps the most explosive political document in modern history. It reveals why the Illuminati financed Hitler and then tried to destroy him, and why Stalin made a pact with Hitler in 1939.

Christian Rakovsky was a veteran Communist insider. Born Chaim Rakeover in 1873, he studied medicine in France before becoming a revolutionary. He was leader of a terror group that attacked government officials.
http://spartacus.schoolnet.co.uk/RUSrakovsky.htm

In 1919, Lenin put him in charge of the Soviet Ukraine government. He successfully kept the area for the Bolsheviks during the Civil War. Stalin appointed him Russian ambassador to Paris in 1925.

Rakovsky belonged to the powerful Trotskyite faction that took their orders from the Rothschilds. Many of this group were shot in Stalin's 1937 Communist Party purge.

**Midnight Interrogation**

Thus, the circumstances of the midnight interrogation

Jan. 26, 1938 were very dramatic.

What could Rakovsky say that would save his life?

Rakovsky appears to use the tactic of "deceiving with the truth." He wins trust by revealing the truth but leaves some of it out. He tries to impress Kus'min that he and Trotsky represent an invincible power he calls the "Capitalist-Communist Financial International."

He confirms that the "revolutionary movement" was designed to enlist support by pretending to serve mankind's moral and collective ideals. The real aim, however, is to divide society, undermine established authority and create totalitarian rule.

"Revolution" really means, "overturning" Western civilization.

"Christianity is our only real enemy since all the political and economic phenomena of the bourgeois states are only its consequences," Rakovsky says. (Griffin, p. 264)

Peace is "counter-revolutionary" since it is war that paves the way for revolution.

Rakovsky refers to the Illuminati as "they" or "them." He claims he does not know them but I suspect he does.

He explains that the "Illuminati" is a Masonic secret society dedicated to Communism. Significantly, its founder Adam Weishaupt took the name from "the second anti-Christian conspiracy of that era, gnosticism." (249)

## How This Gripping Account Surfaced

The interrogator was one of Stalin's cleverest agents, Gavriil Kus'min, known as "Gabriel."

Apart from him and a hidden sound technician, a doctor Jose Landowsky was the only other person present.

Conscripted by the NKVD to help "loosen the tongues of detainees," Dr. Landowsky was sickened by the many tortures he witnessed.

The interrogation of Rakovsky, however, was cordial. Dr. Landowsky doubts if the mild euphoric he put in Rakovsky's drink had much effect at all.

The interrogation, conducted in French, lasted from midnight to 7 a.m. After, Kus'min ordered Landowsky to translate the interview into Russian and make two copies.

The content was so mind boggling that Landowsky made an additional carbon for himself. "I am not sorry that I had the courage for this," he wrote. (279) (The Bolsheviks had shot Landowsky's father, a Tsarist colonel, during the 1917 revolution.)

A Spanish volunteer later found the manuscript on Landowsky's dead body in a hut on the Petrograd front during World War Two. He took it back to Spain where it was published as "Sinofonia en Rojo Mayo," in 1949.

A person with the nickname "Yamaguchi" has posted the first half of "Red Symphony" on the Internet at http://yamaguchy.netfirms.com/symphony/red1.html

The whole transcript was published in English in 1968 as "The Red Symphony: X-Ray of Revolution." You can find it in Des Griffin's "Fourth Reich of the Rich." (1988) I recommend this book.

### Revelations

Rakovsky gives his interrogator an astonishing inside view of modern history in order to prove that his sponsors control the world.

"Money is the basis of power," Rakovsky says, and the Rothschilds manufacture it thanks to the banking system.

The "Revolutionary Movement" was an attempt by Meyer Rothschild and his allies to protect and extend this monopoly by establishing a New World Order using the "revolutionary movement."

According to Rakovsky, "The Rothschilds were not the treasurers, but the chiefs of the first secret Communism...Marx and the highest chiefs of the First International...were controlled by Baron Lionel Rothschild (1808-1878) whose revolutionary portrait was done by Disraeli the English Premier, who was also his creature, and has been left to us (in Disraeli's novel 'Coningsby.')" (250)

Lionel's son Nathaniel (1840-1915) needed to overthrow the Christian Romanoff Dynasty. Through his agents Jacob Schiff and the Warburg brothers, he financed the Japanese side in the Russo Japanese War, and an unsuccessful insurrection in Moscow in 1905. Then he instigated the First World War, and financed the 1917 Bolshevik Revolution. Rakovsky says he was personally involved in the transfer of the funds in Stockholm. (251-252)

The Jewish labour movement or "bund" was Rothschild's instrument. The Bund's "secret faction" infiltrated all the socialist parties in Russia and provided the leadership for the Russian Revolution. Alexander Kerensky, the Menshevik Prime Minister was a secret member. (253)

Leon Trotsky was supposed to become the leader of the USSR. Trotsky, a Jew, married the daughter of one of Rothschild's closest associates, banker Abram Zhivotovsky and became part of the "clan." Unfortunately "national" Communists like Lenin (one-quarter Jewish) got in the way. Lenin overruled Trotsky and made peace with Germany (Treaty of Brest Litovsk, 1918.) This was not the Rothschild's plan.

World War One was supposed to end the way the Second World War did. Russia was supposed to overrun Germany in 1918 and assist local "revolutionaries" in establishing a "people's republic."

Trotsky was responsible for an attempt to assassinate Lenin in 1918 but Lenin survived. When Lenin had a stroke in 1922, Trotsky had Levin, Lenin's Jewish doctor finish him off.

At this critical moment, the unexpected happened. Trotsky got sick and Stalin was able to take power. In the crisis, the Trotskyites pretended to support Stalin and infiltrate his regime. Radowsky characterizes Stalin as a "bonapartist," a nationalist as opposed to an International Communist like Trotsky.

"He is a killer of the revolution, he does not serve it, but makes use of its service; he represents the most ancient Russian imperialism, just as Napoleon identified himself with the Gauls..." (257)

### Containing Stalin

In order to control Stalin, international finance was forced to build up Hitler and the Nazi party. Radowsky confirms that Jewish financiers backed the Nazis although

Hitler was not aware of this.

"The ambassador Warburg presented himself under a false name and Hitler did not even guess his race... he also lied regarding whose representative he was... Our aim was to provoke a war and Hitler was war... (the Nazis) received...millions of dollars sent to it from Wall Street, and millions of Marks from German financiers through Schacht; (providing) the upkeep of the S.A. and the S.S. and also the financing of the elections..." (259-260)

Unfortunately for the bankers, Hitler also proved intractable. He started to print his own money!

"He took over for himself the privilege of manufacturing money and not only physical moneys, but also financial ones; he took over the untouched machinery of falsification and put it to work for the benefit of the state...Are you capable of imagining what would have come...if it had infected a number of other states and brought about the creation of a period of autarchy (absolute rule, replacing that of the bankers). If you can, then imagine its counterrevolutionary functions..."

Hitler had become a bigger threat than Stalin, who had not meddled with money. Rakovsky's present mission was to convince Stalin to make a pact with Hitler and turn Hitler's aggression against the West. The purpose was for Germany and the Western nations to exhaust each other in battle.

Rakovsky urged the Russians to use the tactic of "deceiving with the truth." The Russians were to impress Hitler with their genuine desire for peace. Hitler was not to suspect that he was being set up for a war on two fronts.

Stalin was given a choice. If he agreed to divide Poland with Hitler, the West would declare war on only one aggressor, Germany. If he refused, the bankers would allow Hitler to depose him.

Kus'min demanded some high level confirmation. Rakovsky told him to see Joseph Davies, the US ambassador in Moscow, a fellow Freemason and representative of the International Communist Roosevelt administration.

Someone was sent to Davies who confirmed that

"much would be gained" if Rakovsky got an amnesty. On March 2, 1938 a powerful radio message was sent to Moscow in the cipher of its London embassy.

"Amnesty or the Nazi danger will increase," it said." Davies attended Rakovsky's trial and gave him a Masonic greeting. On the same day, March 12, 1938, Hitler marched into Austria.

Rakovsky's death sentence was commuted. Some believe he lived out his years under an assumed name. See http://www.acts1711.com/red_symphony.htm. Another source has him shot in 1941. http://www.spartacus.schoolnet.co.uk/RUSrakovsky.htm.

Secret negotiations were begun with Hitler. The result was the Ribbentrop-Molotov pact signed in August 1939 just one week before the invasion of Poland.

The interrogation seems to have created an accord between Stalin and the Illuminati.

**Russia Struggles In Rothschild Clutches**

Europe and the United States long ago succumbed to Rothschild Illuminati control. In Russia, there are still some death spasms.

Recently, Vladimir Putin arrested Mikhail Khordordovsky, the head of Russia's largest oil company "Yukos" and "the richest man in Russia."

Putin announced that Russia would seize his $12 billion 26% stake in the oil company, one of many national assets plundered in the reorganization of Communism 15 years ago.

Then we learn the shares already had passed to none other than banker Jacob Rothschild under a "previously unknown arrangement" designed for such circumstances. The two have known each other for years "through their mutual love of the arts." http://washingtontimes.com/world/20031102-111400-3720r.htm

Rakovsky told Kus'min that the Illuminati do not take political or financial positions. They use "intermediaries."

"Bankers and politicians are only men of straw...

217

even though they occupy high places and appear to be authors of the plans which are carried out..." (248-249)

Obviously Khodordovsky is an "intermediary" for Rothschild. So are Richard Perle, Henry Kissinger and Ariel Sharon who each spoke out against Putin's action. Perle, the architect of the Iraq war, called for the expulsion of Russia from the Group of Eight. Sharon expressed concern about "persecution of Jewish businessmen." Khodordovsky is Jewish as is Simon Kukes his successor. And Perle and Kissinger.

Many Jews serve the Illuminati and that is one reason for anti-Semitism. But, Tony Blair and George W. Bush serve it too and are not Jewish. The membership of the Bilderbergers and the Skull and Bones is mostly not Jewish. The Illuminati is an alliance between the Rothschilds, and the world's super rich united by Freemasonry, which consider Lucifer to be God.

Mankind, God's magnificent experiment, has been subverted and compromised. From the U.S. soldier in Iraq, to the taxpayer who pays the debt, we are all "men of straw."

# G Minor - Chapter 34: State-sanctioned Mass Mind Control

It is difficult enough trying to explain government mass mind control. What is more difficult is identifying propaganda. For instance, even if you do prove the whitewashed news on Fox or CNN exists, how do you pin it on, say, the Bush Administration, or the Democratic Party. The answer to that is you don't because it's neither. It is neither George Bush nor Terry McCauliffe that is trying to control you. It is the New World Order. The owners of Clear Channel and similar media monopolies allowed by the Federal Communications Commission are one separate tier of the Illuminati Power Structure. Still, though, most Americans believe that the war is between liberals and conservatives. Maybe that is true, but the government and the Illuminati have learned to play on this ever-present struggle, so that we will not awaken to their true, singular intention of global monarchy. We can see that the foremost objective of the elites is to bring the masses onto the one world bandwagon. The Illuminati would like to simply enforce the global state NOW. They are aware, though, that moving slowly and methodically is a better strategy, in keeping with Fabian's teachings. With this incremental approach, the U.N has become a powerful government on Earth, next only to the U.S. and Russian militaries. They are constantly at work, crafting global legislation that allows them to execute massive land grabs, universal taxation, and absolute gun control. Much of this legislation is in direct conflict with our Constitution and Bill of Rights. Yet, we continue to fund this militarized anti-American U.N. to the tune of approximately $300 million per year. I want to believe that if Americans were given the facts as I have just presented them, our country would not only cease funding the United Nations, it would be necessary for us to behoove them to never again meddle in American affairs, unless they are abroad in a country that is protected by the U.N. (We don't want America to be able to run rampant. We see what that brings about, as in C. and S. Americas and East Timor, etc.) But, most of the Democrats think the U.N. is an august body. Grassroots Republicans don't like the United Nations, generally speaking; but, these GOP constituents are not calling their representatives and demanding that the U.S. stop sending the U.N. our hard earned income tax money.

Why aren't they?

Propaganda.

Another facet of the mass mind control labyrinth is the following. It is not only media we are talking about. Propaganda has been bought and paid for in every sector of Western culture. The list of mind control platforms that the Illuminati has subsumed is seemingly endless: television, radio, billboards, print media, public (government) education, music, movies, fluoride, bio-engineered foods, chemical trails, vaccines, sound frequencies, radio towers, rituals. All these things can either change the way you think or weaken your mind to better accept programming. I read an excellent article from Noam Chomsky. I always add that Chomsky is a U.N. supporter. I agree with his analysis of the U.S. government, but not with his assumption that the U.N. could do better. It was an article by Chomsky entitled "What Makes Mainstream Media Mainstream" in Russ Kick's collaborative book, You Are Being Lied To: The Disinformation Guide to Media Distortion, Historical Whitewash and Cultural Myths. Chomsky was able to break down our relationship to media so simplistically as to be beautifully so. Chomsky suggests that we must identify the buyer of the product. Then, we may be able to find the agenda. The news is the product in this instance. Most people think that the public is the buyer of the news, so the media simply gives us what we, the buyer, want. Chomsky disagrees, and in so doing makes a poignant point. We, the public, are not the buyers; we are the product. The newspaper and the news channel are not a product for us. We are the product, and the main advertisers are the buyers of us. The news, therefore, reflects the wishes of the advertisers, or the buyers.

And who are those advertisers? Energy and oil companies like GE and Exxon, owned by powerful men, including those in our government; pharmaceutical industry giants like Pfizer and Eli Lilly, owned by elite brokers, including those in our government; defense (offense) contractors like Boeing and Lockheed Martin, owned by power barons, including those in our government; plastics manufacturing standards like Dow and Du Pont, owned by toxic polluters, including those in our government. These are the people that are buying us, the product, so they can sell their journalistic wares and retain political dominance. Let's run through the list above.    The largest and most powerful companies want to sell us the energy we work from the earth for them at the highest price possible. They want to build a super one world government so that they can retain possession of their position as overlords. That is not only obvious, it is logical.

News itself reeks of propaganda, whether it be left or right wing. But, how clandestine are the selling techniques? We all learn about celebrity, bandwagon, and visuals as used in advertising. Have you ever heard more than a hum about the Neo Conservatives complicity in the September 11 attacks? It seems that the Democrats would want to air these "conspiracy theories" on CNN or News World International. To their credit there has been a blurb or two. The analysis is that this prior knowledge theory is crazy. Well, what about the "Bush Inc. Did It" Theory. (Six months after I wrote this, Moore's movie was released.) It took two years for the puppet investigative panel to admit that Bush and Co. knew that the attacks were going happen. Hell, we knew that on day one. Howard Dean, during his Democratic Primary campaigning, mumbled something about Bush's prior knowledge.    The conservative mouthpiece, Sean Hannity, exasperated aloud, crying foul from the "crazed" Dean.    Neither Hannity nor Dean ever mentioned that Bush is under investigation for what Dean claimed.    Neither Hannity nor Dean mentioned that the Project for the New American Century was an outline for the war with Iraq written in 1997. Bush's prior knowledge, nay, his involvement, during September 11th has been whitewashed.

That's propaganda, coming from both sides. Spin, as they say. What's more insidious is the Illuminati's supplanting of treasonous doctrine into popular television shows. Take the hit drama *Law and Order*, a show with many offshoots that airs for five or six consecutive hours a day. Here's the routine propaganda employed by the show's writers, including a Guggenheim family member. They spend half the program presenting you with a deranged killer somehow linked with a patriot, or a home-schooler, or a Christian, or a Muslim: in other words, nationalists or the religious. The show represents these groups of people with the 1% minority who are radical. This is during the investigation phase of the program. The second half of the show switches to the legal phase. "Law and Order" has continually painted these "radical" patriots and the religious as being protected by the Constitution. They complain about the Bill of Rights, and how these murderers and rapists get to go free because of the liberal laws. The legal drama rarely, if ever, shows the abuses of power that brought about these protections for the individual in the first place. All we see are District Attorneys who are flummoxed over how to put these rogue, deranged patriots, home schoolers, Christian, Muslims, or what-have-you in jail with the tremendous problems the Constitution presents. Then, at the very end of the show, we realize that these radicals were never guilty in the first place. Unfortunately, all that the dumbed-down American public remembers is the main antagonists, the radical patriot, or whomever. I must admit it is beautifully executed, advanced modern propaganda at work.

Now, when I first began to read libertarian literature, I was somewhat offended at the term 'dumbed-down,' as I somehow thought I might be a part of that group. I was. But, how does one become dumbed-down. The elite's mass mind control is insidious. It is a wonder that anybody knows anything about the truth. I'll explain using an unknown human as my example. It is 2004. A baby is born, and is immediately vaccinated. Mounting evidence shows that elements in vaccines rarely cure diseases. What is shown is that these vaccines cause strange diseases. Mercury in child vaccines have been irrefutably linked to Autism. Gulf War Syndrome was likely caused by military vaccines. There are hundreds of scientific articles, health organizations, and advocates for

222

clean living that insist that these accusations are true. Mega Health published an article, "Vaccines: New Plague for a New Era," by Karen Maidra. Her research links vaccines to childhood asthma, diabetes, autism, and other diseases. The one overused mantra of the pro-vaccination crowd is that vaccines were what saved us from polio, the bubonic plague, and other older diseases. Yet, Maidra also proves this to be false, using the government's own statistics. She expresses, "plagues of disease also disappeared simultaneously in countries which rejected vaccination." Statistical analysis shows that the diseases were on the decline well before the vaccines were even introduced.7 So, we have the case of vaccines being propagandized as being helpful, when any sane person can see that they are harmful. Advanced sanitation has more to do with healthier living than anything else. Also, they can't even cure the common cold. You think they can cure AIDS, or SARS. No. These diseases will just go away because of cleaner living, like using condoms. Or, an 'evolution' in our immune system is possible, which tends to happen. I would not, however, put it past the government to intentionally create a disease and release it, just to study the effects. If our baby survives the vaccination, the mercury levels will at least make sure its IQ has been dropped a few points.

So, the baby is born and vaccinated. Then it is taken home. Mom has been drinking fluoridated drinking water. Fluoride in the drinking water is a scam. Fluoride is toxic. Along with poorer health, fluoride provides the added bonus of creating docility in those that imbibe it incrementally for long periods of time. Mom drinks this water, and baby drinks her milk. That is, until baby is old enough, and as a young kid begins drinking the water directly from the tainted source.8 Subtract a few more points from the Intelligence Quotient.

The infant begins watching television in greater amounts around the age of two to four-years-old. I was fortunate in that my mother limited my viewing to the news and instructional programs on PBS when I was a child. Of course, the news is lies, and PBS is actually funded by the government. PBS is state-sanctioned programming. The

223

child, mentally and physically weakened from the fluoride and vaccinations, begins watching programs like Carl Sagan's Nova, which espouses his theory - although Sagan calls it fact - of evolution.  I believe in some form of evolution (possibly devolution,) though I am sure we are not at the point where we can surmise knowing if we all came from one cell or from apes.   Back to the point, many or most parents use the television as a baby sitter.  We are lucky if the babies are only subjected to the one-worlders at PBS.  Thousands of parents stick kids in front of the most violent adult content without giving it a second thought.   Remember the riotous state-sponsored anti-drug commercial?  "This is your brain.  This is your brain on drugs."  Then it shows some eggs frying.  That's actually what happens to your brain when you watch television.

The next thing you know, the kid is five.  He goes to state-sponsored public school.  He or she will need a new round of vaccines.  It's for their own protection.  Kindergarten is a German word like the U.S. public school system is a German education system.   It is designed as a means of indoctrinating our youth.[9] Trust me, private school kids don't have the financial ills of the middleclass.  The elites' children are getting a real education.  Most religious schools teach acceptance of and intermingling with the system.  I dare anyone to go see what they teach kids in public school.  Except for a select few, the students are taught repetition more than critical thinking.  They learn conformity rather than creativity.  They must obey or suffer the consequences.  And woe to the independent child.  They will snuff out the beautiful spark that our world has created with Ritalin, or some other such drug.  Public school History books devote precious little time to explaining the Founding Fathers and their intentions and philosophies.  Conversely, their affiliation with Freemasonry should be studied.  Shouldn't every American child be able to learn about the Constitution, its intent, its metamorphosis, its current form?  Why do most people not know how many Congressmen or Senators their State has, much less who the representatives are?  The underlying theme that now permeates our school is not learning.  It is collectivism.  Collectivism, my friends, is not an American concept, but it is an American practice. I add that my Mother and Sister are both teachers for government schools. I know there are teachers out there that are independent thinkers that know the system is rigged. These unique teachers are also targeted by the administration and taught to stick to the prescribed doctrines. Also, we have huge problems when a teacher is paid an average wage of $25,000. Yet, these Illuminati-trash administrators make six-figures handily.10

At last, the kid graduates from high school. He or she is lucky to be in the half that is literate beyond a "see Jane run" level. If so, the young adult will attend their finishing education at the public (government) university. More collectivism, more indoctrination. If you are a rebel or one who questions the official statement, there is no room for you. If you are poor, there is probably no room for you. It is funny to me that many of the elite from the Industrial Age, men who would go on to become the inner sanctum of the Illuminati, didn't have more than a third or fourth grade education. It seems the School of Hard Knocks is better for the individual than public schools are.

Then graduation, and a New Age indoctrination training program at your favorite corporation. After all that school, and after a hard day's work conforming, it's back to watching television, and the lies, and the propaganda, for the rest of your life. If you feel bad, here's Prozac or whatever other antidepressant is in-fashion. If they can't get you to take their prescription drugs, they'll get you with the chemical trails, or sonic booms, or the radio towers. You, all of you, will be controlled. Finally, we might understand why it is so difficult for Americans to see the truth, to know of the insidious nature of our world. All the bases have been covered. And, if you do become aware, they have something for you, too. Black Hawk helicopters patrolled Las Vegas and New York City on New Year's Eve, 2003. Masked National Police manned weapons that have never been legal for the law abiding American citizen. I think we will be seeing quite a bit more of the Black Hawks and the National Police in the future. For the 95% of the population, still mired in their socialistic upbringing and weak from toxins and chemicals, the helicopters in our skies are another indoctrination. For those who resist the Black Hawks or the SWAT teams...well, one day soon, the NATO military will come to take you to your (my) new home. This new home is the FEMA internment camps and the American Gulag. That is what awaits those who see through the mass mind control sanctioned by those who sanction our government.

We have three options. One, hide. Two, become political prisoners. Three, be brave and WAKE PEOPLE UP!

# G Minor - Chapter 35: Report Suspicious Activity

By Tom Chittum

I was driving down the Glorious Imperial Beltway a few days ago when I saw a large electronic sign above the road. It said:

**"REPORT SUSPICIOUS ACTIVITY. Call 1-800-XXXX"**

I'll tell you what looks suspicious to me. I'm suspicious that we're living in a mind-control dictatorship because we have large electronic signs over the road that say, "Report Suspicious Activity."

I'm also suspicious that tens of millions of Americans are going to lose their houses to foreigners within the next few years. Yes, I said tens of millions. I've come across another reference to this problem. The following quote is from an article written by Walter Burien.

"As I brought forward in a recent post I put out, the U.S. Political move at this point is to create a garage sale special on all U.S. goods, products, and services, while at the same time transferring the wealth of this country internationally through the devaluation of the dollar. Look for international orders of U.S. goods to jump significantly each month over the next 5 months. Look for a trade surplus over a trade deficit. Look for property and land sales to go up from the interests to buy of foreigners. The foreign buyers can now buy the good old US of A at a 50% discount over last year. EXAMPLE: Your $100,000 home last year if sold for $100,000 this year to a foreigner after currency exchange rates, he gets it for $50,000 in his currency's buying power compared to the dollar last year. This applies also to U.S. cars, equipment, land, stocks, etc. So yes, the U.S. Stock Market will jump. It just became a half price bargain buy to the international crowd."

Here's a fine site I came across recently. It's called Rescue American Jobs. It does a thorough job of documenting our free fall into a snow-covered Brazil. For instance:

"More than 4 million guest worker visas have been issued since the recession began in 2000."

and...

"The total number of U.S. technical jobs is around 8.5 million and we have imported around 3-4 million temporary foreign technical workers. In the year 2001, 9 out of every 10 new job openings for computer/IT were taken by H-1Bs, and despite record unemployment the INS issued 312,000 visas in 2002. L-1 workers are considered employees of a foreign company and paid by the foreign company. This means that they do not have to pay U.S. taxes."

Let's cut to the bottom line. The Permanent Global Super Depression is here right now. There will be no recovery. This Permanent Global Super Depression is permanent because it is meant to be permanent, just like the phony baloney worldwide campaign of slaughter and looting that Beloved Emperor and his fellow pirates call the "War on Terrorism." This Permanent Global Super Depression is also just as phony as the phony baloney permanent police state to protect us from terrorists that our government hires to attack us.

I say again - America will not be spared. Tens of millions will lose jobs, then their houses, then they will starve or die in a civil war. There is nothing in our future except soup lines, mushroom clouds and razor wire FEMA camps. We'll have the economy of Argentina, the blood baths of the Balkans, and the liberties of plantation slaves.

It is impossible to shame the average American zombie. If Beloved Emperor and his neo-con pals set up guillotines on the White House Lawn and started decapitating hundreds of "enemy combatants" every day and broadcasting the whole circus on CNN, absolutely nothing would happen. Well, maybe the ACLU would sue somebody and then fly off to a five-star hotel in Tel Aviv for a convention. But the typical Americow won't so much as go "MOOOO!" until he's evicted from his house and is starving under a privatized toll bridge owned by some aristocrat in Europe. What then?

I'll tell you what we'll have then, we'll have the Knights of the Golden Circle, resurrected and doing their part in a phony baloney Yugoslav-style Second Civil War right here in the continental USA. The secret society known as the Knights of the Golden Circle was founded in 1852 in Cincinnati by a Dr. George Bickley, a Virginian who had moved to Ohio. These so-called "knights" billed themselves as pro-slavery and pro-secession and pro-Southern. More to the point, they were agent of the British Empire and their you-know-who banker pals.

"...the Knights of the Golden Circle have intimate ties to Old World Knights and Scottish Rite Free Masonry, are linked to the highest circles of American Free Masons (through figures as diverse as John Calhoun, Jefferson Davis, General and Mississippi Governor J.A. Quitman, explorer and highest ranking Mason General Albert Pike, Jesse James, Massachusetts politician Caleb Cushing), are interlocked with Cherokee and Choctaw tribal leaders and territories but also with French Rosicrucians, and operated (and may still operate) secretly in a gamut of places such as Charleston, Natchez, Nashville, Missouri, Arkansas, Oklahoma, and Arizona."

Bickley and his fellow so-called "knights" were traitors to the Republic because they were actively conspiring with foreign agents to stir up armed rebellion with the aim of breaking off the Southern states and making them a puppet plantation colony of Britain once again. Bickley and all the other so-called Knights of the Golden Circle were traitors in cahoots with foreign agents. They should have been dragged to the nearest tree and strung up for treason, every last one of them.

And here's something I never knew before - The Knights of the Golden Circle didn't disband after the Civil War, they continued as guerrilla fighters serving the ongoing British attempts to destabilize the Union. They robbed money to finance a second Confederate rebellion. That was the specialty of the James Gang, which was really a lodge of the Knights of the Golden Circle.

"According to the book *Jesse James Was One of His Names* (written by Del Schrader, with Jesse James III), the American Civil War did not really end in 1865, but continued to be fought "underground" for 19 more years. Its highly sophisticated spy network, operated by the Knights of the Golden Circle, continued for even longer and was involved in many subversive activities. One of these was train robbery, a specialty of the James Gang, the purpose being to enrich the coffers of the Confederate underground. As a Confederate agent, James was also involved in smuggling guns and ammunition to the Plains Indians, as well as providing training in guerilla tactics, for use against their common enemy, General George Armstrong Custer and the Union Army."

Some say the Knights of the Golden Circle didn't disband until 1916. Fancy that, a Brit-run guerilla outfit marauding around America from 1852 to 1916 and we Americows weren't told about it in our history books.

These days, we've got organizations just like the Knights of the Golden Circle, and they are still working for the Brits and their you-know-who banker pals, and their aim is still civil war in America and its dismemberment into a series of feeble banana republics under the boots of the Brits and the Zionists.

These Brit/Zionist stooges and traitor organizations are usually pretty easy to spot. They often present themselves as patriots, with American flags and Bald Eagles posted all over their websites. Sometimes, they even disguise themselves as secessionists. Whatever the façade they use to lure the suckers into their tent, they always go along with the Osama hoax. After 9-11, the establishment-run mock opposition groups smoked themselves out. They showed their true colors by endorsing what their leaders knew full well was slop for the tube zombies. To Hell with all of these British and Zionist stooges on parade. To Hell with Americow Patrol. To Hell with the Council of Confused Peasants, and to Hell with Amerizombie Renaissance and The Amerizombie Cause.

## G Minor - Chapter 36: State-sanctioned Individual Mind Control

A chapter that this book would be remiss in not including pertains to the elites' use of mind control techniques on unsuspecting victims. Specifically, American human psychological terror and brainwashing operations will be studied. It has recently become a much easier task to research and write about the government's mind control tactics, because of a new wealth of books, declassified documents, and firsthand testimony that has been forthcoming. It continues to remain difficult to present the growing reams of evidence to the U.S. public. A media cabal controls our news sources. Rupert Murdoch, Ted Turner, and their ilk continually work to suppress the truth. Perhaps my little book can lead new people to revelations of the vast conspiracy.

Mind control is nothing new. The powerful, be they priest or king, chancellor or president, have always used subtle and overt techniques to control the behavior of individuals and the masses in general. Here, we will explore the former, or the Illuminati's search for dominance over the individual and his thoughts. From as far back as Ancient Egypt and Babylon, rulers have controlled us. Until the last century, control over a single human has most usually been in the form of physical torture or the threat of physical pain. Not long after man first raised himself or was created over the animals, he intellectualized the disadvantages of pain. Soon thereafter he saw the control he could wield over others by inflicting pain on a recipient. Even the smallest child learns that by hurting, or even merely threatening to hurt, a sibling or friend, the inflictor of the pain can make the recipient promise or say anything. (Say uncle, or I'll hurt you.) This phenomenon not only allows the inflictor to force admissions and extract promises, it also allows the inflictor to sustain a lasting dominance over the other individual through psychological manipulation.

Torture. Volumes of books are filled with the history

and accounts of the practice. It is woven into our very life, both through oral and written traditions. Jesus was whipped and degraded before his crucifixion. The European Inquisition is not only historically documented, but innumerable fiction books have been set in that time period. In America, when one was simply accused of being a witch, one could expect a severely painful series of tests, which almost always proved guilt. Today, it is terrorists. And here is where our webs begin to get sticky.

So many issues tie into mind control sponsored by the United States Government. One of these issues is not broached often. It is the subject of Satanism, and specifically, Satanic ritual abuse, or SRA. We do know that Satan Worshippers are alive and well in America. This is actually allowed by our own Constitution, through freedom of religion. I believe that Satanists are only one of the several groups that the Illuminati use to out-source their mind control programs. Satanism serves the threefold purpose of creating public chaos, researching and developing new mind control techniques, and providing brainwashed victims to be used in various tasks and operations.

Some people say they can believe that the government used one "Manchurian Candidate" in the JFK murder. Yet, they can't believe that victims brainwashed by the government could have perpetrated three or four high profile murders. And they certainly can't believe that the government was involved in torturing and abusing thousands of Americans, then released them into society with triggers that would eventually have them perform a destructive act or acts. With the thousands of abducted, abused, and molested children America is witness to each and every year, we are looking at potentially hundreds, thousands, maybe millions of brainwashed victims across the country. There have been reports of government facilities warehousing rows and rows of children, living like animals in their own refuse. Only the best are used in high profile assassinations. Oswald was military. Hinckley was involved in the World Vision mind control project. What about Columbine, or all the sniper shootings, or nutty serial killers? I'm not saying that they are all government

232

victims. What I am saying is that psychosis and schizophrenia are almost always caused by abuse, and ritual abuse. What I am saying is that the government has admitted to using Americans as mind control guinea pigs. We must all make our own assumptions. However, as I stated earlier, the mainstream media doesn't tell you all the facts. Therefore, most Americans are unable to make informed assumptions.

Is there a darker, underlying fabric that binds the unfortunate, abused victims together? Has the government really partaken in human torture and mind control? Sadly, the answer is yes, there is and they have. By their own admission, the government has used American citizens as test subjects in sick, sadistic mind control programs. There have been Congressional hearings wherein the military, the CIA, and other groups have stated unequivocally that it is all true. And, let's face it. Whatever they admitted can only be the tip of the iceberg. The U.S. Government only admits what they have been caught red-handed doing. No more, and sometimes much less.

The most notorious mind control experiment in U.S. History was, arguably, a government project called MK Ultra. The story actually goes back further, to the infamous Dr. Mengele and his Nazi human-Pavlovian experiments performed on Jewish 'detainees.' After the fall of the Third Reich, the Nazi mind control scientists were highly sought by governments. The former Soviet Union was able to acquire a few, as were various others. But, as American preeminence was waxing, our leadership, by this time supplanted with Rothschild stooges, was able to accumulate the majority of these vile doctors through Project Paperclip. After the scientists were bought and paid for during Project Paperclip, they launched a psychological testing campaign using Americans as unwitting test subjects. This may seem like a bit of rubbish, but it is true. In 1977, Senators Barry Goldwater and Edward M. Kennedy, along with other leaders, forced the Central Intelligence Agency (CIA), Federal Bureau of Investigations (FBI), National Aeronautics and Space Agency (NASA), and the Department of Defense (DoD) to show their hands. During the "Joint Hearing Before the Select Committee on Intelligence and the Subcommittee on Health and Scientific Research of the Committee on Human Resources, United States Senate, Ninety-Fifth Congress", the Senators were able to obtain admissions from several high-ranking members that they had used American citizens as test subjects. These agencies experimented with psychoactive drugs, radiation, electro-shock, sound waves, brain implants, and various other torturous methods. The goal of the project, dubbed MK Ultra, was to learn as much as possible about how to control people, and specifically how to control individuals. With this admission, it should not be too difficult to imagine Lee Harvey Oswald as some degenerated assassin, programmed by the CIA. Or John Hinckley, Jr. Or the Trench Coat Mafia.

We will never know how many humans were used in tests, but there is some first hand testimony concerning MK Ultra. The most renowned case of an escapee from a state-sanctioned mind control project is the case of Cathy O'Brien. Her book, Trance: Formation of America provides all the grisly details that I won't go into here. To summarize, her story goes something like this. Cathy O'Brien was sold to the project by her father, a child abuser himself. President Ford and then Vice President Bush are implicated. Once enmeshed in MK Ultra, she was ritually tortured and abused. She claims that Dick Cheney raped her repeatedly, beat her, and forced her to sleep with dozens and hundreds of other heads of state, including American and foreign elect. An intelligence insider rescued her in 1988. Even though Congress knows about MK Ultra, Cathy O'Brien isn't permitted to have her day in court because of the tried-and-true reason that all Americans accept - National Security. What is worse, O'Brien's daughter was used in the programming done by Bush, Sr. Cathy O'Brien's daughter will live her remaining years in a mental health institution, her mind collapsed by the intensive brainwashing.

Brice Taylor is another woman whose book, Thanks for the Memories: The Truth Has Set Me Free, gives an account of being a mind control subject for the government and a sex slave for officials, especially Bob Hope and Henry Kissinger in this case. She also names presidents Kennedy and Clinton, as well as many others. Both O'Brien and Taylor's first hand accounts are harrowing stories, and difficult to get through. If these stories are patently false, shouldn't that come out in court. What if these stories are true? Are we not all implicated if we do not insist that Cathy O'Brien and Brice Taylor are allowed to be heard in a court of law? There is a much bigger, more important question, too. How many more Cathy's and Brice's are living the horrid existence of a government sex slave?

Another mind control experiment that has come to light is the Montauk Project. Started around 1976, Montauk is a military facility that is supposedly defunct. However, thousands of children were warehoused there, and intensive mind control was used on them. Al Bielek and Phil Schneider are only two people that are testifying that the government kept up to 250,000 children in stacked cages. These kids, boys mostly, were brainwashed through torture and ritual slayings. What were they trained to do? I can guess that many serial killings, rapes, school shootings, and the like can be traced back to these projects. Remember, we are not speculating. The government HAS ADMITTED to conducting these experiments against Americans in the name of National Security. Much of this experimentation used radio and electromagnetic waves to control individuals. It is now being used on us en masses through radio towers. Montauk probably falls into mass mind control, now. The theory is that most of the radio towers presumably used for cellular phones are actually emitting frequencies that deter the "will" of we humans. This may sound crazy, but with the government's past admissions, I don't see how anyone could NOT believe it is true.

Large-scale abduction of children and experimentation on unwitting subjects actually answers many questions. For instance, brainwashing or insanity are the only two things that explain our country's overabundance of "lone gunmen" and serial killers. Even if the killers are insane, insanity almost always stems from physical or psychological trauma. The abductions also explain why thousands of Americans are sure that aliens took them. The government has recently admitted to "leaking" alien evidence to scare the public, and thereby making it easier for them to conduct military testing. Using aliens to instill fear in Americans goes all the way back to H.G. Wells, a close friend to Cecil Rhodes, both of whom were high-ranking Illuminati and creators of the Council on Foreign Relations. It seems obvious that the government has wanted us to think there are aliens in existence. That is why they made several thousand MK Ultra subjects believe they were abducted by aliens, to brainwash people off track. All of America was off track, chasing Whitley Strieber's Communion. Now, we know it was the government. It put fear into our hearts, which made a whole generation give even more control to the government, all in the name of security. It beats the truth: that the CIA and other government agencies were the actual perpetrators of the rigorous series of tests inflicted on Americans. That would explain the very real needle marks that alien abduction survivors have had recorded by doctors.

A last note about aliens. It is very interesting that one of the families included in this book was instrumental in the study of extraterrestrials. In the volume 11, number 2 issue of Nexus magazine, author Will Banyan explains the Rockefellers part in the whole alien scheme. From the insert of his article entitled "Rockefeller Internationalism" comes these strange indictments. "Laurance Rockefeller has also raised more than a few eyebrows with his much-publicized funding of UFO research during the 1990s, some of which persists to this day." His complete article is very telling, and Nexus magazine is a great source for New World Order information.

With the Freedom of Information Act, citizens have been able to uncover incidents of transgressions by our government as recently as 1988. Projects that were aimed at U.S. citizens have been exposed. Operations such as Cointelpro were targeted specifically against political dissidents (anyone exposing the truth about the Illuminati, like Lyndon LaRouche and Ezra Pound.) MK Ultra used women as political prostitutes, drug mules, and message couriers. In Montauk, boys were tortured into anti-social, crazed killing machines. There are many other projects, all with differing techniques and levels of success.   Why would they have stopped doing this to us when no one was punished?   Does anyone honestly believe that these things are not going on anymore?   Sadly, most people don't believe the government ever did these things in the first place, even though the government has itself, on record, admitted to doing them.

## G Minor - Chapter 37: An Open Letter To
## Christian Conservatives

By Chuck Baldwin

My purpose in writing these columns is to make people think, to confront current events and trends with an intense appreciation for the truth. My desire is also to awaken a lethargic population to an ever increasing societal, cultural, political, and spiritual departure from America's historic Christian roots and from a commitment to constitutional government.

When I confronted the foibles and fallacies of President Bill Clinton, Christian conservatives hailed me a hero. I was deluged with congratulatory emails and letters. Their appreciation for my work could not be expressed loudly or often enough.

However, when I confront the foibles and fallacies of President George W. Bush, those same Christian conservatives call me every dirty name in the book. I am suddenly their enemy. Their songs of praise for my work have turned into a cacophony of hate. But amazingly, I am saying the same things now that I said then. So, what has changed?

I submit that what has changed are the attitudes and principles of vast numbers of Christian conservatives. Where once they stood for truth, they now stand for political parties. Where once they gave their loyalty and allegiance to the U.S. Constitution, the Bill of Rights, the Declaration of Independence, and even the Bible, they now swear loyalty and allegiance to G.W. Bush and the Republican Party. It seems that many Christians have become little more than spineless lackeys for a political machine. They seem to have lost the ability to think critically and objectively.

Scores of readers have chastised me for criticizing President Bush, calling him God's "anointed." Countless numbers of Christians seem to believe that G.W. Bush deserves the kind of unquestioned loyalty that they would give to the Apostle Paul or even to Christ Himself. Of course, such thinking is beyond foolishness; it borders on blasphemy!

G.W. Bush is an elected politician. He was elected President of these United States. Nothing more; nothing less. He has no more divine "anointing" than any other elected politician.

Where was all this "anointing" talk when Bill Clinton was elected President? The same God that permitted Bush to become President permitted Clinton to become President. Yet, Christian conservatives called Clinton the Anti-Christ, whereas they now want to add Bush to the Holy Trinity. However, they can't have it both ways: If Bush is God's "anointed," so was Clinton.

While we are on the subject, it seems lost to most Christian conservatives that G.W. Bush is a member of the same church denomination as Senator Hillary Clinton. Yet, I doubt that we will hear many of them referring to Hillary's divine "anointing."

The fact is, under our form of government, God has given to "we the people" the right and responsibility of selecting our leaders. Therefore, we have the President, the Congress, the courts, and the state and local leaders that we elect.

There is no king or monarch in America! There is no "divine right" to any political party or to any politician to any public office in this country! In America, the people must rule themselves. They do this through their elected lawmakers and elected chief executives.

When the people's elected leaders stray from their oaths of office, when they violate their contracts with the people, when they govern unjustly or unconstitutionally, it is the right and duty of the people to openly criticize them, scold them, and replace them.

One of America's finer presidents, Theodore Roosevelt, said, "To announce that there must be no criticism of the President, or that we are to stand by the President, right or wrong, is not only unpatriotic and servile, but is morally treasonable to the American public. Nothing but the truth should be spoken about him or anyone else. But it is even more important to tell the truth, pleasant or unpleasant, about him than about any one else."

My criticisms of President Bush are consistent with my criticisms of President Clinton. They are based on his policies, statements, and administrative decisions. I never attempt to judge his heart, for only God has judgment and authority there. However, I will continue to judge his actions, or inactions, as is my constitutional right and duty to do.

Accordingly, I charge G.W. Bush with posturing himself as a conservative while giving us bigger government than did even Bill Clinton. I charge him with creating the machinery with which a police state may emerge. Furthermore, I charge President Bush with attempting to take more freedoms away from the American people than any president in modern memory.

I also believe that Mr. Bush has redundantly violated his oath to support and defend the Constitution of the United States and that he has given nothing but lip service to the pro-life and pro-family agendas. It is also my contention that President Bush has jeopardized the security of these United States and has made a mockery of our nation's laws by his treacherous illegal alien amnesty proposal. He also lied to the American people by saying he supported the Second Amendment only later to endorse the Clinton gun ban.

Even worse, I charge Christian conservatives with willingly surrendering their independent thinking as well as their American heritage in order to accommodate President Bush and the Republican Party. I further charge them with selling their spiritual birthright for a mess of political pottage!

We should expect more of our leaders than lip service. Indeed, if any elected office holder talks the Christian talk, he should be held to a higher, not lesser, standard. Beyond that, the one standard that really matters for any elected politician is not his rhetoric, but his loyalty and commitment to America's founding principles. This should be the overriding determinate as to whether he or she is re-elected or un-elected, party affiliation or denominational affiliation not withstanding.

Therefore, I stand by my criticisms of President Bush. And I will continue to warn the American people of his big government, pseudo-conservative policies. I will not be a partaker of his political sins.

Whether readers react with anger or appreciation to these columns is not my responsibility. If, however, these columns can somehow create a hunger for truth, a thirst for freedom, and a reverence for America's founding principles, they will have attained their intended purpose.

## G Minor - Chapter 38: Leni Riefenstahl and Fox News

Joseph Goebbels is often referred to as the father of modern state-sanctioned propaganda, and with his evolved, then-subtle "advertising," he was able to not only get the Germans to accept the patriotic war cry of the National Socialists; Hitler's Minister of Information sculpted a nation of willing accomplices in global destruction. It must be noted, though, that the infamous Leni Riefenstahl, the beloved German actress and director, became intimately involved in Hitler's life, producing one of the most hauntingly beautiful, subliminally subversive films of all time, *Triumph des Willens* or *Triumph of the Will*. Without question, Riefenstahl was one of the most talented filmmakers of her time. Far from being Goebbels lackey, the beautiful Leni Riefenstahl was able to win the affections of Hitler, and reportedly produced her films with virtual autonomy. *Triumph of the Will*, more than any other single piece of Nazi propaganda - perhaps any propaganda, ever - was a case of greatness used for evil.

In America today, there is little doubt within the mind of anyone conscious that American media, and specifically American news, is slanted toward a pro-Federal Government, pro-Israeli (not to be mistaken for pro-Jewish, which the mainstream media is not) viewpoint. While CNN plugged along, moderately liberal, the Fox News Channel (FNC) phenomenon came to pass. Rupert Murdoch owns Fox. Murdoch is a wealthy power broker, selling neo-conservatism in the guise of true conservatism, effectively changing the attitudes of half the political population in America: namely, grassroots Republicans. However, I believe that we can presume that CNN is just as culpable of clandestine mind control, only perhaps to a different audience. It was U.N supporter Noam Chomsky who pointed out in his book, <u>Rogue States</u>, that the Arabs dancing with glee in the streets after the September attacks broadcast by the major news networks were proven shortly thereafter to be Palestinians given candy and then videotaped by Israeli military. A lamentable 'mistake,' but not surprising.

The parallels between Leni Riefenstahl's work - including *Victory of Faith* and *The Blue Light* - and Fox News Channel's propaganda programming are obvious. Just as apparent are the differences. Leni Riefenstahl's masterpieces are seventy years old. Still, they will stir emotion. And, Riefenstahl's artistic talent is irrefutable. That is the most striking difference, as Fox is not, nor could it ever be considered art. Then again, in a slick, corporate way, there are elements of enlightenment, as in Walter Cronkite meets Jerry Springer for the masses. It is the similarities between Riefenstahl and Fox that are worrisome. Both portray military as the central, heroic entity. A brother-in-print for conservatives, Time Magazine, actually heralded the U.S. Military as 'people of the year.' Fortunately, this generation learned from the hippies and has decided to support the troops, and attack the policy. No spitting on returning GIs nowadays. However, our volunteer military will have to make amends, at least to their own selves, for the atrocity that is Operation Iraqi Freedom. People of the Year, spreading depleted uranium, dictating democracy, ignoring civil rights, and otherwise devastating the ancient lands of Babylon.

Which brings me to my point. Are we, as a society, willing to let Leni Riefenstahl deflect responsibility for melding the minds of the German people when she directed her films glorifying the vile Nazi Party and their platforms. If so, then I suppose we cannot take Fox to task for their transgressions. It seems Reifenstahl has received a pass from the world court of opinion. Her excuse? She was only performing a job, and had no idea of what was going on behind closed doors. But, we shall say that this is not correct. Leni and Adolph were very close friends, so much so that Goebbels was often jealous of the relationship she had with the Fuhrer, and jealous of Hitler's relinquishment of control from her projects. If we agree that Riefenstahl almost assuredly knew about the Nazi philosophy and intent, then we must also assume that she knew she was making films to change German attitudes about war and Jews. The question then becomes this:

what should the punishment be for creating propaganda that leads to the death of one, ten million, or more people. *Triumph of the Will* indirectly led to approximately 20 million deaths, very roughly. Should Riefenstahl live in luxury, even winning awards for her work after so many people were brutally slaughtered as a direct or indirect result of it. People were slaughtered by Germans who had been whipped into a killing frenzy by the nationalistic rhetoric disseminated by Germany's federal government, through willing accomplices like Leni. Sadly, it seems that the powers-that-be have decided to let the Nazi director off the hook.

If we mimic the same leniency with FNC, we must excuse Murdoch's network's complicity in "directing" America into war with Iraq. Again, this seems to be a simple procedure of forgive-and-forget on the part of the populace. Example: weapons of mass destruction. Bush and Blair said Hussein had them. David Kay refutes that claim. The premise for war was, at best, a blunder. This has cost the lives of over 900 American soldiers, and between 10,000 and 20,000 Iraqis. Women and children are dead. I grew up with a Vietnam Veteran for a father. I love him, but so help me, that war did a tragic number on his head. The family feels the brunt of that kick. We now have approximately 3,000 disabled Iraqi Freedom Veterans. These men will assuredly have mental scars. Of the remaining men and women who are not physically injured, my uneducated guess is that approximately 25% to 50% will have Post Traumatic Stress Disorder, anxiety attacks, depression, or any number of other mental disorders that we are certain war brings. That's probably a conservative percentage. These men and women will be parents. The mental damage from the war will make the stress upon their families almost unstoppable. It was Fox News, as well as others, that proclaimed the certitude of the "Bush Doctrine," a.k.a. preemptive attack, because of the vast proliferation of WMDs. Fox was behind the allusion that Saddam was behind 9-11 or had ties with al-Qaeda. Maybe he did, but that has yet to be proven. Fox News was even behind the staged toppling of Hussein's statue. That was a fine piece of work. Never pan out, so sixty people look like hundreds. Watch those guys, make sure they don't look around to often for directions. Is not Fox responsible for the deaths, the mental injury, the travesty...at least to some degree? Yet, no mainstream media outlet, not even CNN, is asking the important questions.

In the end, we have let ourselves down once again, by not holding the elite responsible for their actions. Even the respected former Secretary of State, Madeleine Albright, wondered aloud about the staged capture of Hussein, and when might Bush and Co. parade out bin Laden. Fox airs blips admitting that people are spreading these rumors. The mainstream critics scoff at even the assumption that Fox and others might have broadcast according to the Bush/Cheney/Ashcroft/Rumsfeld team. Yet, from the stepping forward of men alleged to have been 9-11 hijackers to the killing of journalists, the DoD seems to be intent on full-scale war. It gives me a very scary feeling about the intellect of my fellow Americans, who accept the Fox mantra. War is Peace. They live, we sleep. I don't give a damn what your actual political ideology is, I only ask that we as a Nation become informed. Even if it hurts.

So one last time, I ask you: are we willing to make rules about what is or isn't said in reporting politics. Even if the report leads to deaths. This author believes that the expectations of free speech, either in words or in visual communications, should be consistent. One can cuss, but one must expect a level of animosity in most circles if one does so. Conversely, one can't yell fire in a crowded theater. Neither can one explain exactly where and how to kill a person to another. The potential for victims would precede a right to free speech in most courts. I hope. This standard should be used as a the precedent for news programmers, movie directors, and television producers. They can give us gunfights, sex, cussing, and base humor. But they can't air directions on how to build a pipe bomb. They shouldn't repeat erroneous intelligence reports from the CIA; an agency known for military coups of democratically elected leaders; known for training and arming vile dictators and then attacking them a decade or two later; known for experimenting with horrendous mind control techniques on unwitting Americans during project MK Ultra.   Fox must be held accountable for transmitting the erroneous intelligence reports from the erroneous CIA, and backed by an erroneous administration that gave us the Project for a New American Century.  At least with Leni Riefenstahl, the case can be made that her films have artistic, historic, and educational value.  Fox is guilty of the worst, lowest, and most potent form of propaganda.

"History is a set of lies agreed upon" - Voltaire (Freemason,) later prodigiously parroted by Napoleon, reinvented by Hitler's "Tell a lie loud enough and long enough...", and taken to new levels by Fox and cable news, talk radio, and our traditionally beloved newspapers.  When do we demand accountability?

## G Minor - Chapter 39: Jewish Hate and the Global Conspiracy

By Dr. Len Horowitz

*The following letter to the editor was sent by Dr. Horowitz to Mr. Clay Douglas, Editor and Publisher of "The Free American" regarding his April 2001 feature entitled, "Jews: Do They Really Run the World? Is it Hate to Ask that Question?"*

Dear Editor:

I am writing you to express my deepest, heart-felt, sadness regarding your April 2001 feature entitled, "Jews: Do They Really Run the World? Is it Hate to Ask that Question?" As someone who has contributed to, and financially supported, your work and magazine for years, I am now suddenly confronted by the use of "The Free American" to promote hatred against the Jewish people, not just the "Jews" alleged to be controlling the world. For this I express my sincere apologies to the intelligent remnant that perceive, as I do, the abuse of the First Amendment (freedom of speech) in this issue.

Above all, I am extremely disappointed in you for publishing such a contextually biased and hate filled article, allegedly by an honest, investigative, anonymous author, who on every page provides egregious distortions condemning the Jewish race in general as people "by their nature, due to their religion and upbringing, are virulently, relentlessly 'specially anti-Christ.'" You abuse our friendship, my support, my name to justify your cause. You used me as an example of one of few "good" Jews in your opening paragraph by writing "there were many Jews who believed in Christ, called Messianic Jews...who were not involved with any anti-Christ movement." These quotes aptly exemplify the ignorance, and subliminal racism, of your publication. The term "nature"

247

implies a genetic predisposition or evolution, but "religion and upbringing" refers more accurately to behavioral and cultural determinants of admittedly biased and likewise hate-filled Jewish ideologues.  The second quote implies the vast majority of Jewish people are taught to hate and fear versus love and respect Christians and/or Christianity.  As a Jewish man and author of "Why it's Time Jews and Christians Unite," I submit this was not my experience during family or religious instruction.  Nor do I believe that Jews, in general, are reared to distrust gentiles any more than other Jews, or any more than gentiles are taught, through works like yours, to distrust Jews.

I was obviously wrong to assume you understood the destructive manner in which populations (we refer to as "sheeple") have been, and with your article are being, divided to conquer the global flock.  For this, I also apologize to my supporters since I suspect your feature has done more to misinform the America patriot community than any "anti-Semitic" publication I have read to date, including The Protocols of the Elders of Sion (the Masonic document that was re-named "Protocols of the Elders of Zion" following its reworking to propagandize, like your article, Jewish hate).  Deceptively, you stated, "The author went to great lengths to point out that all Jews were not necessarily involved" in global fascism and genocides.  Where in the article were these "great lengths?"  Why would you even add the word "necessarily" in the above quote?  This implies your own belief that possibly all Jews participate in this sinister plot, or your desire to raise such suspicions in gullible readers.  Cunningly, stating your own position/bias, you challenged "anyone who could, to dispute the facts" presented by the anonymous author.  Why would anyone bother when you, the editor/publisher-who most readers assume did his due diligence in substantiating the author's claims (suspiciously missing references) - stated, "It was factual, a little frightening, and dead on when put into context with current events."  Regarding current events, your publication fits precisely the "divide and conquer" New World Order protocols.

Time does not permit me to respond to almost every page and paragraph of the article that included gross misrepresentations.  I will focus merely on two glaring deceptions: the alleged Jewish-ness of international bankers, particularly the Rothschilds, and the alleged "Jewish control" over Hollywood and the liberal media in general.  The following is excerpted largely from my forthcoming book, *Death in the Air: Globalism, Terrorism, and Toxic Warfare* (Tetrahedron, LLC; 1-888-508-4787).  I have added "not Jewish (NJ)" to the globalists and international financers who shame other religions.

### Rothschild, J.P. Morgan, and the Rockefeller Banking Axis

The most infamous anti-Jewish document in history - The Protocols of the Elders of Sion was reworked (into the "Elders of Zion") during a meeting in 1773 by Mayer Rothschild, a non-Hebrew Khazar.  The Khazar's ancestry, according to most scholars, stems from Noah's son Yefet (Japheth), predating Abraham's covenant with God, the tribe of Judah, and therefore, the first genetically Jewish people.

Baigent et al in *Holy Blood Holy Grail*, provided a harsh reality check regarding the Masonic, not "Jewish", origin of these infamous Protocols.  Originally a secret document that heralded a deadly totalitarian plot for herding the masses into a "New World Order" run by financial elitists, the document had been turned into an anti-Semitic propaganda piece during the Russian revolution.  "By 1919, the Protocols were also being circulated by Alfred Rosenberg," who later became the chief racial theoretician and propagandist for the National Socialist Party in Germany.  The document was said to have advanced convincing "proof" of an "international Jewish conspiracy."  Hitler referred to it in *Mein Kampf* with vicious conviction as to the document's authenticity.  Today, experts correctly view the Protocols as an insidious forgery distracting from the original globalists' document.

Professor Carroll Quigley (NJ) - President Clinton's teacher and mentor at Georgetown University during the mid-1960's - explained that the financial elite maintained global colonialism among their highest aspirations.  In order to accomplish this, secret societies were administered largely on behalf of the Rothschild (NJ) and Rhodes (NJ) dynasties. The secret societies in which they invested had inner member structures that were shielded by successively larger outer circles. The central part of the structure was established by March, 1891, using Rhodes's money. Rothschild trustee Lord Alfred Milner directed the organization that was called "The Round Table." This organization "worked behind the scenes at the highest levels of British government, influencing foreign policy and England's involvement and conduct of WWI" and later WWII.

According to secret society investigator and author Jan van Helsing, the British Secret Intelligence Service (MI6) evolved largely from efforts of members of the Committee of 300 and The Round Table. Other sources have reported that MI6 has exercised far greater worldwide control than most people realize. More wiretaps in the United States, for instance, have been administered on behalf of MI6 than the CIA. In this regard, Loftus and Aarons reported in *The Secret Wars Against The Jews* (St. Martins Press, 1996), that, "for the last fifty years, virtually every Jewish citizen, organization, and charity in the world has been the victim of electronic surveillance by Great Britain, with the knowing and willing assistance of the intelligence services of the United States."

To set the stage for the first World War, The Round Table directors developed the "Royal Institute for International Affairs," or RIIA. It was also known as "Chatham House" and had among its members Lords Albert Grey (NJ) and Arnold Toynbee (NJ). The latter was known as the eminence grise of MI6.

Apparently the Masonic influence in the affairs of the world's leading intelligence organization has been striking and esoteric. Even the name "MI6" reflected knowledge of the ancient mystical arcane, as discussed in my earlier book *Healing Codes for the Biological Apocalypse* (Tetrahedron, LLC, 1999).

It was Lord Toynbee of the MI6 who, following "brainstorming" sessions conducted at the Wellington House into ways to condition the public into accepting World War I, delivered the orders from the Committee of 300. Dr. John

Coleman, a retired MI6 agent, documented this in his excellent book, *Conspirators' Hierarchy*. Other famous members of the Committee of 300, past and present, included many non-Jewish leaders including George Bush, George Schultz, J.P. Morgan, John M. Forbes, David Rockefeller, and Cardinal Spellman.

Another leading committee member, Lord Rothmere, used his newspapers to test the Wellington House "social conditioning" strategies. Following a six-month test period, it was learned that eighty-seven percent of the public had formed their opinions without using critical or rational judgment - the intended result - much like the risk posed by The Free American Jewish-hate article. Thereafter, the English working class, according to van Helsing, "was subjected to sophisticated propaganda methods to convince them that they had to send their sons by the thousands to their deaths" in WWI.

In response, Teddy Roosevelt, the 26th President of the United States, complained during his 1912 election campaign, "Behind the visible government there is an invisible government upon the throne that owes the people no loyalty and recognizes no responsibility. To destroy this invisible government, to undo the ungodly union between corrupt business and corrupt politics is the task of a statesman."

## From Shadow Governors to Rockefeller High Finance

The solidification of secret society power in America began in 1776 around the time Adam Weishaupt was establishing the Order of the Bavarian Illuminati on behalf of the Rothschilds. The anonymous Free American author correctly detailed how Weishaupt, genetically Jewish "converted to Catholicism and became a Catholic priest..." before he formed for the Rothschilds the Illuminati organization. Thus, how "Jewish" was he?

Your article, and Freemasons, obviously wish to pin the blame for global genocide and agendas on "Jews" rather than Freemasons currently seeking the deception of patriotic America, yet the founding of the United States was the result of the secret plan carried out by Freemasons beginning in the

17<sup>th</sup> century.  Freemasons had organized the America War of Independence.  The U.S. Constitution was penned and signed by Freemasons.  Almost a third of American Presidents have been Freemasons.  The Great Seal of the United States with the pyramid and all seeing eye, the bald eagle that replaced the phoenix, the original thirteen states, stars and stripes, were all adopted symbols of Freemasonry.  Though they had been put in place by Weishaupt to convey Rothschild wishes, the symbolism dated back to the Masons of ancient Egypt.  The Illuminated pyramid on the American dollar bill was the design of Philip Rothschild (NJ) as Ayn Rand, his lover, divulged in *Atlas Shrugged*.

Although early American political leaders Benjamin Franklin (NJ) and Thomas Jefferson (NJ) heavily favored private centralized banking, in 1790 Alexander Hamilton (NJ) was appointed secretary of the treasury, and reformed policy heavily favoring his silent benefactors Mayer Amschel Rothschild and his sons.  A year later, Hamilton established the "First National Bank of the United States" fashioned after the "Bank of England."  The Rothschilds controlled it.

After Mayer Rothschild's death in 1812, Nathan took control over the family fortune and opened the "Nathan Mayer Rothschild & Sons Bank" in London, Vienna, Paris, and Berlin.  In America it was represented by J.P. Morgan (NJ) & Co., August Belmont (NJ) & Co., and Kuhn Loeb & Company.

During the American Civil War, the Rothschilds financed both sides of the conflict.  "The reasons leading to this civil war," van Helsing wrote, "were almost completely due to the actions and provocations of Rothschild agents."  One of the troublemakers, founder of the "Knights of the Golden Circle," was George Bickley (NJ).  Bickley extolled the advantages of succession from the Union by the Confederate States.  On the other side, the Rothschild-J.P Morgan and August Belmont banks financed the Union.  In addition, Rothschild's London bank supported the North, while its Paris bank funded the South.  It was a glorious business.

President Lincoln finally caught wind of the scam and

withheld immense interest payments to the Rothschilds. He
then petitioned Congress to print "greenbacks" - dollars over
which only the Union held printing power. In response, the
furious Rothschilds are said to have arranged his assassination.
John Wilkes Booth murdered Lincoln on April 14, 1865.
Booth was freed from jail due to the efforts of the Knights of
the Golden Circle. He spent the duration of his days living
comfortably in England, funded by the Rothschilds.

By the early 1900s, the Masonic-linked "secret
societies," including the CFR, held a stranglehold on
America's leading social, economic, and political institutions.
In 1913, American banking mogul William Avery Harriman
(NJ) was initiated into the Skull & Bones fraternity. During
the "Roaring Twenties" Harriman became the chief of Western
financier of communism, the Russian governments, and the
Ruskombank - where Max May, a Skull & Bones brother of
Harriman, was vice-president. May was simultaneously vice-
president of the Guaranty Trust Company, controlled by J.P.
Morgan and by extension the Nathan Mayer Rothschild Bank.
Other Skull & Bones members partnered with J.P. Morgan at
that time included Harold Stanley and Thomas Cochran
(NJ).The Capital used to create the Guaranty Trust came from
the Harrimans, Rockefellers, Vanderbilts (NJ) - all families
with blood kin in the Skull & Bones. Percy Rockefeller (NJ)
represented his family's interest in the Skull & Bones as well
as Guaranty Trust, which he directed from 1915 to 1930.
Rothschild and Bavarian Illuminati representatives helped
establish the Rockefeller's European Standard Oil empire as
well as Carnegie's steelworks and Harriman's railroads.

Many ignorant "patriots" have claimed the
Rockefeller family is Jewish. This stems largely from an
article spread in "Christian" circles by Richard Darcy, Jr.
entitled "Rockefeller's Jewish Ancestry!" (The misspelling
of Ancestry was Darcy's.) He referenced Stephen
Birmingham's book *The Grandees* in which the author stated
the Rockefellers, and other elite American families, were
surprised to learn of the Sephardic ancestry. The fact is that as
early as 1904 Silas Hubbard self published from New York a
book exposing John D. Rockefeller's various frauds citing his

Sunday      church-going/Bible-carrying      behavior      and
alternatively Monday through Friday criminality.

The introduction of the "Federal Reserve System" in
1913 enabled the Rothschild-Rockefeller banking axis to
consolidate their American financial powers.  Banking chiefs,
who were largely supported by the Rothschilds, became the
chairmen of the first Federal Reserve Bank of New York.

Following passage of "The Federal Reserve Act,"
Warburg led the U.S. Congress to fraudulently forward the
16th Amendment to the Constitution that granted Congress the
power to levy personal income taxes on American citizens.
The legislation was required since the United States
government could no longer print money to finance its
operations due to the controlling forces of the international
banking cartel.

The Warburg family, admittedly Jewish, is said to
have heavily financed Hitler's rise to power and I.G Farben's
operations along with the Rockefellers and others.  In Sidney
Warburg's *Hitler's Secret Backers* (CPA Book Publisher,
1933, reprinted 1983), prominent Nazi officer Franz von
Papen credit's the book for accurately detailing Hitler's
financial backers wherein "all the bankers named are gentiles,
not Jewish."

*With No Apologies: The Personal Memoirs of U.S.
Senator Barry Goldwater*, the obviously Jewish Senator
expressed the insider's view that The Round Table's cover
organization, the CFR, tightly controlled the American
political scene with Rockefellers at the helm.  "I believe the
Council on Foreign Relations and its ancillary elitist groups
[referring to the other "secret societies" such as Skull &
Bones] are indifferent to communism.   They have no
ideological anchors.  In their pursuit of a New World Order
they are prepared to deal without prejudice with a communist
state, a socialist state, a democratic monarchy, oligarchy - it's
all the same to them.

"...Their rationale rests exclusively on materialism,"
Senator Goldwater added.  "When a new president comes on
board, there is a great turnover in personnel but no change in
policy.  For instance, as stated earlier, during the Nixon years

Henry Kissinger, a CFR member and Nelson Rockefeller's protégé, was in charge of foreign policy. When Jimmy Carter was elected, Kissinger was replaced with Zbigniew Brzezinski (NJ), CFR member and David Rockefeller's protégé.

Henry Kissinger, hailed as a hero by unwitting Jewish organizations, and recently exposed as a war criminal in Harper's magazine (Feb. and March, 2001), was excommunicated from the Jewish religion on June 20, 1976 during a religious ceremony presided over by five member Rabbis of the Supreme Rabbinic Court of America, partly for helping top Nazi war criminals to escape Germany at the close of the war.

Thus, the Bible correctly counsels, "Beware of those that call themselves Jews who are not." In regard to the above, and the repugnant Free American article, readers are urged to "Beware of those that call non-Jews "Jews" in an effort to create inter-racial and inter-religious hatred." In the anonymous author's case, it might also be wise to "Beware of those that call themselves Christians who are not."

Concerning the repeated allegation that Hollywood, and the general media, is "controlled by Jews," Dr. Coleman more accurately detailed the Committee of 300's control over the American media by way of the CFR. He likewise recognized Zionism, and virtually all major religions, heavily infiltrated, if not completely controlled, by primarily British globalists.

America's mainstream magazine chief, for instance, Henry Luce (founder of Time, Life, and many other periodicals), helped, along with the Rockefeller family to engineer the "National Purpose" for all Americans during the early 1950's. This included linking "guns, butter, and the new technology" for "weapons production to the cause of Freedom and the Free World." Henry Luce, according to his biographer, W.A. Swanberg, was "the son of missionaries and one of America's leading Presbyterian laymen."

Moreover, intelligent persons would glean from the Halpern/Jacobovici documentary "Jews, Movies, Hollywoodism and the American Dream" more of the truth. Each of the movie studio founders were Jewish immigrants

255

who toughly fought their way to the top of an industry controlled by the White Anglo-Saxon Protestant (WASP) elite who maintained support from bankers - the old money. The Jewish film financiers were unable to compete in New York where the Edison Corporation had monopolized the movie industry early by producing films that degraded Jews and Blacks as the stagnant underclass. The Jewish moviemakers, thus, moved to Hollywood, California to circumvent this political snag. Here they found fertile soil, what America was supposed to provide, for their creative and imaginative productions. Increasingly successful with the development of films that consistently relayed the struggles of "little guys" against various establishments and odds - their own story reflected in many, if not most, of the Westerns and musicals they produced - they largely (some historians claim totally) created the fantasy culture in which we as Americans currently live.

Shortly before World War II, some of the Hollywood Jews began to speak out against fascism on American shores. They likely realized that old money, including the Rothschilds' and Rockefellers', had largely engineered Hitler's rise to power, and that America too was threatened in the same way pre-Nazi Germany had fallen. Harry Warner, Warner Brothers Studio chief, for instance, gave an anti-fascist speech before the American Legion in which he clearly referred to the secret racist societies and apparently the Liberty Lobby's neo-Nazi "propaganda machine" in America. He urged:

"Drive them out. Make America unsafe for those who seek to tear down what others have built through the generations from 1776. Drive them from their secret meeting places. Destroy their insidious propaganda machines. Drive out their "[Skull &] Bones," and their leagues, the [Ku Klux] clans and the black legions, the silver shirts, the black shirts, and their dirty shirts. Help keep America for those who believe in America."

As a result of this perceived threat, Former Ambassador to Britain, Joseph P. Kennedy, met secretly in Los Angeles with officials representing the international bankers and shadow governors. He reportedly argued that

256

Jews would be blamed if America entered the war, although there were other secret matters discussed. It is likely that Harry Warner's American Legion speech alarmed America's elite that they may be vulnerable to Hollywood exposes.

Hypersensitive to Jewish persecution, and their own continued immigrant status and insecurities, the movie moguls refused to produce any films heralding the Nazi threat prior to the Pearl Harbor attack and America's declared war with Germany. The two anti-Nazi films that were produced in Hollywood before that time came from non-Jews.

With the war, and the American government's urging, Hollywood went into full-scale production of propaganda films. Roosevelt had personally requested the moguls produce Russian films depicting the communists as our friends. This was later used against the Hollywood filmmakers during the McCarthy era.

By World War II, the "Hollywood Jews" had worked to become totally secular with similar themes in their films reflecting mass integration, including intermarriages. Though the American military was racially segregated completely at that time, Hollywood movies depicted our armed forces as fully integrated.

The Jews in Hollywood had done such a superb job on behalf of the American war effort that following armistice the studio bosses received military awards. They were also escorted to Europe to tour the concentration camps courtesy of the U.S. Government. Historians remain perplexed as to why no films were produced depicting this genocidal horror. The consensus of critics hold that the "Hollywood Jews" were simply too afraid to project any pro-Jewish sentiments that might lift their thin veil as seculars and integrated Americans.

Following the war, Louis B. Meyer, MGM Studios chief, called for the creation of a "new human type," liberated from the fears and persecutions of racism in America. "We gather here today," He said, "not as Catholics, Protestants, or Jews. All of the ancient bloods have contributed to those who meet here today. This great country is itself the result of the unity of all of these ancient bloods. We are all here as Americans."

257

Soon after these words were spoken, the Hollywood Jews were called before the U.S. Congress's Hearings on Communism directed by the vicious and openly anti-Jewish John Rankin, who like The Free American article, blamed Jews for virtually every social woe.  During the hearings, a number of persecuted movie executives stated the obvious - the shadow governors' efforts to regain control over the silver screen and American culture by wrestling it away from the Hollywood Jewish cartel.   The media moguls folded precipitously beneath this political pressure.  Then they helped facilitate what we recognize today was a virtual witch-hunt, a total ruse, given the international bankers' creation of communism and subsequent funding of its leaders.

In summary, there is nothing new under the sun, or in The Free American Jewish hate diatribe by Clay Douglas and an anonymous co-author.  I, for one, would like to know the source of the article.  Suspiciously, it appears perfectly timed and suited for a contemporary political agenda that insidiously includes resurrecting Jewish hate.  Let the primary author reveal himself and his political/financial affiliations.  Does he maintain connections to the Liberty Lobby, publishers of The Spotlight?  Is he affiliated with other groups that selectively relay half-truths to fully deceive well-meaning largely susceptible populations such as American patriots and Christians?  Free American readers deserve to know the whole truth.  Will Clay Douglas provide it, along with an apology? Time will tell.

## G Minor - Chapter 40:
## Congressman Ron Paul On Guns, Money, and
## the New World Order

Interviewer, Erik Forman - *Congressman Paul, thank you for providing time for this interview. I must say I have been one of your constituents since you took office in the seventies. I have grown up knowing your name and later, being proud that I could claim you as my representative. With your permission, Dr. Paul, I would like to skip the formalities, as my readers are fully aware of your Libertarian ideology and your platform. I would specifically like to talk about certain powers in our government that, to the thinking of a growing band of Constitutionalists, seem to have taken control of the political system itself. First question: do you believe there are secret forces at work that are attempting to dismantle the Constitution and the Bill of Rights?*

Congressman Ron Paul - I don't know what the best word is, but secret is pretty good. They're certainly not known to a lot of people; it's actually what their doing. But then again, it's not absolute secrecy. If you look around you can usually get the information. There was a time when nobody even knew who was a member of the CFR or the Trilateral Commission. I think it's a bad sign that they're not as secret as they used to be. They're bolder now. They get on television and they give interviews. But there is an agenda. They're behind the scenes in many way - very secretive. And, that was certainly the case on those individuals who planned and pushed us into the Iraqi War.

*EF - I've read in The New American that you are aware of the Round Table Groups, Skull & Bones, and other "secret societies" that have actively participated in the dismantling. In your essay "Neoconned", you went so far as to align the*

259

*Bush Administration with Trotskyites. However, it seems that the Bush/Skull & Bones guys are perpetually fighting the United Nations, the CFR, the Bildebergs. Are the Bohemian Grove Republicans on the same team as the Rockefeller Round Table members, or are they at war?*

RP - You know, their rhetoric suggests they might not like the United Nations, and you hear that often. They'll be complaining about the United Nations, and this and that. But, we have to remember, when it came time to get authority and a reason to go to war, they mentioned the United Nations twenty-one times in the authority, when we voted for the authority for the President to go to war when he felt like it. Even in his last State of the Union message, he once again brought up the subject - we had to go, we had to defend the United Nations. "We don't want a weak United Nations."

I think what's going on, they're not anti-U.N., they're anti-U.N. if they don't do exactly what they want. So, it's human nature not to have a monolith. Everyone at the U.N. doesn't agree. Because there is a fascist-type faction that wants to keep the military/industrial complex going, and the oil control. Then there's the Kofi Anan-type guys. They are Socialists. They like world government.

I don't think they (Republicans) are really going to be on our side on getting rid of it, although at times they say things. Richard Perle, not too long ago, made a statement that he thought we should get out of the United Nations. Well, I think that's, sort of, to pacify some of our supporters. They figure, "Oh, this is great. We've never had a President so sharply critical of the United Nations." But in his mind, they may well be believing they are saving the United Nations or transforming the United Nations, rather than being opposed to world government.

*EF - You have also written (and I have quoted you) that the U.N. is actively working to criminalize the $2^{nd}$ Amendment. Who do you think the men at the top are, and what is their ultimate plan?*

260

RP - Anybody in Washington that likes big government, authoritarian government, which is most of them…deep down, the $2^{nd}$ Amendment is their greatest obstacle, in the physical sense. Their other greatest obstacle is the right of free speech. The FCC is always coming in to do good things. Just recently, they had that little scandal that went on at the football game, and they had to express an outrage. What they're claiming is that we need the FCC to make sure that everything that comes out on the airwaves is proper and prim and moral. At the same time, those same individuals are the ones who would probably get rid of radio shows they don't like.

Same way with guns. I think that they haven't been able to be as aggressive with guns because it's a healthy sign of this country. I think our people defend the $2^{nd}$ Amendment better than they defend the $1^{st}$ Amendment. Which is sort of a twist, I think. Twenty years ago that probably wasn't the case. But, they do a pretty good job, now. I think in the year 2000, the Democrats didn't get anywhere.

Once again, what they say and what they really want are two different things. They criticize the U.N, yet they want to build it up. They can say they support the $2^{nd}$ Amendment. At the same time, they wouldn't mind curtailing that freedom. Because that is the ultimate freedom.

I kid a lot at my speeches and say, you know, I believe in gun control. I want to take the guns away from those 100,000 federal bureaucrats who own them. The Al Gores of the world, Schumer, these people…they want a monopoly of the guns. They never talk about getting rid of the guns from the bureaucrats. But, they want to get rid of the guns from the people who can't defend themselves.

So, it's a pretty important right that we better remain vigilant. Although, we haven't seen a vicious attack here recently, and I think behind the scenes, it's there. Also, we have the United Nations at times talking about gun registration. We do things in our country under orders of the international community. Like, we pass tax laws for the WTO. So, if there's going to be a tax law or gun law, for us to be a part of the world community, there's going to be a feeling of obligation to do it. So, we have remain very vigilant in defending this right.

*EF - Going off that, Americans are still reeling from the '95 Clinton ban? How many Congressmen and Senators would you estimate are actually directly involved with these plans of destruction? Or can most claim ignorance?*

RP - You know, it's weird.  From outside and observing it objectively it looks like that's what they are dedicated to. Many are sort of dupes.  Even as bad as John Ashcroft is, he doesn't sit around and say "What am I going to do to destroy the Constitution."  He probably believes in his heart that he's doing the right thing.  I think he believes, even with the Patriot Act, that he's doing his very best.  "Yeah, a little bit of infringements, but how could our country survive if I don't have this authority to make people safe."  So, there's a tremendous amount of rationalization.

There may well be very, very dedicated leftists and one world government people who are very deliberate.  They feed the information and play on the sensitivities of people who say "giving up a little bit isn't too bad."  They look at the Constitution and say "it's a changing and evolving document. We shouldn't take so long to amend it.  We should just reinterpret it."  They don't go to bed with guilt feelings.  In their own minds I don't believe...they think they're still doing the best thing.

It's sort of like us on our side, who believe in pure liberty.  We have a lot of support and a lot of help.  But, a lot of people aren't as dedicated.  They go along with our logic, and they agree with us on many issues.  On the left, there's probably just a few who really believe in totalitarian government completely and totally.  So, it's the propaganda that you have to watch out for.

Just look at how the propaganda machine gets busy when they decide the country must go to war.  It's really a powerful force.

*EF - Do you think the, say, Rhodes Scholars know what's going on?*

RP - I don't think everybody who got one is going to be one of the bad guys. But, I think they are talented people, and they have close connections, and it is...I would say that if you get a Rhodes Scholar, the propaganda is pretty powerful, they're going to lean away from our position and lean toward a one world government position. I don't think there's any doubt about that.

*EF - You have sponsored legislation that would get America out of the United Nations. Some Americans believe that if we must go to war, that the United Nations would be the people to fight. You have claimed that the U.N. is actively working to destroy American sovereignty. Can you list of the main bullet points that support that theory?*

RP - Well, just everything they've done. Everything the U.N. does from day one, you give up a certain amount of your sovereignty. And, the worst giving up is this notion of going to war under U.N. resolutions, which we did very quickly after we got in the United Nations. There was a U.N. resolution and we sent off all those men to get killed in Korea.

Whether it's that, or the WTO that manages trade, or the IMF that we subsidize with our taxpayers' money and then they go off and play games with their special interests. They rarely ever help poor countries. The World Bank isn't any better. That's an international welfare scheme. It's sold as a scheme that's going to help poor people in poor countries. But, all these programs end up helping the very wealthy, connected corporations and banks.

*EF - You talk about the WTO, the IMF, the World Bank. With these groups, the American Government has been complicit in many atrocities. We've used our troops to overthrow democratically elected leaders, massacred tribes and dissenters. I am against the United Nations. But, if they don't stop our government from committing these acts, whom does it fall to?*

RP - The American people have to be responsible. And yet, they don't have much clout, and they're not as well informed, and they respond to the propaganda. But then the most important branch is the U.S. Congress, because we're there, we're sworn to uphold the Constitution. If they - if the executive branch or the United Nations - oversteps their bounds, our moral and Constitutional responsibility is to restrain them.

But, Congress never seems to and the people don't seem to hold it against too many. We're going through this right now with Iraq and Afghanistan, spending these hundreds of billions of dollars, not doing any good at all. At the same time, we're going broke.

*EF - About the police state and the seemingly endless assault on civil liberties: Can you recall a time in American history when the common, blue-blooded American was more in danger of losing the powerful right of life, liberty, and pursuit of happiness than he or she is today? Or have we always been clandestinely oppressed, and every generation thinks their loss of liberty is the worst?*

RP - It has been going on a long time. In fact, we shouldn't be totally pessimistic. I think the Internet and radio shows have awakened a lot of people. The fact that we stirred up opposition to the Patriot Act is pretty good, because nobody of significance as yet has been pulled out of their bedrooms in the middle of the night and hauled off. Though, we have the Guantanamo-type arrests. That's a little different than what we are afraid of.

I would say it's been especially bad since the Civil War. The Civil War probably did more to undermine the principle of the Republic than any other one particular war. But, if you look at the violation of civil liberties in World War I, I mean, they were atrocious. And that war was unnecessary as well, and all the things that have been done. They have all these kinds of controls.

So, it seems like all those things are bad now, and there's more internationalism. There's probably more awareness, too. It's just that those who have become aware and would like to stop it...we're still in the minority. We don't have control.

*EF - Many Libertarians agree that our right to bear arms is the only thing that assures a defense against martial law, and the insurance for the other nine Amendments. Do you believe that the Clinton-sponsored assault rifle ban (currently supported by President Bush) is unconstitutional? If so, what do you say to the millions of Americans who believe in the 2^{nd} Amendment, yet support the ban?*

RP - Ha...Well, you mean go along with the ban. That's a personal choice on what you do. It is unconstitutional, and that's why I have a bill that would repeal it. I think what you're leaning to is they go along with it and the question is whether or not you should practice civil disobedience and just ignore it. People do that at their own risk.

Sort of like, I don't think much of what the IRS does as being legal or constitutional. I mean, it's pretty abusive. Especially if you compound it on the way they collect taxes, and then what they do with the money. They then take your money and they enforce bans on automatic rifles. It's all pretty bad.

But, when it comes to what somebody would do, we shouldn't be complacent to go along and say well it's not so bad and we'll just play this game. But, I take the position that I should do whatever I can to change it, so that's why I get involved in politics. Others, who have chosen another route - whether it's taxes, or guns, or whatever - they do it at risk because they practice civil disobedience.

You can be absolutely right on the Constitution, but the Constitution is no longer a defense in court. So, the federal laws and the judicial system is very biased against us. I could conceive of a time where if they came and curtailed, they took everyone off the radio that they didn't like. They are now monitoring the Internet, since the Patriot Act was passed.

If they came and said that not only do we register guns indirectly with these purchases, and they seem to have a lot of information. Uh, if they did that, curtailed our freedom of speech, curtailed our right to own a weapon. They then came and said you can't even protect yourself economically. We'll print money and we'll make you use it, and you can't even use gold or silver, like they did. You talk about times when they were worse, the '30's were pretty bad. It's hard to think about that you couldn't go buy American gold coins.

I would think then, that would be a tougher decision for everybody. I think there's going to be more people fed up. Some may do it quietly, and some may do it more boldly. But, that's risky business. Because our government is very powerful.

*EF - Will our government eventually make handguns illegal?*

RP - Well, I think that's where they've had their set back. That's why I think Schumer and others backed off a little bit. But, that's what they do. They work on the automatic rifles and then the handguns. They do it incrementally.

If they do it and they get away with it, it means we didn't do a very good job. Because, you know, the Saturday Night Special is a wonderful weapon. Because they should be legalized in every    household, especially the inner city. Because, that's where the greatest amount of crime is. People who are poor and minority, live in the city, have the least amount of protection. And, they're getting robbed and killed. They could afford a cheap handgun, and they should be allowed to do it.

So, I think it's our job to try to try to neutralize that, and to some degree to do it. But, we need to do a lot better.

*EF - There has been some rumors surrounding the National Rifle Association lately. Do believe that the NRA is still an entity that defends our right to bear arms; or have they become a victim of their own success? Alex Jones recently reported that the NRA was willing to make some back door concessions  pertaining to gun registration.  When does it become more beneficial to a club that makes its money fighting gun laws to make sure there are gun laws on the books to fight?*

RP - That depends on their membership. They have to be awake. I don't think everything they do is bad, but I'd agree that they're weak. I agree that that's the case with my old medical association, the AMA. Went up their, working hard to pass socialized medicine, and they're a lobby now to get their fees raised. They're not a lobby up there to protect the patients through the free market, which is how I believe they would get better care. So the AMA is not very good at that, and the NRA isn't either. They get too big, too bureaucratic, but the members should say something about it.

You know, when we passed that Medicare Bill, a lot of people objected. It didn't bring the AARP down, but I think they lost, what, 60,000 members or something. So, a lot of members just flat-out quit. So, that's why, as long as there's competition in these types of organizations, then you have Larry Pratt, Gun Owners of America, and Gottlieb(?) with the other group out of Washington. So that's what we have to do. We have to sort it out, make sure people know the differences.

I don't think the NRA will be our saving grace. Although I wouldn't argue the case they're there purposely to...I just think their compromisers.

*EF - Changing lanes here. Congressman Paul, anyone who has followed your career knows that you are a strong proponent of the Gold Standard. The Federal Reserve seems to have been the main vehicle for driving America from a nation of savers to a nation of borrowers. Everywhere in America, especially with the economic downturn of 2000 and 3 million jobs lost, American citizens are having to turn to bankruptcy as the answer to their inability to kick the habit of credit. Now, with our national deficit estimated at half a trillion dollars...*

RP - It's seven trillion. Oh, you mean the deficit. It's at $600 billion.

*EF - Do you believe that America will one day have to file a global Chapter 13? What would that mean for us?*

RP - Well, they do, but not in the sense of a business or even a State, where they just renege on paying. Sovereign nations always have control of the money, but they shouldn't go bankrupt through the destruction of their money. People lose confidence in the money.

    In our case, if the world lost confidence in the dollar, you would have interest rates soaring, a lot of price inflation. You would have upheaval in the financial markets. And, I think that's what's coming. It's slowly starting now. But, I think it will accelerate, because we've been given a free ride.

    Since World War II, we've been the beneficiaries of having, to be able to issue the reserve currency. So, it's almost like us being able to issue gold. Because we've been so rich and powerful, there's been a lot of trust in the money. But, you can't do it forever. So, when we can't pay our debt, and when we can't reverse this annual deficit...how government's pay that debt off is, let's say we owe $7 trillion dollars, and over the years we have to pay it off. If you inflate so much in the next five years that the dollar's only worth fifty cents, you only have, you only owe, in real terms, 3.5 trillion. So, that's what we're doing continuously.

    But, what finally happens, it becomes so rapid, everyone starts dumping the dollar. That can be very dangerous, very chaotic, and I think it would be a political mess, and an economic mess. But, they don't really file any papers. Because, I think that they will always pay the paper. They wouldn't pay when they owed it in gold. They reneged on that. They will always pay the bond holder, and they're always going to pay the Social Security recipients. It's just with money that's worth a lot less.

*EF - I've heard said that "if" is the biggest word in the dictionary. Nevertheless, I'd like to go down that theoretical road for a moment. What if Congress were able to regain control of our money supply from the bankers and the Federal*

*Reserve? What if our Federal Government backed currency with gold again? What would that do to the American economy? Would there be an initial recession or depression as we learned how to save for the future instead of borrowing against it?*

RP - If you did it with the stroke of a pen, it would be very, very chaotic. And, uh, even I, who have bills in to get rid of the Federal Reserve, I don't advocate that. It's sort of like the Medicare system. There are so many people dependent on Medicare and Medicaid. If you just said, "well, we're not supposed to be doing this," and you just close the door. Just think of the chaos there. But, to introduce a free option like medical savings account, let people assume responsibility and gradually move out. That's what makes the most sense.

Same way with money. We've made one major step, because in 1976, I had a little bit to do with it, that was to re-legalize gold. And, the fact that you can buy gold or silver is real important. But, the next step is to repeal the legal tender laws. Say you and I have a contract in gold and I default. You go to the court and I have to pay you, they'll settle the debt in dollars. They won't do it in gold. Gold is not legal tender according to our courts.

It would be chaotic. But, I would like to see a, more of a voluntary transition. Now, of course, if you have runaway inflation and the dollar collapses, you won't need a law. People will know what they'll trade for. It will be survival. You'll trade anything, but gold and silver will be the money that people will trade. And, they're starting to do that a little bit more. But, it would be pretty chaotic just to do it in one moment.

*EF - I'd like to turn your attention to propaganda, and state-sanctioned mind control. It is common knowledge that the CIA and military have conducted mind control experimentation on American citizens. The most notorious case was Project MK Ultra in which Goldwater sat in on the Senate Hearings against the accused. Each time these agencies have been caught performing experiments, they*

269

*shrug it off and say the activity was done a few decades ago, and that they have stopped. Yet, more evidence surfaces, and we become aware that the mind control projects went on at least until the eighties. Now, when we hear rumors that the government has abducted children or sponsored sex slavery, we don't want to believe it, but we must not discard it because of the government's past history. Do you believe that members of our government are still actively involved in individual mind control experimentation?*

RP - Probably, but the tragedy is I don't know. The tragedy is that I'm in the Congress, and even when those bills come up you can't get much information. I would assume to some degree they are. You know, what is official and what is not official? Some of the CIA gets caught trading drugs and financing some corrupt regime, which they have been caught. That individual, "We don't even know who you are, buddy." They disown you. And, that's why the CIA in particular is a very, very dangerous organization.

Although, we made a major step in the wrong direction when this administration made it clear that we would fight preemptive wars, even though we hadn't been attacked. We have been doing that for a long time. But, this time it's bolder, because they're announcing it, and saying this is policy.

Look at the government under Johnson. No, it was under Kennedy, and murdered Diem. And, that was part of the CIA. The CIA's been involved in coups for years. The CIA put the Shah of Iran in power, and that led to the radicalization of Iran. We're suffering from that since. So, that's the heinous stuff.

They're capable of it. There's certainly been a record of it in the past, and then they deny it. There's no easy way to solve that problem. Because, like I say, even I, who is right there, can't get the information we should have. That makes it an easy no vote for me, to vote against all that funding.

*EF - What about mass mind manipulation. Do you think that Clear Channel and other media outlets are intentionally trying*

270

*to manipulate us?*

RP - I think they're propagandists, you know, and they're propagandists for the administration. That's pretty significant. But, uh, hopefully, we have to be careful exactly how you define it, because what if they want to make the same accusation against everybody on our side that resorts to radio and Internet. "Oh, see that Internet stuff. These are bad people, and they're lying, and they're passing this horrible propaganda." And, that's why we all have to try as hard as we can to stick to the facts and the things that we know.

But, throughout the whole 20th Century, even before Clear Channel, the media is owned by big business that owns the corporations who make a lot of money. They always support the war: WWI, WWII. And they do. They control public opinion.

*EF - Take Bush's claim for Iraq/WMDs, now proven false. Fox News and CNN are both guilty of spreading that lie over and over again for months on end. Are they as guilty as say, Leni Riefenstahl, the director of the Nazi Party's "Triumph of the Will"? Or are they guilty, but not guilty enough to be held accountable?*

RP - Well, I think the people behind the scenes, the people that I've written about, that you're talking about - the Neocons - who have a strategy to sort of push this on. Those individuals, I think it's pretty clear what their ulterior motives are. But, even a guy like Bush, he's gone along with it, but you don't know whether he's naïve. I think it's a judgment call on looking into their souls, and there are times when I can't do that.

I think, if you look at Fox, I think they're naïve. I think they consider themselves patriotic Americans. They so often say, "they're trying to kill us, and all we're trying to do is save our lives." They come around to believing their own propaganda. So, sorting that all out is pretty difficult, and I don't pretend to know. If what their doing is wrong, I don't think it's crucial that I know deep down in their heart what they're thinking, because I can't. We'll never know.

We'll never know why we were manipulated through the back door into WWII, and how consciously they did it. There are a lot of books written about that but, the individuals who do it always have, you know, a rationalization. "Well, war's tough, but we need it. It's a tough war to go, but we have to get rid of this bad guy. We need the oil." They go on and on, to the point where…the funny thing is they don't have much guilt about it.

*EF - Congressman Paul, I want to thank you for your time. I have just a couple of more questions. These are of a more personal nature, but your fans want to know, so I have to ask. Is there any possibility that you would run for President again under the Libertarian or Constitution Party mantle?*

RP - Probably not. It just doesn't look like that. I think what I'm doing now, you know I've worked hard to try and prove that you can believe in something, you can stick to it, and vote that way, and you won't be penalized by the voters. And, I think, at the moment that seems to be a pretty good goal. And, it's not, it doesn't go unnoticed.

Most people in Washington think, "How did he ever get here? How does he stay?" Yet, each time I've gotten a higher percentage, and this time, of course, I ended up without an opponent. So, I would like to think that what I've done on this very local level has popularized the views that we hold. And, I haven't been penalized. And, other members of Congress notice that.

Because there are a lot of members of Congress who are more sympathetic than the way they vote. They'd like to do better, but they don't think they can buck the system. They know I'll buck the system, but they keep thinking that they'll get hit. But, I think freedom is a popular idea. If you work at it, you convince them.

*EF - Finally, DeLay created a fire storm down here in Texas when he gave the orders for the Republican Party to go against tradition and redistrict the State in a non-census year.*

272

*The Democrats hightailed to New Mexico to protest the impending loss of seats. After September 11, the country united in a very positive manner, yet the redistricting brought us back to Republican versus Democrat. Now that the new Texas map has been shuttled out for all to see, it is evident to some Republicans that the redistricting may not be what they wanted. You, yourself, have been affected, and will no longer be the Congressman for the same cities that you have represented for the last seven years. I personally believe that your change was an intentional move on the part of the Republicans to punish you for not toeing the party line. Do you agree with that assessment, or do you think your district being moved was purely coincidental?*

RP - Yeah, because they gave me the worst Republican seat. You know, they have twenty-two Republican seats, mine is the twenty-second worst one. I think they probably wanted me to work hard, and they probably figured I could win. They probably rationalized and said, "Well, we need him to help beat this guy next door," and all these kind of things. And, that I would be able to get Independent people to vote for me, and some Democrats, and I can.

That, in combination with, we're not going to give him a freebie. But, the irony of it is everyone else got an opponent, and I didn't. So, sometimes their plans don't go quite the way they think they're going to go. Maybe we'll have the last laugh.

# Bibliography

Chapter 1
1.       irs.gov
2.       Ross, Robert Gaylon Sr. *Who's Who of the Elite: Members of the Bilderbergs, Council on Foreign Relations, Trilateral Commission, & Skull & Bones Society* RIE, 1996
3.       Mullins, Eustace *The Secrets of the Federal Reserve* John McLaughlin, 1993
4.       "The Golden Isles: Jekyll Island" History Channel International, 2004
5.       Mark, Christopher *The Grand Deception: The Theft of America and the World I* American Achievement Seminars, Inc., 28 February 2003
6.       Jefferson, Thomas "Jefferson's Opinion of the Constitutionality of a National Bank" 1791
7.       McFadden, Louis T. "Congressman McFadden on the Federal Reserve Corporation: An Astounding Exposure" remarks made in Congress, 1934
8.       "Inner City Federal Reserve Beat" innercitypress.org, 14 April 2003
9.       McBride, Greg CFA "Deflation: Real Threat, or Convenient Whipping Boy" bank rate.com, 23 May 2003
10.      Russbacher, Gunther "The Short Road to Chaos and Destruction: An Expose of The Federal Reserve Banking System" rumormillnews.com, 1992
11.      Ross, Robert Gaylon Sr. *The Elite Serial Killers of Lincoln, JFK, RFK, and MLK* RIE, 2001
Chapter 2
1.       usda.gov
2.       Viadero, Roger C. Congressional Testimony commdocs.house.gov/committees/ag/hag10658/hag10658_0f.html, 27 July 2002
3.       Palmer, Eric "Pork Producers Group Considers Suing USDA" Kansas City Star, 12 January 2001
4.       Kennedy, Joanne "Family Farmers Fight Against Unjust Pork Tax" The Progress Report, 2001
5.       Williams, Tad "The Corruption of American Farms and Agriculture" pbs.org, 2003
6.       Farm Security and Rural Investment Act of 2002 usda.gov, 2002
7.       Study On Discriminatory Practices by the USDA

Commissioned Under President Johnson  pbs.org, 1964
8.        Green, Che "Not Milk: The USDA, Monsanto, and the
U.S. Dairy Industry" LiP Magazine, 9 July 2002
9.        "End Inhumane Slaughter - Tell the USDA To Do Its Job"
Animal Protection Institute, 2004
10.       freemasonry watch.org
11.       USDA Forest Service "Hostile Work Environment for
Christians" SCRC Issue Form, April 1994
12.       Lavello, Randy "The Great Deception"  prison planet.com
2003
Chapter 3
1.        fema.gov
2.        Martin, Harry V. "FEMA: The Secret Government" Free
America, 1995
3.        Rivero, Michael F.  FEMA Executive Order List
FreeRepublic.com, 2003
4.        Turley, Jonathon "Camps For Citizens: Ashcroft's hellish
Vision" L.A. Times, 14 October 2002
5.        "Who Is Al Cuppett?" geocities.com/cuppett, 2003
6.        Jones, Alex Police State 2000 Alex Jones Productions,
2004
7.        Paul, Ron "Ron Paul on Guns, Money, and the New World
Order" Erik Fortman, interviewer, 21 February 2004
8.        Bowman, Rob X Files: The Movie Twentieth Century
Fox, 1998
9.        Dominick, Brian A.  rootmedia.org, 2003
10.       Bovard, James Feeling Your Pain St. Martin's Press,
2000
11.       Armstrong, Ari "NRA-Endorsed Politician Calls For
Expanded Gun Registration" The Colorado Freedom Report, 4
October 2002
12.       Senate Bill H.R. 3162 Uniting and Strengthening America
By Providing Appropriate Tools Required to Intercept and Obstruct
Terrorism (PATRIOT) Act, 26 October 2001
13.       Moyers, Bill "Patriot Act II" PBS, 7 February 2003
Chapter 4
1.        defenselink.mil/
2.        Dobbs, Michael "Oil In Iraq: Role of Halliburton"
washingtonpost.com, 28 August 2003
3.        Stone, Oliver Salvador MGM/UA, 2001
4.        soaw.org/
5.        hrw.org/
6.        History Channel International The Fifties

7.      Is This Justice? "The United States Vs. The International Criminal Court" themailactivist.org/icc,htm

8.      Colvin, Jeff "Interview with Robin Hanson" Wall Street Week, 20 February 2004

9.      Hertzberg, Hendrick "Too Much Information" The New Yorker, 2 December 2002

10.     Singel, Ryan "Bill: Down With Citizen Databases" Wired News, 17 January 2003

11.     Total Information Awareness Resource geocities.com/totalinformationawareness/, 2004

12.     Bush Budget Request FY2003

Chapter 5

1.      immigration-Bureau.org

2.      justice-denied.net

3.      Hayes, Matt "INS Plagued With Corruption" Fox News, 23 May 2002

4.      "INS Inspectors Arrested in Border Corruption Case" cannabisnews.com/news/thread404/shtml

5.      "Drug Control: INS and Customs Can Do More To Prevent Drug Related Employee Corruption" The Schaffer Library of Drug Policy, 20 March 1999

6.      55% in Federal Prison, 25% in State Prisons drugwarfacts.org/prison.htm, 2004

7.      Baum, Dan Smoke and Mirrors: The War on Drugs and the Policy of Failure Little, Brown and Company, 1996

8.      Burnett, John "Corruption at the Gates" NPR, 12 & 13 September 2002

9.      Hiaasen, Chris The Miami Herald, 2003

10.     Weisman, Robyn "U.S. Proposed Anti-Terror Border Tracking Technology" News Factor Network, 31 January 2002

11.     Bovard, James Lost Rights Palgrave, 2000

Chapter 6

1.      cia.gov

2.      "9/11 Redux: Anniversary of Treason" prisonplanet.com, 2004

3.      Cantelon, Jessice "Corrupt CIA Ensures U.S. Vulnerability to Terrorism" CNSNews.com, 15 July 2002

4.      ciadrugs.com

5.      Tarpley, Webster G. and Chaitkin, Anton George Bush: The Unauthorized Biography Executive Intelligence Review, 1991

6.      "Enron-FedGov Corruption: CIA Used in Int'l Corporate Espionage, Racketeering!" Free World Alliance freeworldalliance.com/newsflash/2002/02newsflash0273.htm, 17

February 2002

7.      Best, Ben *A Covert History of the 1960's* Ben Best, 1999

8.      Stockwell, John "The Secret Wars of the CIA", 2003

9.      Xymorpha *Ali Mohammed - U.S. Agent, Al Quaeda Spy...or Both?* Guerrilla News Network, 24 February 2003

10.     Henderson, Leonard "The Stratton Family" Family Rights Association, 2004

11.     Johnson, M Raphael "Media Leviathan, U.S. Intelligence Form Secret Cabal" American Free Press, 2004

12.     PATRIOT Act

Chapter 7

1.      fda.gov

2.      "Need To Reform The FDA" Life Extension Magazine, May 2001

3.      Seguin, Larry "Drug Deaths?" mapinc.org/drug news/v01/n121/a04.html, 14 January 2001

4.      Hubbard, William K. International Prescription Drug Parity: Are Americans Being Protected or Gouged? The Committee on Government Reform; Subcommittee on Human Rights and Wellness, 20 March 2003

5.      "Drug Mix-ups Prompt FDA Action" Associated Press, 5 Jan 2002

6.      Consumers Against High Drug Prices (CAHDP), stopfda.com, 2004

7.      "A Glorious Victory Over FDA Tyranny" CAHDP, stopfda.com/july99-glorious victory.htm

8.      Sheran, Ariana "We Are In This Together" newciv.org/nl/newslog.php/_d35/__show_article/a000035_000062.htm

9.      Cohen, Robert "Bush and Monsanto" Alkalize For Health, 18 March 2001

10.     Fox News Channel, January 2004

Chapter 8

1.      Baum, Dan *Smoke and Mirrors: The War on Drugs and the Policy of Failure* Little, Brown and Company, 1996

2.      usdoj.gov/dea

3.      Herer, Jack *The Emperor Wears No Clothes* Ah Ha Publishing, 2000

4.      alternet.org

5.      Stitch, Rodney *Defrauding America: Encyclopedia of Secret Operations by the CIA, DEA, and other Covert Agencies* Diablo Western Press, 1998

6.      Conroy, Bill "DEA supervisor claims he is a target of

reprisal, discrimination" San Antonio Business Journal, 13
December 2002
7.       Shaffer Library of Drug Policy "Congressional Reports on
Drug Corruption and the Federal Government" druglibrary.org, 2004
Chapter 9
1.       irs.gov
2.       Edwards, Chris "Cato Scholar cites 10 surprising facts
about the income tax" Cato Institute News Release, 14 April 2003
3.       "Update on IRS Seizure in Indianapolis"
warroom.com/rage church.html, 2003
4.       O'Reilly, Bill O'Reilly Factor Fox News, extensive
coverage approx. 1999-2001
5.       Davis, Shelley L. *Unbridled Power: Inside the Secret
Culture of the IRS* Harper Business, 1997
6.       irs.gov
7.       trac.syr.edu
8.       givemeliberty.org
9.       Schiller Institute "IRS Corruption Fueled Operations of
'Get LaRouche' Task Force" Executive Intelligence Review, 5 June
1998
Chapter 10
1.       Quotes from elites such as Ted Turner and Prince Phillip
2.       Jones, Alex Live from Alex Jones Radio Program, 8
November 2002
3.       Clinton, William Jefferson Associated Press and ABC
News, 28 December 1999
4.       fbi.gov
5.       Rowley, Colleen *Memo to FBI Director Robert Mueller"*,
21 May 2002
6.       Skousen, Joel "FBI Continues to Cover Up Pilot
Communications Related to September 11"
rense.com/general18/sep.htm, 3 January 2001
7.       "9/11 Redux: Anniversary of Treason" prisonplanet.com,
2004
8.       Wolf, Paul compiler "Cointelpro: The Untold American
Story" Presented by U.N. High Commissioner for Human Rights
Mary Robinson, 1 September 2001
9.       Streissguth, Tom *J. Edgar Hoover: Powerful FBI Director*
Enslow Publisher, Inc., 2002
10.      Spannaus, Edward "'Black Like Me?' The Strange Saga of
J. Edgar Hoover" Executive Intelligence Review, 4 August 2000
11.      Marrs, Jim *Rule By Secrecy* Harper Collins Publisher,
Inc., 2000

12.      School of the Americas Watch
13.      Farrell, Perry "1%" *Jane's Addiction*

**Part 2 - Shadows of Power**

Chapter 11
1.       "FCC adopts media ownership rules" CNN Money, 2 June
2003  1:10EDT
1a.      TRIO Channel March 2004
2.       Genesis, *Holy Bible*
3.       Bay, David "Secret Societies Killed Jesus Christ - Part 1"
The Cutting Edge Radio Program, 2004
4.       Missler, Chuck "Notes and References on Islam"
ldolphin.org/missler.html  2004
5.       Regular, Arnon "'Road map is a lifesaver to us' PM Abbas
tells Hamas" Haaertz, 10 March 2004
6.       Icke, David *Children of the Matrix* Bridge of Love, 2001
7.       Ziggler is based on an acquaintance, Zamarath the
Interdimensional Wizard. He first told me names like Icke and
Rothschild.
8.       davidicke.com
9.       Goldstein, Paul and Steinberg, Jeffrey "Skull & Bones and
the New World Order" A New American View, April 1991
10.      atlantisrising.com
Chapter 12
1.       Washizu, Bro. Yoshio "Critical Reading of Masonic
Literature" freemasonry.bcy.ca/aqc/reading.html, 2003
2.       Waite, Arthur Edward *New Encyclopedia of Freemasonry*
Wings Press, 1994
3.       freemasonrywatch.org
4.       Leadbeater, C.W. *Freemasonry and Its Ancient Mystic
Rites* Gramercy, 1998
5.       trosch.org
6.       Alex Jones Radio Program, February 2004
7.       Lause, Mark "Antimasonic Party"
geocities.com/CollegePark/Quad/6460/dir/827anti.html, 2004
8.       "Rosicrucians" Americanreligions.org
9.       McDonnel, Patrick J. "Judge Grants Political Asylum on
Claims of French Persecution Courts" L.A. Times, 15 June 2001
10.      O'Brien Cathy *Trance: Formation of America* Reality
Marketing, Inc., 1995
11.      templarhistory.com
12.      Baigent, Michael *Holy Blood, Holy Grail* Dell Publishing,

1982-83

13.       Pike, Albert *Morals and Dogma of the Ancient and Accepted Scottish Rite of Freemasonry* Reprint Services Corp

Chapter 13

1.        Marrs, Jim <u>Rule By Secrecy: The Hidden History That Connects the Trilateral Commission, the Freemasons, and the Great Pyramids</u> Perrenial, 2001

2.        Melanson, Terry "Illuminati Conspiracy, Order of the Illumined Wise Men" conspiracyarchive.com/NWO/Iluuminati.htm, 2004

3.        Fagan, Myron "A Satanic Plot for a One World Government - the World Conspirators: The Illuminati" survivalistskills.com/illumin.htm

4.        Chomsky, Noam *Rogue States* South End Press, 2000

5.        "Illuminati History: 1901-1970" geocities.com/lord_visionary/illuminatihistory19011970.htm, 2004

6.        Zukeran, Patrick "Jehova's Witnesses: Witnessing to the Witnesses" probe.org/docs/jehovah.html, 1994

7.        Springmeier, Fritz *Bloodlines of the Illuminati* Spring Arbor Distributors, 1998

8.        Darst, G. Albert "Satan's Method of World Dominion" seekingchrist.net/satan%27s.htm, 2004

9.        Marrs, Texe *Mystery Mark of the New Age: Satan's Plan for World Domination* Crossway Books, 1988

10.       Segel, Benjamin W. and Levy, Richard S. *A Lie and a Libel: The History of the Protocols of the Elders of Zion* University of Nebraska, reprint 1996

Chapter 14

1.        Ross, Robert Gaylon Sr. <u>*The Elite Serial Killers of Lincoln, JFK, RFK, and MLK*</u>

2.        Makow, Henry PhD. "Do Jews Suffer From False Consciousness" resne.com 28 April 2003

3.        Jewish Virtual Library "A Definition of Zionism" us-Israel.org/jsource/Zionism/Zionism.html

4.        Hooker, Richard "The Diaspora" wsu.edu:8080/~dee/HEBREWS/DIASPORA.HTM

5.        Kadary, Nili "1897: At Basle I Founded the Jewish State" Jewish Agency for Israel jafi.org.il/education/100/port/time/1897.html 2004

6.        Palestine Facts "How did the Zionists acquire land in Palestine?" palestinefacts.org/pf_early_Palestine_Zionists_land.php

7.        Icke, David "Was Hitler a Rothschild?" davidicke.com 2004

8.        Propaganda Matrix "The New World Order-Nazi Connection" propagnadamatrix.com/archivenaziconnection.html
9.        Amanullah, Shahed & Mohaiemen, Naeem "Mindless 'Martyrs': Muslims against Suicide Bombings" press action.com/pablog/archives/001059.html 13 October 2003

Chapter 15

1.        *World Newsstand* "The Roadshow of Deception" wealth4freedom.com/truth/6/roadshow.htm 1999
2.        Rivera, David Allan  Final Warning: A History of the New World Order  Conspiracy Books, 2004
3.        Watch Unto Prayer "The Rhodes-Milner Round Table" watch.pair.com/roundtable.html, 2004
4.        Icke, David "The Round Table-Bilderberg Network" davidicke.com/icke/article2/rd-table.html, 2004
5.        Fisher, Marc "Vernon Jordan introduces Governor Clinton to world leaders at 1991 German Bilderberg gathering" *Washington Post* 27 January 1998
6.        Nyquist, J.R. "Why some of us fear Clinton?" cutting edge.org/news/n1315.cfm
7.        Skolnick, Sherman H. "Bill Clinton and the Rockefellers" *Conspiracy Nation* geocities.com/CapitolHill/8425/CLINROC.HTM 2004
8.        Steingberg, Jeffrey "Open Conspirators Behind September 11 Coup Plot" Executive Intelligence Review, 25 January 2002

Chapter 16

1.        Goldstein, Paul & Steinberg, Jeffrey "George Bush, Skull & Bones and the New World Order" *A New American View - International Edition*, 1991
2.        Tarpley, Webster G; Chaitkin, Anton; Wertz, Marianna  George Bush: the Unauthorized Biophraphy, 1991
3.        Millegan, Kris "The Order of the Skull and Bones: 4. Name Roster of the Secret Establishment" conspiracy archive.com/NOW/Skull_Bones_2.html
4.        Draheim, Richard N. Jr. "The Bush Nazi Connection" lpdallas.org/features/draheim/dr991216.htm, 2000
5.        Sutton, Anthony  Secret Cult of the Order  Concord Books, 1983
6.        Robbins, Alexandra  Secrets of the Tomb: Skull and Bones, the Ivy League, and the Hidden Paths of Power  Little, Brown and Company, 2002
7.        Shore, Josh "Skull and Bones (Part 1): Interview with Alexandra Robbins" Guerrilla News Network, 2003
8.        LaRouche, Lyndon "Expose of Skull and Bones"

LaRouche Campaign, 1980
Chapter 17
1.        Overbeck, Charles "The Council of Foreign Relations and the Trilateral Commission" truedemocracy.net, 2004
2.        Perloff, James The Shadows of Power: The Council on Foreign Relations and the American Decline American Opinion Books, 1988
3.        cfr.org
4.        Reid, Tim "How U.S. helped Iraq build deadly arsenal" London Times, 31 December 2002
5.        Baker, Joe "Attack panel still bogus" The Rock River Times, 11 January 2003
6.        "Clinton suggested as next NATO boss" Aftenposten News Wire, 8 July 2003
7.        Robertson, Pat The Collected Works of Pat Robertson: The New Millennium/The New World Order/The Secret Kingdom Budget Book Service, 1999
Chapter 18
1.        Wisdom and Freedom "Bohemian Club" World Newsstand, 1999
2.        Various sources "World Leaders Engage in Symbolic Pagan Worship of Molech-the 'god' of Child Sacrifice" propagandamatrix.com/world_leaders_engage_symbolic_pagan_wors hip.htm, 2004
3.        Kick, Russ ed. You Are Being Lied To: The Disinformation Guide to Media Distortion, Historical Whitewashes, and Cultural Myths The Disinformation Company, 2001
4.        Mathison, Dirk "Inside Bohemian Grove: The Story People Magazine Won't Let You Read" Extra!, Nov/Dec 1991
5.        Weiss, Philip "Inside Bohemian Grove" Spy Magazine, November 1989
6.        Jones, Alex Dark Secret: Inside Bohemian Grove Alex Jones Productions, infowars.com
7.        Tarpley7, Webster G; Chaitkin, Anton; Wertz, Marianna George Bush: the Unauthorized Biophraphy, 1991
8.        International Action Center "Who's Coming to Bohemian Grove" CorpWatch, 13 July 2001
9.        Lee, John ed. "Club Bohemian" geocities.com/bohemian_grove_dirt/, 2004
Chapter 19
1.        Ross, Robert Gaylon Sr. Who's Who of the Elite: Members of the Bilderbergs, Council on Foreign Relations, Trilateral Commision, and Skull & Bones RIE, 1996

282

2.      Gosling, Tony  bilderberg.org
3.      A-Infos News Service  ainfos.ca/
4.      Harding, Gareth  "Four anti-war states to create EU army"
upi.com/view.cfm?StoryID=20030429-105505-3460r, 29 April 2003
5.      Zobel, Gibby  "Bilderberg Papers: Leaked minutes from
confidential meetings of world's Elite"  *The Big Issue*, 19 November
1999
6.      Brandt, Daniel  "Clinton, Quigley, and Conspiracy: What's
going on here?"  *NameBase NewsLine*, April-June 1993
7.      Quigley, Carroll  *Tragedy and Hope: A History of the
World in Our Time*  Gsg & Assoc., 1975

Chapter 20

1.      Ross, Robert Gaylon Sr.  *Who's Who of the Elite: Members
of the Bilderbergs, Council on Foreign Relations, Trilateral
Commision, and Skull & Bones*  RIE, 1996
2.      Marrs, Jim  Rule By Secrecy: The Hidden History That
Connects the Trilateral Commission, the Freemasons, and the Great
Pyramids  Perrenial, 2001
3.      trilateral.org
4.      Shoup, Lawrence  Jimmy Carter and the Trilateralists:
Presidential Roots  South End Press, 1980
5.      Evans-Pritchard, Ambrose  The Secret Life of Bill Clinton:
The Unreported Stories  Regnery Publishing, 1997
6.      Brzezinski, Zbigniew  The Grand Chessboard: American
Primacy and Its Geostratic Imperatives  Basic Books, 1998
7.      Various Authors  The Triangle Papers #'s 8-14, 32, 35, 38,
41, 54
8.      Gun Owners of America  "Australian Crime Statistics and
Analysis" gun owners.org/sk0703.htm, 2004
9.      Rise Phoenix  "Trilateral Commission: World Shadow
Government"  geocities.com/CapitolHill/8425/TRI-SPT.HTM, 2004
10.     Goldwater, Barry  The Coming Break Point  MacMillan
Publishing Co., 1976
11.     Goldwater, Barry  With No Apologies  Berkley Pub Group,
1980

Chapter 21

1.      Griffins, Des  Descent Into Slavery  Emmissary, 1980
2.      Ferguson, Niall  The House of Rothschild: The Money
Prophets, 1798-1848  Penguin, 1998
3.      Martin, Willie  "American Wars and Military Actions - 8"
christianlinks.com/forums/archive/topic/56122.html, 2004
4.      Ferguson, Niall  The House of Rothschild: The World's
Banker  Penguin, 2000

5.      Ross, Robert Gaylon Sr.  The Elite Serial Killers of JFK, RFK, and MLK  RIE, 2001
6.      Mitchell, J.V.  "The Federal Reserve Scheme" Jefferson Review  effersonreview.com/articles/2003/081803/federal.htm, 18 August 2003
7.      Freeman, David T.  "Economic Rape"  Personal Empowerment Resources, 1997
8.      Reuters  24 September 2002
9.      International Herald Tribune  "Immigrants for President" 2003
10.     Associated Press  "Records: Arnold's father was member of Nazi storm troops"  USA Today, 24 August 2003
11.     Alex Jones Radio Program  March 2003
12.     Stone, Olver  JFK: The Director's Cut  Warner Home Studio, 2003

Chapter 22
1.      Rockefeller.org
2.      Chernow, Ron  Titan: The Life of John D. Rockefeller Sr. Vintage, 1999
3.      West, Woody  "The Truth About Robber Barons"  Policy Review, 2004
4.      Baum, Dan  Smoke and Mirrors: The War on Drugs and the Policy of Failure  Back Bay Books, 1996
5.      Lederman, Robert  "Chase Manhattan Banks Right-Wing Relationship"  sonic.net/`doretk/Issues/00-12%20Winter/chaseman.html, 2004
6.      Segall, Grant  John D. Rockefeller: Anointed With Oil Oxford University Press, 2001
7.      Wycliffe Bible Translators  "Rockefeller Connection"  seek god.ca/Rockefeller, 2003
8.      The Christian Alert Network (TCAN)  "United Nations Set to Impose 'One World Religion'"  vvm.com/`ctomlin/a96.htm
9.      unesco.org
10.     Kjost, Bert  Brave New Schools  House Publishers, Inc., 1996
11.     Pierson, James  "Under God"  Weekly Standard, 18 October 2003
12.     Griffins, G. Edward  Fearful Master  American Opinion Books, 1964
13.     Wake Up America  "The Rockefeller Bloodline" geocities.com/lord_visionary/the_Rockefeller_bloodline.html, 2003
14.     Collier, Peter  The Rockefellers: An American Dynasty Summit Books, 1991

15.     Cloud Rider "Laurance Rockefeller and Sean Morton"
ufomind.com/misc./1997/fed/d01-001.shtm, 31 January 1997
16.     Icke, David <u>Tales From The Time Loop</u> Bridge of Love,
2003
17.     "Rockefeller Internationalism" Nexus Magazine

<u>Chapter 23</u>
1.      H.R. 2473 Medicare Prescription Drug and Modernization
Act of 2003
2.      Farm Security and Rural Investment Act of 2002 usda.gov,
2002
3.      Americans for the Arts "President Bush's FY'04 Arts
Funding Budgets" artsusa.org/issues/advocacy_article.asp?id1101
4.      Baldwin, Chuck "As I Predicted, George W. Bush Is
Backing Bill Clinton's Gun Ban" Free Republic 15 April 2003
5.      O'Neill, James "Dum...and Dummer: Can George W.
Bush match wits with a typical community college student?" *San
Francisco Chronicle* 2 September 2001
6.      Adams, Cecil "Did George W. Bush go AWOL During his
time in the National Guard?" straighdope.com/columns/030411.html
11 April 2003
7.      Tarpley, Webster G; Chaitkin, Anton; Wertz, Marianna
<u>George Bush: the Unauthorized Biography</u>, 1991
8.      Briody, Dan <u>The Iron Triangle: Inside the Secret World of
the Carlyle Group</u> John Wiley & Sons, 2003
9.      Bowen, Russell S. <u>The Immaculate Deception: The Bush
Crime Family Exposed</u> American West Publishing, 2001
10.     Bush Watch "How Bush Really Made His Millions"
Politex, 1999 & 2002
11.     Citizens for Legitimate Government "Breaking News"
legitgov.com, 31 July 2002
12.     danconsulting.com/dumpjeb/jeb_lies.cfm
13.     Golden, Daniel; Bandler, James; Walker, Marcus "Bin
Laden Family Could Profit From a Jump in Defense Spending Due to
Ties to U.S. Bank" *Wall Street Journal* 27 September 2001
14.     Foust, Michael "Christians, Muslims worship same God,
Bush tells reporters" Baptist Press News, 20 November 2003
15.     Draper, Theodore <u>A Very Thin Line: The Iran-Contra
Affairs</u> Hill & Wang Pub., 1991
16.     freemasonry watch.org
17.     Blumeberg, Nathaniel "Neil Bush (And His Family)"
*Treasure State Review*, 1December 1991
18.     North Star Zone "Hincley: Hit Man for the Shadow
Government?" geocities.com/northstarzone/HINCKLEY.html, 2004

19.      Martin, Al  The Conspirators: Secrets of an Iran-Contra Insider  National Liberty Press, 2002

20.      Phillips, Kevin  American Dynasty: Aristocracy, Fortune, and the Politics of Deceit in the House of Bush  Viking Press, 2004

21.      Marrs, Jim  Rule By Secrecy: The Hidden History That Connects the Trilateral Commission, the Freemasons, and the Great Pyramids  Perrenial, 2001

22.      Loftus, Mark & Aarons, Mark  The Secret War Against the Jews: How Western Espionage Betrayed the Jewish People  St. Martin's Press, 1997

Chapter 24

1.      Springmeier, Fritz  Bloodlines of the Illuminati Ambassador House, 1998

2.      Gates, John D.  The Du Pont Family  Doubleday, 1979

3.      "Reader's Companion to American History"  Houghton Mifflin, 2004

4.      Pile, Lawrence A.  "The Siren Call of Modern Pied Pipers" *Employee Assistance*, January 1993

5.      Fager, Wesley M.  "A Clockwork Straight: Rehabilitation, Thought Reform, and the Destruction of Young Minds" wesfager.com/book/index.htm

6.      Baum, Dan  Smoke and Mirrors: The War on Drugs and the Politics of Failure  Back Bay, 1997

7.      Bryson, Chris and Griffiths, Joel  "Fluoride, Teeth, and the Atomic Bomb" *Waste Not*, 1997

8.      Sutherland, Donald  "Most of U.S. Liquid Toxic Waste Injected Underground" *Environmental News Service*, 1999

9.      Herer, Jack  The Emperor Wears No Clothes  Ah Ha Pub, 2000

10.      Balko, Radley  "William Randolph Hearst and the Criminalization of Marijuana" *The Agitator*, 29 September 2002

Chapter 25

1.      Virtual American Biographies  "Junius Spencer Morgan" virtualology.com, 2001

2.      Jones, Alan B.  How the World Really Works  ABJ Pr, 1997

3.      Griffin, G. Edward  The Creature From Jekyll Island: A Second Look at the Federal Reserve  American Media, 2002

4.      Chernow, Ron  The House of Morgan: An American Dynasty and the Rise of Modern Finance  Publishers Group West, 2001

5.      U.S. Securities and Exchange Commission report  "SEC Settles Enforcement Proceedings Against J.P. Morgan Chase and

Citigroup", 28 July 2003

6.      Freedom From Fiats Foundation "It's Time to Indict the Fed" knology.net/'bilrum/fed.htm, 2004

7.      Blase, William "The Council on Foreign Relations and the New World Order" *The Courier*, 1995

8.      "How Governments Manipulate the Gold Market - A Primer" *Freemarket Gold & Money Report*, 6 October 2003

Chapter 26

1.      Isaacson, Walter <u>Kissinger</u> Simon & Schuster, 1993

2.      Hitchens, Christopher <u>The Trial of Henry Kissinger</u> Verso Books, 2002

3.      Ellsberg, Daniel <u>Secrets: A Memoir of Vietnam and the Pentagon Papers</u> Viking, 2002

4.      Sauter, Mark A. et. al. <u>The Men We Left Behind: Henry Kissinger, the Politics of Deceit, and the Tragic Fate of POWs After the Vietnam War</u> National Press Books, 1993

5.      Foner, Philip S. <u>The Black Panters Speak</u> DeCapo Press, 2002

6.      Komisar, Lucy "Kissinger Encouraged Chile's Brutal Repression, New Documents Show" *Albion Monitor*, 8 March 1999

6.      Bernstein, Carl & Woodward, Bob <u>All the President's Men</u> Simon & Schuster, 1998

Chapter 27

1.      Mosley, Leonard <u>Dulles: A Biography of Eleanor, Allen, and John Foster Dulles and Their Family Network</u> Hodder & Stoughton, 1978

2.      Arend, Anthony Clark <u>Pursuing a Just and Durable Peace: John Foster Dulles and International Organization</u> Greenwood Pub Group, 1988

3.      Moreno, Jonathon <u>Undue Risk: Secret State Experiments on Humans</u> Routledge, 2000

4.      Tarpley, Webster G; Chaitkin, Anton; Wertz, Marianna <u>George Bush: the Unauthorized Biography</u>, 1991

5.      Marrs, Texe <u>Dark Secrets of the New Age: Satan's Plan for a One World Religion</u> Crossway Book, 1987

6.      Samples, Charlie "The Greatest Hoax" sweetliberty.org/issues/hoax/greatest hoax.htm, 2004

7.      *Joint Hearing Before the Select Committee on Intelligence and the Subcommittee on Health and Scientific Research of the Committee on Human Resources, United States Senate*, 3 August 1977

8.      Freedom Magazine "Government Reform" 30th.freedommag.org/page17.htm, 2004

Chapter 28
1.      "Vice President Richard B. Cheney" whitehouse.gov
2.      Skolnick, Sherman H. "The Enron Black Magic"
skolnickreport.com, 2001
3.      Scheer, Robert "Cheney's Grimy Trail in Business: His
Career Offers a Textbook Example of Shady Doings" *Los Angeles
Times*, 16 July 2002
4.      Lindorf, David "Secret Bechtel Documents Revealed: Yes,
It Is About Oil" counterpunch.org, 9 April 2003
5.      Fox News Channel (I watched the Haliburton scandal
unfold on Fox)
Chapter 29
1.      infowars.com "Skull & Bones archives"
2.      Drudge Report "Kerry On Imus: There's Nothing to
Report" 13 February 2004
3.      WorldNet Daily "Kerry's Intern Tells All To TV Network"
rense.com/general49/krr.htm, 16 February 2003
4.      John Edward's campaign finance plan, given in February
during a stump speech
5.      Issel, Bernardo "Extended Discussion of John Kerry's
Enron Hypocrisy" freerepublic.com/focus/f-news/1065673/posts, 26
January 2003
6.      Owens, Mackubin Thomas "Vetting the Vet Record"
*National Review Online*, 27 January 2004
7.      Perez, Jennifer Anne "A Jewish Czech in John Kerry's
Court" Reform Judaism Online, Fall 2003
Chapter 30
1.      Springmeier, Fritz Bloodlines of the Illuminati
Ambassador House, 1998
2.      Baigent, Michael; Leigh, Richard; Lincoln, Henry Holy
Blood, Holy Grail Dell. 1982
3.      Marrs, Texe Dark Secrets of the New Age: Satan's Plan
for a One World Religion Crossway Books, 1987
4.      Hislop, Alexander The Two Babylons Chick Pub, 1998

# Index

United Nations, 20, 94,
131, 142, 175, 186, 219,
260
United Steel, 165

**V**
Vaccines, 220-224
Viadero, Roger C., 11
Vietnam, 106, 110, 167,
171-175, 180
Vietnam Veterans
Against the War, 188

**W**
Waco, 20, 41
Warburgs, 141, 214,
216, 254
War of 1812, 8, 140
Warner, Harry, 256, 257
Watergate, 154, 180,
181
Weishaupt, Adam, 85,
89-95, 137, 213, 251
Wells, H.G., 105, 236
We The People, 61
Whiskey Rebellion, 58
Whistleblowers, 32, 55,
122
Wilensky, Gail R. Dr.,
47
Wilson, Woodrow, 168
WMDs, 36, 116, 244
Wolfowitz, Paul, 126

**X**
X Files, 21

All Items Come With 100% Money Back Guarantee!
Select Titles and Mail to Van Cleave Publishing

| | | |
|---|---|---|
| *Webs of Power* | *5.5x8.5* | $14.95 |
| *Webs of Power* | *Audio CD* | $14.95 |
| *Moonstone* | *Tribe CD* | $ 9.95 |

**Free Shipping and Handling!**
All prices include taxes, and shipping and handling
charges for United Postal Service mailing (7-9 days).

**Receive a signed and numbered copy of *Webs of
Power* - Add $10**

**Total** of your order:$_____ Signed copy of
Webs: Yes____No____

Your Name: _____

Address: _____

City: _____ State: _
Zip: _____

Refer Credit Card payments to Amazon.com.

Please make check or M.O. (U.S.$) to
**Van Cleave Publishing**, and send payment to:

**Van Cleave Publishing**
1712 Riverside Dr.  #93
Austin, TX  78741

**Van Cleave Publishing** appreciates your business and
extends a
**Complete Discount For ANY Reason!**